Medievalisms

MW00489734

From King Arthur and Robin Hood, through to videogames and jousting-themed restaurants, medieval culture continues to surround us and has retained a strong influence on literature and culture throughout the ages.

This fascinating and illuminating guide is written by two of the leading contemporary scholars of medieval literature, and explores:

- the influence of medieval cultural concepts on literature and film, including key authors such as Shakespeare, Tennyson, and Mark Twain;
- the continued appeal of medieval cultural figures such as Dante, King Arthur, and Robin Hood;
- the influence of the medieval on such varied disciplines as politics, music, children's literature, and art;
- contemporary efforts to relive the Middle Ages.

Medievalisms: Making the Past in the Present surveys the critical field and sets the boundaries for future study, providing an essential background for literary study from the medieval period through to the twenty-first century.

Tison Pugh is Professor of English at the University of Central Florida, USA.

Angela Jane Weisl is Professor of English at Seton Hall University, USA.

Medievalisms

Making the Past in the Present

Tison Pugh and Angela Jane Weisl

Routledge
Taylor & Francis Group

LONDON AND NEW YORK

First published 2013
by Routledge
2 Park Square, Milton Park, Abingdon, Oxon OX14 4RN

Simultaneously published in the USA and Canada
by Routledge
711 Third Avenue, New York, NY 10017

Routledge is an imprint of the Taylor & Francis Group, an informa business

© 2013 Tison Pugh and Angela Jane Weisl

The right of Tison Pugh and Angela Jane Weisl to be identified as authors of
this work has been asserted by him/her in accordance with sections 77 and 78
of the Copyright, Designs and Patents Act 1988.

All rights reserved. No part of this book may be reprinted or reproduced or
utilized in any form or by any electronic, mechanical, or other means, now
known or hereafter invented, including photocopying and recording, or in any
information storage or retrieval system, without permission in writing from
the publishers.

Trademark notice: Product or corporate names may be trademarks or
registered trademarks, and are used only for identification and explanation
without intent to infringe.

British Library Cataloguing in Publication Data
A catalogue record for this book is available from the British Library

Library of Congress Cataloging-in-Publication Data
Pugh, Tison.
Medievalisms : making the past in the present / Tison Pugh
and Angela Jane Weisl.
p. cm.
ISBN 978-0-415-61726-0 (hardback) — ISBN 978-0-415-61727-7
(paperback) — ISBN 978-0-203-10828-4 (ebook)
1. Medievalism. 2. Medievalism—Social aspects. 3. Medievalism—Political
aspects. 4. Popular culture. 5. Commercial products—Social aspects.
6. Middle Ages in art. 7. Middle Ages in literature. 8. Middle Ages
in motion pictures. I. Weisl, Angela Jane, 1963- II. Title.
CB353.P74 2012
909.07—dc23
2012001437

ISBN: 978-0-415-61726-0 (hbk)
ISBN: 978-0-415-61727-7 (pbk)
ISBN: 978-0-203-10828-4 (ebk)

Typeset in Sabon
by Taylor & Francis Books

MIX
Paper from
responsible sources
FSC
www.fsc.org   FSC® C004839

Printed and bound in Great Britain by the MPG Books Group

To David Dean and Bob Squillace, non-medievalists who, not very surprisingly, make all things, medieval or not, more fun.

Contents

Acknowledgements

Chapter 2, "A Case Study of Dante: Naked Icons of Medievalism," is also published in *Medieval Perspectives*; we thank the Southeastern Medieval Association and Dan O'Sullivan, the editor of *Medieval Perspectives*, for permission to reprint this essay. Also, our sincere thanks to Jello Biafra and the Guantanamo School of Medicine for permission to quote "The New Feudalism" in its entirety, and to the Metropolitan Museum of Art for permission to reproduce images of the Antioch Chalice and the Annunciation Triptych.

Our understanding of medievalisms would not be nearly so rich without the assistance of many others who offered their expertise, understanding, and time to help our project succeed. Helen Evans, Curator of Medieval Art at the Metropolitan Museum and the Cloisters, Melanie Holcomb, Associate Curator of Medieval Art, and Dita Amory, Acting Associate Curator-in-Charge of the Robert Lehman Collection, The Metropolitan Museum of Art, spoke to us in great detail and candor about medieval art and the way it is displayed, as well as giving us great insight into museum culture and current ideas about exhibit design. The world of Viking Metal was opened up to us in all its eccentric glory by Gesina Phillips, DJ and Promotions Director, and Michcella Tiscornia, DJ and Technical Operations Director of WSOU-Radio, South Orange, New Jersey. Medieval gamers and enthusiasts Matt Honig and Gesina Phillips (whose understanding of medievalisms is all-encompassing) discussed many different videogames and answered multiple questions at length, and Kevin Stevens played the *Dante's Inferno* videogame for us; without their expertise, our sense of the world of the electronic Middle Ages would not be nearly so rich. Eveleena Fults, a long-time princess at Medieval Times® Dinner and Tournament, Orlando, provided insights that even a pilgrimage there could not. Cathryn Wiatroski and Kevin Stevens visited the Metropolitan Museum and the Cloisters and took copious notes on the differences between the Medieval Hall, the Old Master Paintings Galleries, and the Greek and Roman exhibits. Mary Balkun, Elizabeth Centanni, A. J. Cunder, Ashley Lorenzo, Bob Squillace, and Michcella Tiscornia attended the New York Renaissance Faire in Sterling Forrest and the Fort Tryon Park Medieval Festival and shared their experiences and commentary, and A. J. Cunder is particularly to be commended for his own act of medievalism: wearing a sword on the New York City subway. We also benefited from the support of several research assistants at Seton Hall: Jamie Rooney and Christine Mallon provided support at the end of the project, while Kevin Stevens proved himself boundlessly helpful and unceasingly useful, including undertaking research, participating in various medieval activities, reading chapters and offering commentary on them, and bringing us interesting examples we would not have found on our own. He has been an invaluable part of the project from its inception, and his input can be found on many of these pages.

Additional thanks are due to our institutions, the University of Central Florida and Seton Hall University, for their support of our scholarship. Audiences at many conferences, including the Southeast Medieval Association, New Jersey College English Association, and the Plymouth Medieval and Renaissance Forum provided commentary on early drafts of chapters, and we have benefited as well from thoughtful readings by our colleagues, including Mary Balkun, Jonathan Farina, and Karen Gevirtz. The editorial and production team at Routledge has been a joy to work with, including Emma Joyes, Polly Dodson, and Niall Slater. The support of our students, and the patience of our families and friends, throughout the project has been legion.

The "Antioch Chalice" and The Annunciation Triptych (Merode Altarpiece) by Robert Campin images © The Metropolitan Museum of Art. Image source: Art Resource, NY.

1 Medievalisms

The Magic of the Middle Ages

The magic of the Middle Ages: the phrase should collapse in its inherent ridiculousness, yet it holds firm in the cultural imaginary, as it has held firm, in multiple and contradictory permutations, for the many centuries since the Middle Ages was created by Renaissance thinkers determined to establish a break with the past. Distinguished as the "Dark Ages" by Petrarch in the 1300s to set it apart from the classical period that preceded it, and defined as "medieval," or "Middle" by Leonardo Bruni in *History of the Florentine People* (1442) and by Flavio Biondo in *Historiarum ab Inclinatione Romanorum Imperii* (1483), the "Middle Ages" emerges as an invention of those who came after it; its entire construction is, essentially, a fantasy.[1] Set apart both from the rational classical period and from the ostensible return to these values in the Renaissance, the Middle Ages by definition encodes a kind of magical thinking, in which both cultural difference and continuity can be cordoned off from prior and subsequent eras. The ostensible allure and magic of the Middle Ages should implode as a cultural fantasy for multiple reasons, beginning with the prosaic realization that the various wars, plagues, diseases, turmoil, and strife of the period rendered life rather miserable for much of its populace, and extending to the observation that not many of even the most devoted of today's "medieval" aficionados would surrender the comforts of the twenty-first century for the uncertainties of the fourteenth. Also, life in the western European Middle Ages offered harsh restrictions on individual freedom and autonomy, particularly for any person not granted the status of the normative, including but not limited to women, Jews, homosexuals, and Muslims. And yet, despite the unpleasantness of historical reality, the Middle Ages is magic: it is continually reborn in new stories, new media, new histories. It continues to enthrall for its pageantry and its manners, for its ideals of courtly love and chivalry, for its literary and artistic accomplishments, in such plenitude that, although the Middle Ages did in fact end, medievalisms, it appears, will never cease to be reborn.

In its simplest sense, *medievalism* refers to the art, literature, scholarship, avocational pastimes, and sundry forms of entertainment and culture that turn to the Middle Ages for their subject matter or inspiration, and in doing so, explicitly or implicitly, by comparison or by contrast, comment on the artist's contemporary sociocultural milieu. Numerous scholars have put forth definitions of this term, including Leslie Workman, a leading figure in the field of medievalisms due to his role as the founding editor of the journal *Studies in Medievalism*. In his editorial published in its first volume, he defined the field as:

> the study of the scholarship which has created the Middle Ages we know, ideals and models derived from the Middle Ages, and the relations between them. In terms of these things medievalism could only begin, not simply when the Middle Ages had ended, whenever that may have been, but when the Middle Ages were perceived to have been something in the past, something it was necessary to revive or desirable to imitate.[2]

As Workman observes, a sense of nostalgia for a lost past percolates throughout many medievalist endeavors, in that the turn to history often reveals a sense of discontentment with the present. Workman also focuses on the connection between scholarship and medievalism, in that even academic studies of the Middle Ages become implicated with such nostalgia. Pauline Stafford likewise sees a scholarly component to medievalisms, suggesting that the term refers to the "use of and responses to the medieval past ... and the scholarly study of these responses,"[3] and Clare Simmons posits that medievalism is "the later reception of the Middle Ages," noting also its "reputation as an aberration from scholarly Medieval Studies."[4] As Simmons posits, the scholarly study of the Middle Ages is often seen as distinct from its re-creation in various artistic and entertainment media, yet as medievalisms themselves increasingly become the focus of scholarly study, this distinction may fade. Summarizing such sentiments, Tom Shippey affirms that medievalism includes "[a]ny post-medieval attempt to re-imagine the Middle Ages, or some aspect of the Middle Ages, for the modern world, in any of many different media; especially in academic usage, [it is] the study of the development and significance of such attempts."[5]

Perhaps the most famous theorist of medievalisms is novelist and social critic Umberto Eco, the author of the murder mystery *The Name of the Rose* (1983) but also widely acclaimed for such works as *Foucault's Pendulum* (1989), *Baudolino* (2003), *On Ugliness* (2007), and *The Prague Cemetery* (2011). In his groundbreaking study of medievalism, included in his collection *Travels in Hyperreality* (1986), Eco identifies "Ten Little Middle Ages," each of which captures a particular trope of post-medieval re-creations of the medieval past. His "Ten Little Middle Ages" include: Middle Ages as a pretext; as a site of ironical revisitation; as a barbaric age; of Romanticism; of the *philosophia perennis* or of Neo-Thomism; of national identities; of Decadentism; of philological reconstruction; of so-called Tradition; and of the expectation of the Millennium. Among this plenitude of converging and diverging Middle Ages, Eco urges his readers to openly declare their allegiance to the particular fantasy of the past to which they subscribe: "we have the moral and cultural duty of spelling out what kind of Middle Ages we are talking about. To say openly which of the above ten types we are referring to means to say who we are and what we dream of."[6] Eco's sense of moral duty, however, may not be adopted by practitioners of medievalism, who often blend multiple "Little Middle Ages" in their productions, as the examinations in this volume will demonstrate: for example, full-contact jousting, as explored in Chapter 8, embodies both the barbaric and the Romantic Middle Ages, while also being a site for a kind of revisioned nationalism. Like the Middle Ages themselves (real or imagined), such medievalisms prove both ripe for categorization and resistant to it.

Complementary to Eco's "Ten Little Middle Ages," medievalisms may be organized in a somewhat simpler fashion by chronology (medievalisms of the various centuries), by influence (e.g., Shakespeare's medievalism, or that of the Pre-Raphaelite Brotherhood), and by media (e.g., literary, cinematic, or video-game medievalisms), yet in each instance, the medievalism under scrutiny will expand beyond any core definition to reflect the artistic energies impelling a creator to look to the past for the creation of the new. As Kathleen Davis and Nadia Altschul wryly note, "Medievalism, it soon becomes apparent, can only be considered in the plural,"[7] and this astute observation stresses the necessity of looking at the various intersections of medievalisms uniting in a given work. For example, in a twentieth-century film version of the Arthurian legend, as told and retold by such authors as Chrétien de Troyes, Alfred, Lord Tennyson, and T. H. White, and then scripted and filmed by the screenwriter and director, multiple and contradictory medievalisms reflect and refract one another, and to understand their functioning in an organic artwork necessitates understanding them in their individuality as well.

If the above definitions of *medievalism* are admirable in their simplicity and utility, the tempest raging over the term *neomedievalism* exemplifies how taxonomic debates can inhibit rather than encourage the analysis of their subject matter. For the most part, attempts to define neomedievalism focus on its ostensibly greater distance from the Middle Ages than the distance between the Middle Ages and medievalism, whether due to irony, humor, postmodern pastiche, or deployments of newer media forms. As Amy Kaufman argues, "Neomedievalism is thus not a dream of the Middle Ages, but a dream of someone else's medievalism. It is medievalism doubled upon itself," an intriguing view that posits neomedievalisms as twice removed from their medieval sources.[8] It nonetheless seems difficult to determine in many instances whether one is dealing with a dream of the Middle Ages or of someone else's dream of medievalism doubled upon itself, for many medieval tropes are themselves fantasies of the period: are not courtly love and chivalry both realities of the Middle Ages (as the numerous treatises on these subjects attest) as much as they are dreams of what medieval people believed their world should be? What emerges is a recognition that reimaginings of the Middle Ages are essentially fantasies built upon fantasies, for many medievalisms draw more firmly from medieval ideas about fictionality than they do from medieval history. A distinguishing feature of much medievalism, its anachronism, must be seen both as authentically medieval and as fantastic, for many medieval narratives revel in their own anachronistic constructions of past and present. Chaucer's Troy in *Troilus and Criseyde* is no more authentically like the classical world it claims to represent than the Middle Ages of most "medieval" films are like the historical period in which they claim to be set, but *Troilus and Criseyde* is no less a masterpiece for its anachronistic mishmash of time, place, and cultural setting.

Carol Robinson and Pamela Clements espy in neomedievalism a disingenuousness in the artist's position vis-à-vis the past, in which the temporal and sociocultural parameters of the Middle Ages are untethered from any historical foundations. They define the term and use the film *Monty Python and the Holy Grail* (dir. Terry Jones and Terry Gilliam, 1975) to make a key point about the disregard for history evident in much neomedievalism:

> [N]eomedievalism does not look to the Middle Ages to use, to study, to copy, or even to learn; the perception of the Middle Ages is more filtered, perceptions of perceptions (and of distortions), done without a concern for facts of reality, such as the fact that The Knights Who Say "Ni" never existed. This lack of concern for historical accuracy, however, is not the same as that held in more traditional fantasy works: the difference is a degree of self-awareness and self-reflexivity.[9]

The observation that the Monty Python troupe created some of its characters out of whole cloth for *Monty Python and the Holy Grail* is hardly surprising, but it is not then apparent why this artistic decision should reflect the film's neomedievalism rather than its medievalism. For it is readily apparent in numerous scenes of the film, such as in its "Tale of Sir Galahad" that parodies Gawain's seductions in the medieval masterpiece *Sir Gawain and the Green Knight*, that the Pythons used medieval texts and ideas as direct sources for their ideas. Indeed, one could argue that the Knights Who Say "Ni," despite the brash ridiculousness of this plotline, encourage viewers to consider the linguistic confusion coincident with the Great Vowel Shift between 1350 and 1500: when King Arthur's companion Sir Bedivere cannot pronounce "Ni" correctly, repeatedly stumbling over the syllable and saying "Nu" instead, such levity carries a very learned joke about the difficulties in pronouncing Middle English, both for medieval and modern speakers. At the very least, *Monty Python and the Holy Grail*, within the context of debates of medievalism versus neomedievalism, exhibits traits of both schools. What is more interesting in the study of medievalisms, then, is not whether a particular treatment, trope, or text should be prefixed with *neo* before its *medievalism*, but how and why the artists looking back to the Middle Ages create this particular past, in whichever historical, semi-historical, or magical incarnation they desire. As David Marshall cautions, "the categories of medievalism could likely proliferate to pointlessness with individual perceptions and preferences on the parts of both producers of medievalia and scholars of it,"[10] and his words posit that the study of medievalisms need not concern itself as much with a semantic tempest but instead focus on why medievalisms flourish long past the Middle Ages and on how and to what purpose they function in a given text. In so doing, it is possible to uncover a series of relationships of past and present, of longing and transcendence, that medievalisms reveal in the relationships produced between their own contemporary world and the medieval world they envision and revision.

The *Oxford English Dictionary* constructs the word "medieval" in a series of definitions that highlight the multiple functions of medievalisms. Etymologically drawn from the Latin *medium aevum*, "medieval" in its current form may be constructed on analogy with "primeval," an unwitting suggestion of many of the assumptions of primitivism so often assigned to the period. The first definition, "Of or relating to a period of time intervening between (periods designated as) ancient and modern; spec. of, relating to, or characteristic of the Middle Ages. Also, of art, religion, etc.: resembling or imitative of that of the Middle Ages," is relatively objective and unbiased in its assessment,[11] yet such an understanding becomes vague and problematic in its usage. The "in-between" quality of the period that makes it so challenging to fix, as well as the assumption that the Middle Ages is neither one era (ancient) nor another (modern) but something amorphous and unclear, is balanced against the idea that medieval also constitutes a set of productions ("art, religion, etc.") that not only exist within their own historical era but which can be imitated. As the meanings proceed, these cultural productions become associated with a series not of facts but of stereotypes as further definitions expand from the objective to the subjective: "Exhibiting the severity or illiberality ascribed to a former age; cruel, barbarous." Thus the medieval past quickly becomes a period of primitive irrationality, and the *OED* offers examples from 1883 to 1988 using "medieval" to allude to various specimens of violent behavior. The dictionary also adds a usage it determines to be particular to the United States: "to get medieval: to use violence or extreme measures on, to become aggressive,"[12] further cementing the connection of the Middle Ages to unbridled violence and "frenzied, berserker-like behavior."[13] Finally, readers are offered, "A person who lived in the Middle Ages. Also: a person whose outlook or perspective is (regarded as) characteristic of or resembles that of the Middle Ages,"[14] from which we might assume that someone "medieval" is someone imbricated in irrational, primitive, and destructive behaviors.

Revealing in themselves, these converging definitions become even more pointed in comparison to the *OED*'s discussion of the word "Renaissance," which is first defined as "The revival of the arts and high culture under the influence of classical models, which began in Italy in the 14th cent. and spread throughout most of Europe by the end of the 16th; (also) the period during which this was in progress."[15] The notions of stasis implied in the discussion of "medieval" contrast sharply with the idea of progress imbued in this notion of the Renaissance, which is further defined as "any period of exceptional revival of the arts and intellectual culture" and "a revival of, or renewal of interest in, something; (also) the process by which this occurs."[16] The problematic nature of both definitions is evident: classical models are hardly innovative intellectual and artistic specimens in the fourteenth century (despite the need to rediscover many of them), and art, culture, and philosophy abounded throughout the Middle Ages as vibrant traditions in their own right, as visiting museums with medieval collections, attending early-music concerts, and reading throughout the medieval section of the library asserts with confidence. What can be teased out from these definitions, apart from persistent attitudes about both periods of history that contemporary scholars have interrogated at length, is that the Middle Ages showcases unique qualities that make medievalism possible (and perhaps also make "renaissancism" less likely). Its amorphousness and its imitable nature, far more than its associations with violence and aggression, enable creative revisions and imaginings of the period. There are certainly other kinds of historical fantasies that engage the popular imagination—Jane Austen versions of Anglophilia, Civil War (British and American) re-enactors, and Steampunk all have avid followers—but none is as persistent, varied, or multi-genred as the medievalisms, operating in both high and low culture, in forms as diverse as videogames, high art, Viking heavy metal, and political discourse, among many, many others.

Medievalisms: Making the Past in the Present, then, is a study of how the Middle Ages is continually reborn in subsequent centuries and of the persistent tropes that create this magical past. It is not a chronological survey of the field, as such an undertaking is beyond the scope of this rather slender volume. Nor is it a genre survey of various medievalisms, although we focus on patterns within converging yet discrete traditions, including literary, cinematic, and experiential medievalisms. Rather, our hope is, that by examining the multiple ways that medievalisms operate in disparate media and in a divergent array of examples, we focus this critical conversation on the aesthetic functions, narrative effects, and pervasive allure of medievalism as a whole. Understanding medievalisms, thus, becomes a methodology for understanding the production of cultural and historical fantasies out of the fragments of real material, and looking at contemporary examples of the genre can bring one closer to understanding the ways in which the Middle Ages operates as its own cultural fantasy. Indeed, we readily admit (indeed, embrace) the eclectic nature of this study, in which we have selected idiosyncratic examples of medievalisms from diverse genres and historical periods—ranging from Shakespeare's deployment of Chaucer to Sarah Palin's use of the phrase *blood libel*, from the poetry and artworks of the Pre-Raphaelites to the exuberant cacophony of Viking Metal—to sample the wide range of medievalisms over the centuries but also to seek similarities and convergences among these disparate cultural artifacts. Each of the chapters of this book, and possibly each of the artifacts examined in these chapters, could well stand as the subject of its own monograph, and so the goal of *Medievalisms* is not to write the definitive study of distinct and discrete medievalisms but to theorize complementary modes of meaning in play with divergent medievalisms. To quote the Major League Baseball Network's lead-in to its popular show *Prime 9*, "our goal is to start arguments, not to end them."[17] Like Eco's "Ten Little Middle Ages," we offer the following chapters as extended rhapsodies over the allure and charm, dissatisfactions and limitations, of engaging the medieval past.

Following this Introduction, *Medievalisms* continues with the chapter "A Case Study of Dante: Naked Icons of Medievalism," which analyzes Dante Alighieri as an icon of the Middle Ages and of its subsequent re-creation. It is essential to see, however, that Dante is also a naked icon, one stripped of his literary accomplishments and then remolded to become the author whom his descendants wish him to be. As much as one may think of authors as historical figures, as men and women grounded in their history and culture and recognizably similar over the years due to their literary accomplishments, Dante models the vagaries of identity that authors undergo as their readers reinvent and rewrite them. From the crowning genius of the medieval literary tradition to a character in a videogame, Dante shifts in each retelling, and such transitions highlight the power of medievalisms to use multiple and contradictory visions of the Middle Ages as semiotic shorthands that communicate critical ideas while simultaneously enlarging or diminishing the icon in view. To condense Dante into an icon is itself an interpretive move, but one that highlights the power of medievalisms to shift cultural visions of complex histories. Such shifts are not necessarily to be lamented, as there are certainly various pleasures available in a videogame Dante, yet such shifts should not pass unremarked, as Dante's malleability in the cultural imaginary testifies to the heady play possible in the miscellany of contradictory medievalisms that resignify him into an icon of the past.

Literary medievalisms, which serve as the focus of the following chapter, "Literary Medievalisms: Inventing Inspirations," allow authors to look to the past as they create new works in the present, and thus literary medievalisms cannot be divorced from an individual author's relationship to his or her forebears. Harold Bloom believes that such relationships carry with them "the anxiety of influence," as writers must situate themselves vis-à-vis their forebears, but the weight of past authors must be considered in tandem with the weight of past historical periods. Literary medievalisms compel authors to consider their places within various and contradictory traditions: of medieval authors and their artistic achievements; of fantasy, chivalry, and courtly love; of the rigors and demands of historical accuracy (or the pleasures of anachronism); and of the contradictory impulses emerging from various combinations of such factors. In all such instances, whether in Shakespeare's praise of Chaucer or in Mark Twain's denigration of Walter Scott's medievalism, descendant authors establish their positions in the literary pantheon by inventing the necessary avatar of medievalism from the past for their own unique ends.

The medievalisms of children's literature frequently construct the Middle Ages as a lost time of innocence, which corresponds with a widespread cultural desire to view children themselves as avatars of innocence, but both of these desires for innocence are cultural fantasies. As explored in the chapter "'Medieval' Literature for Children and Young Adults: Fantasies of Innocence," the Middle Ages is no more "innocent" a time than those preceding and following it, and children's "innocence" often reflects parental and cultural desires to misread their offspring as undefiled by knowledge deemed taboo for the young. These converging fantasies of innocence trouble the meaning of medievalisms in children's literature, for the didactic impulse of much such literature, at least tacitly, encourages its readers to grow in their understanding of the world, while nonetheless perpetuating the innocent image of the child and of the Middle Ages. At the same time, the Middle Ages can also serve as a locus for the coming-of-age story, particularly in Young Adult literature, as the traditions of the quest narrative merge with those of the *bildungsroman*; because events such as adoption, fosterage, and monasticism take children out of traditional family structures, medieval literature for older readers becomes an opportunity to investigate avenues of making one's own way in the world and constructing one's own family. If the innocence of childhood is preserved in literature for younger children, the Middle Ages also becomes a place to lose that innocence and find one's self.

As Dante exemplifies the ways in which artists and artifacts from the Middle Ages come to serve as icons of the past, King Arthur and Robin Hood exemplify the continued appeal, and the continued rebirth, of medieval masculinities in the modern world. In the chapter "King Arthur's and Robin Hood's Adventures in Medievalism: Mythic Masculinities (and Magical Femininities)," we examine the ways in which the legendary king and the equally legendary outlaw tap into powerful fantasies of medieval masculinity, and, through their relationships with female characters, of medieval femininity as well. By examining pivotal moments in these men's respective corpora, this chapter traces shifts in their depictions that nonetheless, perhaps paradoxically, strengthen their role in the cultural imaginary. Medieval ideals of chivalry, courtly love, and masculinity, as they are continuously reborn in modern novels, films, videogames, and other media, prove intransigent tropes of desire for the past, and King Arthur and Robin Hood exemplify this allure over the centuries, while also exemplifying the limitations of transhistorical genders. These characters' traditions are also rewritten in ways to challenge the appeal of historical masculinities, opening views of femininity that are both rooted in the medieval past yet refreshingly modern in their outlook.

Cinematic medievalisms portray the Middle Ages on the silver screen, and many filmmakers stress their quest for authenticity throughout the filming process. Anachronisms, however, enter into all films depicting the Middle Ages, no matter how carefully such solecisms are warded off through archival research, simply due to the necessary technologies of the filmmaking enterprise. Due to this ultimately liberating exigency, anachronisms create additional levels of meaning in a given medieval film. In this chapter, "Movie Medievalisms: Five (or Six) Ways of Looking at an Anachronism," we address the varying ways that anachronisms can function in a film, employing Thomas Greene's rubric of anachronisms as naïve, abusive, serendipitous, creative, and tragic to demonstrate how filmmakers, whether they admit it or not, rely on such anachronisms to create meaning in their film. The chapter concludes by considering the essential nature of anachronism to any filmmaker's dream of the magical Middle Ages.

Many patrons of music and the fine arts seek transcendent pleasures through them, and the chapter "Medievalisms in Music and the Arts: Longing for Transcendence" addresses the ways in which medievalism intersects with such a longing to escape one's very self through the rapturous pleasures of music and art. Performances of medieval music and displays of medieval art also become enmeshed with a desire to re-create the Middle Ages, to stage the art in a setting somehow temporally separate from today, while still finding a way to speak in the present. Music, whether authentically medieval, such as Hildegard of Bingen's compositions, or imaginatively medieval, such as Viking heavy metal, becomes a conduit to join past and present in a reimagining of values that leads to the transcendence of compartmentalized notions of space and time; the display of medieval art, and the myths made about it, also reauthorize the works' ritual significance that connects viewers with a greater world of spiritual meanings.

For some aficionados of the Middle Ages, it is not enough to enjoy the past vicariously through a novel, film, or artwork; instead, they must (re)live this past themselves. The chapter "Experiential Medievalisms: Reliving the Always Modern Middle Ages" examines various ways in which people can relive the past, including through videogames, live-action role playing, jousting, the Society for Creative Anachronism, and travel destinations such as Medieval Times® Dinner and Tournament. Recreational opportunities to experience the past abound, and these pastimes encourage their fans to escape the chronological coincidence of their lives—why is any person born in the particular time in which they are born?—to live anew in a past deemed intrinsically more satisfying than the present, where they can live as avatars and alter egos distinct from their daily existence in school, work, or other institutions. The lost past serves as a present escape, when and where one can be who one wants to be—a knight, a princess, a jouster, a sorceress—rather than who one is.

In "Political Medievalisms: The Darkness of the Dark Ages," we trace a more pessimistic view of the Middle Ages than these other fantasies suggest. If medievalism can generally be cast as an optimistic understanding of the past, in the realm of politics, medievalism casts a darker shadow, invoking the violence of the Crusades and the static, limiting nature of feudalism. Even chivalric values, put to positive use in other areas of medievalism, are rendered problematic when they inspire the Ku Klux Klan and its particular brand of segregation and violence. The post-9/11 language of crusade and barbarity, in which the "medieval" language used against Al-Qaeda ultimately casts the West as engaging in a new Crusade, reconstructs the lexicons of difference and exclusion, of "Christian right" (as in correctness) and "pagan wrong" found in the *chanson de geste*. If in most other arenas the medieval period is recast as a colorful, unitary, and positive fantasy, in politics it lives again as the Dark Ages. Also, while the preponderance of examples of political medievalisms cast the Middle Ages in a negative light, illuminating visions of medievalism in political discourse mitigate this overarching vision, such as the Kennedy White House, which was configured as Camelot in the prosperous 1960s and offers an optimistic vision of political medievalism. In addition, rhetorics of globalization construct the Middle Ages as a time of multiple centers of economic strength and political influence, a more shared dynamic of power than anything found since the rise of the city-state in the Renaissance. In politics, medievalism is both instructive and problematic; it can point to a past of shared economic power and global understanding, but it cannot escape the violence and conflict inherent in that vision of the world.

As a whole, the chapters of *Medievalisms: Making the Past in the Present* explore the allure of the past, and how meaning is created in various media that re-create this past. Much of what we analyze is typically considered art, entertainment, and play, but the ludic nature of such medievalism should not eclipse its unique position in contemporary culture. No other historical period can lay claim to such an inspired following so many centuries after its passing: there is no comparable pastime as the Medieval and Renaissance Fair for the Classical or Victorian Era, or for the Long Eighteenth Century. The Middle Ages continues to speak in the present, and although the messages of various and contradictory medievalisms may at times be garbled, the quest to understand the appeal of the past stands at the heart of this inquiry. As many studies of history and historiography proclaim, the past is the present, for the past never dies but is continually reborn in the present moment of consideration and consumption. But the past is also the present in the punning sense that it is a present, a gift, that builds meaning and community for its descendants, albeit with some rougher edges that merit scrutiny as well. It should never be overlooked that a magical and Golden Age medievalism is a charming fantasy, yet one that glosses over the profound historical pains of the period. Through their various modes of meaning, medievalisms invite us both to explore and to ignore history, to create a magical Middle Ages reflective of our unique desires, building our very selves through a relationship with history that is simultaneously the past and the magical past that we wish it might have been. In making the past, we make the present, and thus remake the meanings of both.

Notes

1 Petrarch repeatedly called the period in which he lived "nova" but also "tenebra," dark; his apparent concern was with the breakup of classical Latin into the Romance languages and the loss of texts this linguistic shift entailed. Both Bruni and Biondo adopt a tripartite historical structure (Classical, Medieval, Renaissance), although their specific dates differ somewhat from those understood by contemporary historians.

2 Leslie Workman, "Editorial," *Studies in Medievalism* 1.1. (1979): 1–3, at 1.

3 Pauline Stafford, "Introduction," *The Making of the Middle Ages: Liverpool Essays*, ed. Marios Costambys, Andrew Hamer, and Martin Heale (Liverpool: Liverpool University Press, 2007), 1–14, at 1. Studies that focus on academic medievalisms include Marina Brownlee, Kevin Brownlee, and Stephen Nichols, ed., *The New Medievalism* (Baltimore: Johns Hopkins University Press, 1991); Howard Bloch and Stephen Nichols, ed., *Medievalism and the Modernist Temper* (Baltimore: Johns

Hopkins University Press, 1996); and Kathleen Biddick, *The Shock of Medievalism* (Durham: Duke University Press, 1998).

4 Clare Simmons, "Introduction," *Medievalism and the Quest for the "Real" Middle Ages*, ed. Clare Simmons (London: Cass, 2001), 1–28, at 1.

5 Tom Shippey, "Medievalisms and Why They Matter," *Studies in Medievalism* 17 (2009): 45–54, at 45. It should be noted that Shippey criticizes his definition because, "in its effort to be comprehensive, it lacks clarity" (45); on the contrary, we find the definition admirable for its very comprehensiveness, and believe that any lack of clarity in it should be ameliorated within the context of a specific study that moves from the comprehensive to the particular.

6 Umberto Eco, *Travels in Hyperreality*, trans. William Weaver (New York: Harcourt, Brace, 1986), 68–72.

7 Kathleen Davis and Nadia Altschul, ed. *Medievalisms in the Postcolonial World: The Idea of "the Middle Ages" Outside Europe*, (Baltimore: Johns Hopkins University Press, 2009), 1–24, at 7.

8 Amy Kaufman, "Medieval Unmoored," *Studies in Medievalism* 19 (2010): 1–11, at 4.

9 Carol Robinson and Pamela Clements, "Living with Neomedievalism," *Studies in Medievalism* 18 (2009): 55–75, at 62.

10 David Marshall, "The Haze of Medievalisms," *Studies in Medievalism* 20 (2011): 21–34, at 32.

11 "Medieval, adj. and n.," *OED Online*, accessed 31 December 2011.

12 "Medieval, adj. and n.," *OED Online*.

13 This useful phrase is taken from J. P. Mallory's description of the Indo-Europeans in his book *In Search of the Indo-Europeans* (New York: Thames & Hudson, 1991), 110. However, that a phrase associated with cultures that predate the classical world remains useful to describe the Middle Ages as they appear in the popular imagination is deeply telling of the ways in which the medieval period has been constructed and understood as an undifferentiated "past" separated from the "modern" but not from the "primitive," from which it remains more temporally distant.

14 "Medieval, adj. and n.," *OED Online*.

15 "Renaissance, n.," *OED Online*, accessed 31 December 2011.

16 "Renaissance, n.," *OED Online*.

17 "Prime 9," Major League Baseball Productions/A&E Entertainment; Major League Baseball Network.

2 A Case Study of Dante
Naked Icons of Medievalism

"Signs are small measurable things, but their interpretation is illimitable," writes George Eliot in *Middlemarch*,[1] and although her masterpiece of Victorian manners and mores should not be construed as a textbook in semiotics, she nonetheless captures with lapidary precision an important truth of sign theory: symbols and signs connote as well as denote, and thus their interpretations, despite any intentions of the individuals deploying them, vary widely and, at times, wildly. Representations of the Middle Ages, both in high art and in popular culture, depict not a recognizable Middle Ages—whether this would entail approximating some sort of historical, literary, or sociological accuracy— but the particular Middle Ages necessary for the cultural work undertaken through the act of signifying medievalism. Common iconic signifiers of the Middle Ages include kings, queens, and the aristocracy, ranging from fictional rulers (such as King Arthur) to historical figures (such as Henry II and Eleanor of Aquitaine), as well as historical rulers whose exploits are treated as legend (such as Charlemagne). Dress can also be used to code medievalism, particularly chain mail and armor, as well as other clothing suggestive of a pre-modern state, varying from rags to codpieces, from wimples to chastity belts.[2] Despite their abstract nature, emotions and values, such as courtly love and chivalry, also serve as iconic representations of the Middle Ages; for instance, visual depictions of a knight fighting in a tournament for his beloved make concrete an inchoate sense of what the Middle Ages "really were." Architecture (especially castles, dungeons, and gothic cathedrals) and a variety of other items, objects, artifacts, and persons denote the Middle Ages in the popular imagination; as Vivian Sobchack perceptively points out, even dirt can fill this role, for it constructs the past as the soiled counterpart to modernity.[3]

In this manner, icons of medievalism signify an illusory Middle Ages—never that amorphous yet tantalizing view of a "real Middle Ages"—by stripping both the Middle Ages and the signified itself of any intrinsic meaning. These naked icons nonetheless succeed in signifying the Middle Ages precisely because they need signify nothing beyond the barest parameters of the period, which is to say, something indeterminately old, or wonderfully romantic, or dashingly chivalrous, or unspeakably treacherous, or any other characteristic that reflects contemporary issues but must do so by refracting the past. Medieval icons signify in the present moment of interpretation rather than in the past period of their being, and thus they cannot be divorced from the dual temporality of their medievalism.

Because icons communicate so amorphously, they are subject to manipulation by those seeking either to reinforce or to resist the ideological superstructures of a given society. As Klaus Rieser explains, icons "are in an ambivalent, tension-fraught position between on the one hand a suturing function, as hegemonic tools of dominant groups to control the shifting identities and interests of the mass of people and, on the other hand, as democratic elements in the media age, as symbols of popular identities and interests."[4] Icons build a common culture of shared values and traditions, yet they can be manipulated either to strengthen the ideological hegemony of a ruling class or to question their prior cultural significations. Within capitalistic economies, icons communicate commercial values and are often denuded of extraneous significations. Konstantinos Blatanis argues that icons cannot be extricated from signifying within capitalistic discourse: "Popular-culture icons are recognized and accepted as representations proper but also as 'ultimate surfaces' signifying no other entity than themselves. However, in all cases they are rendered effective only on the condition that they sell a product, an idea, or just an image as such."[5] The semiotic power of medieval icons powerfully connotes the past alive in the present. One need only think of Walt Disney's iconic and defiantly anachronistic castles, rising up among landscapes celebrating Main Street USA. and Tomorrowland, to grasp the power of a medieval icon to commemorate the past while it is nonetheless stripped of any intrinsic meaning or context; it is inscribed within capitalistic discourses that cite the past to profit in the present. How else is one to understand the appeal of such cultural and culinary oddities as Chaucer's Choice Shortbread Rounds or Chaucer's Mead,[6] other than as a citation of the author's iconic status in order to increase food and drink sales in the present?

The inherent tensions of medieval iconicity within literary and popular culture are evident in the treatments, both past and present, of Dante Alighieri (1265–1321), Italy's great medieval poet and author of the *Divine Comedy*, *La Vita Nuova*, and various philosophical and rhetorical tracts. To declare that Dante registers as an icon of the Middle Ages is itself an interpretive statement, for it reduces a complex human being and acclaimed literary genius into a symbol of his era. Furthermore, to argue that Dante is stripped of a particular meaning when he is deployed as an icon implies, at least somewhat, that he should signify in a particular manner and that if he were used properly, he would signify differently. In this regard, it appears that all uses of Dante and other icons of medievalism must in some manner denude them of their essence in deploying them to other ends. The most fervent praise of Dante from his most devoted admirers cannot free these citations from complicity in his re-creation and re-signification: even when the objectives behind such commentary are simply to praise him, such praise then redounds to the benefit of the speaker who is proven to be a kindred spirit appreciative of Dante's artistic accomplishments. Whether through Boccaccio's allusion to Dante's genius or through a T-shirt or coffee mug bearing his image, Dante's iconic status reveals the motivations of the person who cites his name more than any inherent truth about Dante, literature, or the Middle Ages.

One of the first creators of the iconic Dante who has been handed down to the present day is his countryman Boccaccio. In his first exposition on Dante's *Divine Comedy*, Boccaccio builds Dante's moral character in relation to his predecessor's literary masterpiece:

> We now must consider who the author of this book was. This is an important step not only for the book at hand but necessarily for all other books as well. We must not injudiciously put our faith in anyone who does not deserve it. ... What could be worse than believing in humanity and compassion on account of a patricidal killer? in chastity because of a lecher? in the writings of an envious man, or in the Catholic faith thanks to a heretic?[7]

In posing these questions, Boccaccio initiates a literary canonization of Dante—the elaboration of a poet who is clearly not a patricidal killer, lecher, envious man, or a heretic but a man worthy of the reader's deepest trust and the iconic status Boccaccio wishes to bestow upon him. He further celebrates Dante as a "man of noble birth from our own city" whose life "was not at all routine" but was "given over to the study of the liberal arts"; to humanize his icon, Boccaccio adds that "he was not free from the incitements of that passion we generally call 'love.'"[8] Beyond these endearing traits, Boccaccio's exposition on Dante's name adds a mystical quality to the man and his work:

> Something still could be said about his name. First of all, its meaning, "one who gives," is quite clear at a glance; anyone who gives liberally what he has received by the grace of God can deservedly be called "dante." That he gave freely is plainly clear from the effects of his masterpiece, this unique and precious treasure that he offered to all who desire it. His work evenly combines pleasure and healthful usefulness for anyone who seeks them with loving intelligence.[9]

Boccaccio's excursus creates someone of special gifts and generosity, someone who created "with immense effort through sleepless nights and in continuous study," capable of "excelling in divine things."[10] Such descriptions of Dante as a man of study, emotion, generosity, and genius come to define him throughout the ages.

This iconic image of Dante as a committed artist edifying his readers circulates throughout the literary imagination of the western world. However, while Boccaccio clearly viewed Dante as a man of his time and geography, in many ways Dante has been seen less as a medieval figure than as a timeless one. This quality detracts from the specific details of his theology and his politics, treating him instead as a poet of transcendent genius born in the Middle Ages yet somehow surpassing the temporal boundaries of his lifetime, and making him accessible to both literary and popular culture. T. S. Eliot, for instance, famously proclaimed, "Dante and Shakespeare divide the modern world between them," suggesting an interpretation of both authors that separates them from their chronologies in their ability to communicate across time.[11] Eliot's praise of Dante echoes Boccaccio's, and he celebrates the poet's talent for illuminating his readers through the written word: "in making people comprehend the incomprehensible, [Dante] demands immense resources of language and in developing the language, enriching the meaning of words and showing how much words can do, he is making possible a much greater range of emotion and perception for other men, because he gives them the speech in which more can be expressed."[12] The long-dead Dante metaphorically metamorphoses into his literature in such assessments, resulting in a blend of man and masterpiece that invites readers to contemplate an image of Dante as a learned and generous pedagogue.

For such a revered and iconic figure, Dante is nonetheless protean in his multiple literary avatars. As Nick Havely points out, "Dante's afterlife ... has undergone a multiplicity of reincarnations and reinventions."[13] The *Divine Comedy* is also used in multiple ways: as Havely suggests, its "mythic journey from self-destruction to self discovery" has been "continuously appropriated as a means of confronting personal and political crises," with prominent figures taking on "powerful contemporary guises."[14] The upshot, therefore, is that Dante proves a mobile and versatile resource, adaptable beyond his time because of the timelessness attributed to him by such followers as Boccaccio and Eliot. Certainly, numerous canonical authors turned to Dante for inspiration for their literature: Samuel Taylor Coleridge lectured on Dante in 1818, and his Romantic colleagues frequently cited Dante as a source of inspiration. Percy Bysshe Shelley affirmed in admiration, "The *Divina Commedia* and *Paradise Lost* have conferred upon modern mythology a systematic form,"[15] and William Blake illustrated a series of prints to the *Divine Comedy*, which were incomplete at the time of his death in 1827.[16] The Pre-Raphaelites, particularly Dante Gabriel Rossetti, engaged Dante as a source of ideas and imagery; and poetry and literary fiction by Thomas Gray, Ezra Pound, Seamus Heaney, Samuel Beckett, Robert Penn Warren, Walker Percy, and Gloria Naylor, among numerous others, showcase the pervasive literary uses of Dante. In many of these cases, the image of Dante is primarily Boccaccio's, the learned, dedicated genius of poetic craft. Dante's translators, including Henry Boyd, Henry Francis Cary, Henry Wadsworth Longfellow, Dorothy Sayers, John Ciardi, Robert Pinsky, and Mark Musa, also contribute to the literary celebration of Dante by making his genius accessible to English-speaking audiences.

The continued turn to Dante raises questions about how to understand these reconstructions, and what the deployments of Dante as an iconic figure reveal about medievalism. An examination of the way Dante has been imagined physically illustrates how he has come to mean and to perform iconically as an always contemporary representative of both the Middle Ages and a transcendent poetic tradition, as a figure tied profoundly to the past but able to walk into the present in a form recognizable to today's readers. This iconic figure might well be unrecognizable to the poet himself, who saw himself as "a Florentine by birth but not in character"[17] and engaged in a journey very different from the "cammin di nostra vita" ("journey of our life") he imagined in the *Inferno*.[18] The *Divine Comedy* itself provides little sense of Dante's appearance; *Purgatory* mentions that he wears a reed around his waist,[19] and readers are also told that Virgil cleans the Pilgrim's face, "ivi mi fece tutto discoverto/quel color che l'inferno mi nascose" ("he made my face clean, restoring its true color,/once buried underneath the dirt of Hell").[20]

Visual representations of Dante in a particular period often point to the ways he negotiates present and past in the various reconstructions, translations, and inventions that make use of him and his art. In making a visual icon of poetic greatness, these artists strip Dante of some meanings while imbuing him with others. Perhaps Dante recognized the significance of pictorial representations of authors for their subsequent reputations, as his poetic praise of the artist Giotto di Bondone (c. 1267–1337) in *Purgatory* was reciprocated in the visual arts. Dante extols Giotto's palette and suggests that he surpasses the accomplishments of his forebear Cenni di Pepo (Giovanni) Cimabue (c. 1240–c. 1302):

> Credette Cimabue ne la pittura
> tener lo campo, e ora ha Giotto il grido,
> sì che la fama di colui è scura.

> Once Cimabue thought to hold the field
> as painter; Giotto now is all the rage,
> dimming the lustre of the other's fame.[21]

Giotto painted the only extant image of Dante dated to his lifetime, a fresco in the Bargello Museum of Florence, presumably created before Dante's exile in 1301.[22] This image portrays Dante wearing a red cloak—a standard feature of subsequent paintings—but without the laurel wreath that symbolically celebrates his poetic achievements, which, indeed, Boccaccio says Dante desired but never received. (Boccaccio wrote that Dante died "without ever having obtained a title or doctorate degree, for though he wished to receive the laurel crown in his native Florence ... death prevented the realization of this desire."[23]) In Giotto's masterpiece, Dante is a person of his place and time. Images that follow, notably those from late-medieval and early Renaissance paintings and manuscripts, depict a single persona, a stern and serious poet, crowned with a laurel wreath and sporting an impressive nose.

Although created approximately 150 years later, Domenico di Michelino's 1465 painting commonly known as "Dante and the Three Kingdoms," in the Duomo Cathedral in Florence, positions Dante in the center of his divine universe, depicting a poet very much in a medieval mode.[24] Domenico's vision of Dante defines his numerous subsequent images in the popular consciousness, as do Sandro Botticelli's illuminations of the *Divine Comedy* and Luca Signorelli's portrait of Dante in his study.[25] John Flaxman (1755–1826) undertook a series of engravings of the *Divine Comedy*, rendering the complexity of the narrative into a series of elegant and spare images.[26] Gustave Doré's illustrations for the *Divine Comedy* (1861) show a very traditional Dante in an untraditional landscape,[27] and even in Henry Holiday's 1884 painting "Dante and Beatrice," the poet inhabits his austere self, despite being overwhelmed by stomach pains at the sight of Beatrice crossing the Arno.[28] A similar Dante is carved on the front of the National Arts Club in New York City, appearing in a series of roundels with Goethe, Shakespeare, Milton, and Benjamin Franklin. This Dante is fully dressed in poetic robes, hat, and wreath, all symbols of the high seriousness and emotional distance traditionally expected from such a revered figure. This example of American medievalism canonizes Dante as first Italy's, and then the world's, greatest poet. Commemorated on the front of the (American) National Arts Club, Dante transcends geography as much as he transcends temporality.[29] Salvador Dali's illustrations of the *Divine Comedy* accentuate the surreal qualities of Dante's masterpiece, and his bronze busts of Dante and Beatrice capture an austere sense of beauty and grace, while nonetheless modernizing them: for example, Dante's head is perched above a circuit board, linking the medieval poet to Dali's nascent computer age.[30]

These visual depictions of Dante by revered artists cannot circumscribe his subsequent appearances in high or low culture, and more recent images of Dante divest him of these symbols of poetic greatness. One of the more striking of these representations, and one of the more striking popular-culture appropriations of Dante, appears in the *Dante's Inferno* videogame, created by Electronic Arts. In this avatar and its accompanying action figure (see Figure 2.1), Dante stands stripped to the waist with a crusader cross embroidered on his chest, which apparently signifies his penitence in the opening sections of the game. The National Entertainment Collectibles Association (NECA), producer of this seven-inch action figure, describes his deadly accoutrements:

> To celebrate this slab of videogameular awesomeness, NECA is proud to unveil our first Dante figure. Boasting 30 points of articulation, Dante is truly one of a kind. He carries a Cross in a sheath on his right hip, has an interchangeable right hand, and then, of course, there's the scythe …
>
> An imposing sight in itself, Death's scythe stands over eight inches tall! Not only that, but the blade is detachable for hand-held use. It might just be the coolest videogame weapon ever, and it's definitely given its due with the Dante figure. The *Inferno* will never be the same.[31]

Pointing out the inaccuracies and anachronisms of a videogame Dante does not require deep knowledge of medieval culture. For example, Dante's body armor is, at best, superficially medieval. He wears chain mail only on his helmet, which resembles a cross between a crusader helmet and the Sutton Hoo/*Beowulf*

Figure 2.1 NECA Toys, *Dante's Inferno* videogame action figure.

helmet, and this warrior's helmet is oddly crowned with the obligatory laurel wreath. This visual cue of Dante's poetic career is a provocative remnant of his earlier images, a small nod to his historical representation and his identity as a poet (although prying the helmet off does reveal a suitably impressive nose). This fabricated Dante emerges from a fabricated *Divine Comedy* as well. If this videogame becomes a source for experiencing Dante's literature, the *Inferno*, indeed, will never be the same:

> In the upcoming third-person adventure, <u>Dante's Inferno</u>, you are Dante. Death has come to steal your love Beatrice's soul and take her to Hell—but on his way out, you grab his scythe and follow behind. As in Dante Alighieri's epic poem, the <u>Divine Comedy</u>, the poet Virgil guides Dante through the circles of Hell, encountering the embodiments of the seven deadly sins along the way. In the video game, he rides on the backs of demons and slashes his way through each circle on his way to Beatrice, who is being held by Lucifer himself.[32]

This is Dante as action hero rather than as penitent pilgrim, on a quest more like what viewers might encounter in a Hollywood adventure film of kidnap and rescue than in Dante's literature. The creators at Electronic Arts melded together an essentialized and mostly medieval icon ("Dante") as crusader, as penitent, and as anachronistic Rambo; divorced him from his intellectual and historical milieu; deployed him on a militarized version of the love quest coupled with allusions to the Orpheus legend; and embedded some science-fiction trappings as well. In so doing, the videogame collapses the Middle Ages into a unitary project in which any one element can be imposed on any other.

Certain elements of Dante's poem are nonetheless present in the videogame. For example, the seven deadly sins, which govern Upper Hell and Purgatory, are featured prominently; instead of punishing transgressive souls, however, they merely serve as monsters for Dante to fight on his descent. The game quotes John Ciardi's translation of the poem, and a voice-over on the website offers background on Dante (the poet, not the mercenary Italian soldier who stars in the game) and the *Divine Comedy*. In an attempt to develop the connections between the historical Dante and his videogame avatar, the game site comments, "but what starts out as a rescue mission quickly changes into a redemption story, where Dante must confront his own dark past and the sins he carries with him into Hell. He faces the epic inhospitable terrain of the underworld, huge monsters and guardians, sinister demons, the people and sins of his past, and the ultimate traitor: Lucifer himself."[33] Throughout the game, Dante's crusader past is revealed, various criticisms are leveled at priests, and Dante (the gameplayer) absolves numerous souls along the way, which then allows him and Beatrice to be saved at the game's conclusion.[34] Visually, symbolically, historically, and narratively, this Dante shares little in common with earlier visions; the many identifying factors that contribute to earlier pictures of the artist and lover have been removed, and a new identity of mythic warrior stitched onto the naked space of his iconic status.

Surely such a representation of Dante strips him of his status as a high-culture icon of literary greatness, but this naked icon nonetheless captures key aspects of Dante's narrative strategy in line with his theological mission. The game synopsis comments, "you are Dante,"[35] and so why would one expect this

"Dante" to be the historical or literary Dante, if he is you? The *Divine Comedy* begins "Nel mezzo del cammin di nostra vita" ("While halfway through the journey of our life"),[36] casting the Pilgrim as an everyman whose story is as much each reader's own as it is Dante's, and so too does the videogame require its players to participate in the unfolding allegory. If some contemporary readers find it difficult to muster empathy with the austere poet Dante presented by Renaissance painters and their descendants, they must nonetheless accept Dante's call for a participatory experience in his masterpiece of damnation and salvation; gamers must likewise cast aside any hesitation to identify with Dante if they are to enjoy the game they have purchased. They must merge themselves with an iconic representation of Dante throughout the game, and thus the naked icon of literary genius is subsumed, at least imaginatively, within the gamer's consciousness.

In contrast to the vision of Dante as a superhero in a videogame, other popular-culture efforts to update his image cast him as a prosaic figure of modern angst. These re-creations of Dante might initially appear in contrast to the high-culture citations of Dante in literature, but their overall meanings are strikingly similar: by refashioning Dante and his iconicity in high culture, artists assert their unique vision of the past while stressing their affinity toward their forebear, and popular-culture appropriations similarly employ Dante to contemplate life's spiritual challenges. In their illustrated version of the *Divine Comedy*, Sandow Birk and Marcus Sanders offer a slacker's vision of a "Dante" whom readers might see walking down the street. Dressed in jeans and a hoodie, this "Dante" opens his story in the voice of a streetwise and somewhat jaded twenty-something:

> About halfway through the course of my pathetic life,
> I woke up and found myself in a stupor in some dark place.
> I'm not sure how I ended up there; I guess I had taken a few wrong turns.[37]

In Birk and Sanders' adaptation, the worlds of Hell, Purgatory, and Paradise are surprisingly familiar: Hell is Los Angeles, Purgatory is San Francisco, and Paradise is New York City. Remaining faithful to the ideology of Dante's poem, Birk and Sanders rewrite his masterpiece in contemporary language. For instance, they replace Dante's metaphor of his feelings of confusion in *Inferno* with a self-deprecating assessment of slackerdom. Dante describes his inner turmoil as:

> E qual è quei che disvuol ciò che volle
> e per novi pensier cangia proposta,
> sì che dal cominciar tutto si tolle,
>
> tal mi fec' ïo 'n quella oscura costa,
> perché, pensando, consumai la 'mpresa
> che fu nel cominciar cotanto tosta.

For the pilgrim, this is a moment of self-reflection and introspective meditation, and Musa's translation captures the inherent paradox of being and creation, of exhilaration ebbing into trepidation:

> As one who unwills what he willed, will change
> his purposes with some new second thought,
> completely quitting what he had begun,
>
> so I did, standing there on that dark slope,
> thinking, ending the beginning of that venture
> I was so quick to take up at the start.[38]

Birk and Sanders rework this moment of inner reflection as:

> Like some flaky, burnout Deadhead who
> changes his mind every two seconds,
> spacing out on everything and paranoid,
> I stood there in the dark,
> thinking of calling the whole thing off,
> even though I had been so keen at the beginning.[39]

Birk and Sanders's contemporary language provides access to a poem that often requires a more careful reading of the notes than the text itself. Furthermore, by updating the cast of characters among the damned, the authors contemporize Dante's poem while remaining true to its vilification of famous sinners. If some readers do not remember why Cleopatra, Helen of Troy, or Achilles are in the circle of the Lustful (especially given contemporary cinematic portraits of these characters that glorify their dalliances), contemporary figures, such as fallen televangelist Jimmy Swaggart, who is "condemned here for committing sins of lust and sex," are nonetheless recognizable.[40]

In addition to their illustrated and updated translation of the *Divine Comedy*, Birk and Sanders contributed further to Dante's popular-culture iconicity by film-ing the first part of their trilogy: *Dante's Inferno* (2007) was directed by Sean Meredith, with Dermot Mulroney and James Cromwell voicing Dante and Virgil.[41] This modernization of the *Divine Comedy* continues beyond the achievements of their textual adaptation. Some of the language of the film is taken from their books, and the background drawings, against which two-dimensional cardboard cut-outs of Dante, Virgil, and the souls and monsters of Hell operate, are familiar from Birk's illustrations. Nonetheless, there is much less of Dante's context and fewer of Dante's own characters. Some of the adaptations are undeniably hilarious and often quite pointed: Friar Alberigo, who in Canto 33 is so evil that a demon inhabits his body on earth while his soul already suffers in Hell, becomes Dick Cheney, and Fillipo Argenti, whom Dante rebukes and Virgil pushes back into the Styx in Canto 8, becomes "Mr. Argenti, my old swim coach. I hated that bastard." Director Sean Meredith summarizes the film's balance of the authentic and the novel:

> Dante and Virgil's chronicles are set against a familiar backdrop of used car lots, strip malls, gated communities, airport security checks, and the U.S. Capitol. Here, hot tubs simmer with sinners, and the river Styx is engorged with sewage swimmers.
>
> Also familiar is the contemporary cast of presidents, politicians, popes, and pop-culture icons sentenced to eternal suffering of the most cruel and unusual kind: Heads sewn on backwards, bodies wrenched in half, never-ending blow jobs, dancing to techno for eternity, and last, but certainly not least, an inside look at Lucifer himself, from the point of view of a fondue-dunked human appetizer. Each creatively horrific penance suits the crime, and the soul who perpetrated it.
>
> As Dante spirals through the nine circles of hell, he comes to understand the underworld's merciless machinery of punishment, emerging a new man destined to change the course of his life. But not, of course, the brand of his beer.[42]

Anyone familiar with the *Inferno* will agree that a cast of politicians and popes accords with Dante's design, as are punishments designed to match the evils of the souls who endure them, although questions such as who precisely would spend eternity dancing to techno music and what the medieval equivalent would be (pastourellas?) can provide endless and fascinating speculation. The sense that Dante must transform into "a new man destined to change the course of his life" is authentic to the *Divine Comedy* in concept if not in articulation. If Dante emerges from Purgatory, "rifatto sì come piante novelle/rinovellate di novella fronda,/puro e disposto a salire a le stelle" ("reborn, a tree renewed, in bloom,/with newborn foliage, immaculate,/eager to rise, now ready for the stars"[43]), in the film Dante ends with the realization that "I have to watch what I do," a more prosaic revelation, less tied to a specific religious rhetoric and understanding of what salvation from Hell might mean, but nonetheless in keeping with Dante's view of personal reformation.

This tense balancing between the present and the past appears in most contemporary explorations of Dante, his work, and his history, in which the medieval then becomes a metaphor for the present and his iconicity is further bleached of deeper meanings. The metaphor can nonetheless shift its tenor dramatically, such as in Matthew Pearl's *The Dante Club*, another popular-culture rebranding of Dante in which nineteenth-century Americans pay tribute to the poet through the eponymous club celebrating his literature, while a murderous psychopath also pays tribute by dispatching his victims in the style of the suffering souls of the *Inferno*. *The Dante Club* participates in a recent trend in detective fiction in casting canonical authors as figures in or inspirations behind mysteries, such as Philippa Morgan's Chaucer novels, Stephanie Barron's Jane Austen novels, Peter Heck's Mark Twain novels, Gyles Brandreth's Oscar Wilde novels, and J. Barton Mitchell's Edgar Allan Poe graphic novels. In response to these Dante murders, the members of the Dante Club, who are in part responsible for raising interest in the Italian's work in America, must relive the poet's descent into the violence of Hell in their own lives. As Pearl says, "while they [the Dante Club] were translating Dante into ink, someone else was translating Dante into blood," making literal what in the work itself is figurative.[44] Pearl borrows Dante's tripartite organization, and although his references are primarily taken from *Inferno*, he creates a structural tribute to the poet from whom he borrows and whose work he clearly sees as an appropriate locus for examining issues of the present—particularly the influence of literature on human behavior—in a fictional American past, and in a fictional medieval past as well. Cosetta Gaudenzi praises Pearl's *The Dante Club* for its "genuine scholarly interest in the Medieval poet and his attempt to alert readers to the dangers of reading Dante's poem as a mere sensationalistic illustration of punishments."[45] Her sense is that the novel "explores whether, but also how one should read the *Commedia*, and it illustrates the social and political relevance that Dante's work may still have in the modern world,"[46] and Pearl comments that he "wanted to arrange a parallel descent for the Dante Club, to force them to confront the abyss present in their own day and society." This, according to Pearl, "brings the fiction back to history: directly after the Civil War, crime and murder rapidly increased in American cities. So while the Dante murders are fictions, they reflect a very real, new sense of violence that had to be confronted at all levels of American culture."[47] These jostling histories of Dante's Middle Ages and of post-bellum America distort the very meanings of history, yet should one expect history either from Dante or from Pearl? For the medieval poet and his modern-day admirer, history is a palimpsest on which fiction is overwritten, and Pearl merely expands on this dynamic by rewriting Dante into a dual icon of literary genius for both aesthetes and serial killers.

If Pearl's *The Dante Club* makes Dante's translators its main characters, Nick Tosches's *In the Hand of Dante* instead re-creates Dante, poet and pilgrim, for a more skeptical world of his own devising, an angst-ridden, postmodern environment in which Dante proves himself prescient to modern-day alienation. Revolving loosely around the discovery of an autographed manuscript of the *Divine Comedy* in a cellar in the Vatican Library, and switching between the main narrator, Nick, and Dante himself, the novel disassociates Dante from the overall meaning of his literature. *In the Hand of Dante* participates in a recent trend of popular-culture works that links canonical authors and artists to modern-day intrigues surrounding their artifacts, which are ruthlessly sought for their commercial potential rather than for their aesthetic merits, including Dan Brown's *The Da Vinci Code* (2004), Ian Caldwell and Dustin Thomason's *The Rule of Four* (2005), and J. L. Carrell's *The Shakespeare Secret* (2007). Tosches's antihero Nick explicitly argues for a reformulation of iconic views of Dante:

In the course of those years, I had come to perceive something of Dante the man—not the unquestioned, infallible god that centuries of reverent scholarship had made of him, but the man whom his contemporaries had remembered in none too glowing a light—and, more so, to perceive the

Commedia's great flaw. It was a flaw of form. Dante had chosen a cage of rhyme and meter so confining that no majestic creation could survive within it, so often did it necessitate unnatural affectation to accommodate structure, so often were soul and beauty and power sacrificed to sustain the structure of the work, as might be done by one so cold as to value artfulness above art. As no beautiful wild bird born to soar free could survive in a cage, so it was with the beautiful wild bird of his poem.[48]

Tempting as it is to ask what scholarship Tosches has been reading, it is clear that it did not provide him with much understanding of medieval poetics, as the creation of "wild birds" devoid of artifice hardly matches the sense of artistic creation understood by Dante and his compatriots. The task of this novel, then, is to distance Dante both from the form and content of his poem, to suggest that what Dante really believed was not the Christian doctrine of his period, but a much more mystical, cabbalistic vision of divine unity, taught to him by Jacob, an old Jewish philosopher schooled in multiple languages (Greek, Hebrew, Arabic, French, Latin, Italian) and gematria (which, it is suggested, comes from *geometria*), which then explains the numerical interests expressed in the *Divine Comedy*. Tosches affirms, near the end of the novel:

> On his return voyage to Venezia, the poet swore he would make a poetry that truly would sunder the artifice of all verse: a poetry that would destroy and discard that artifice for the natural, indwelling meters of breath and the elements; a wild, free, and powerful rhythmus beyond all meters devised; a poetry that ran *sans entraves*, a poetry that roared as he had roared into the waves of the sea, and as the sea itself had roared; a poetry whose dactyls blossomed in the soft, gentle, imperceptible sough and sigh of the All.[49]

Here one finds a medieval poet and a Middle Ages whose preoccupations are not remotely those of his own historical time: Dante's interest in the politics of his age, which adds significant irreverence to the *Divine Comedy*, his understanding of medieval philosophy, theology, and allegory so eloquently put forward in the "Epistle to Can Grande," and his engagement with a medieval form of craft are cast onto the breeze. This medievalism eradicates everything a modern reader might find challenging in Dante's work and invents a Dante who mirrors him or herself (essentially himself; women have no place other than as sexual objects in Tosches's novel), a Dante preoccupied not by his accomplishments but by a series of textual failures (both in the *Vita Nuova* and the *Divine Comedy*) and impulses to destroy that which he had created because of their supposed flaws.

Such a characterization of Dante does not take into account one of the challenges that many readers encounter in his literature—his inherent arrogance and faith in the rightness of his understanding, which is nonetheless combined with a profound humility. Dante's understanding of the ineffability of Paradise is evident. He says, in Canto 1,

> Nel ciel che più de la sua luce prende
> fu' io, e vidi cose che ridire
> né sa né può chi di là sù discende;
>
> perché appressando sé al suo disire,
> nostro intelletto si profonda tanto,
> che dietro la memoria non può ire.
>
> Veramente quant' io del regno santo
> ne la mia mente potei far tesoro,
> sarà ora materia del mio canto.
>
> I have been in His brightest shining heaven
> and seen such things that no man, once returned
> from there, has wit or skill to tell about;
> for when our intellect draws near its goal
> and fathoms to the depths of its desire,
> the memory is powerless to follow;
> but still, as much of Heaven's holy realm
> as I could store and treasure in my mind
> shall now become the subject of my song.[50]

Dante understands the limits of his project, but Tosches constructs him more as a medieval incarnation of Ezra Pound finding that "Paradise lay beyond words."[51] Tosches assigns the authorship of large sections of the *Paradise*, those he does not like, to Dante's son, who seeks revenge against his father for writing about his beloved Beatrice while married to his mother. Indeed, the emphasis on the wind (which also represents the breath of God and the soul in the old Jew's teachings) is taken directly from Pound's "Do not move/Let the wind speak/that is paradise."[52]

Tosches's novel condemns Dante for not imagining a place for himself in Hell, conveniently forgetting Dante's exposition of his own likely posthumous history, elucidated in *Purgatory*:

> "Li occhi," diss' io, "mi fieno ancor qui tolti,
> ma picciol tempo, ché poca è l'offesa
> fatta per esser con invidia vòlti.
>
> Troppa è più la paura ond' è sospesa
> l'anima mia del tormento di sotto,
> che già lo 'ncarco di là giù mi pesa."
>
> "My sight one day shall be sewn up," I said,
> "but not for long; my eyes have seldom sinned
> in casting envious looks on other folk.
> It is a greater fear that shakes my soul:
> that of the penance done below—already
> I feel on me the weight those souls must bear."[53]

These lines also suggest a place in Paradise for Tosches's narrator, someone who in the course of the novel kills or is accessory to the murders of eleven people and a dog; steals priceless historical documents; fornicates with "the wife, girlfriend, mistress, mother, and daughter of every guy I knew";[54] and, despite an extensive screed against the publishing industry's lack of interest in great literature (presumably his own), divides into pieces and sells off to the highest bidder an irreplaceable and priceless historical treasure, using the money to gamble, extort, and fornicate further. In a sense, then, this medievalism offers a Dante and a *Divine Comedy* with less connection to its time even than the *Dante's Inferno* videogame, which at least retains the seven deadly sins, if not in a form that Dante Alighieri would recognize.

Although Dante's life and literature may not appear to be fodder for children's literature, as works such as Pearl's *The Dante Club* and Tosches's *In the Hand of Dante* implicitly demonstrate, the potential to appropriate the poet respects no boundaries between juvenile and adult fiction. In Daniel Handler's *A Series of Unfortunate Events*, a series of thirteen books that begins with *The Bad Beginning* and ends with *The End*, the narrator and purported author Lemony Snicket dedicates each tome to his beloved but deceased Beatrice: "To Beatrice—darling, dearest, dead," he laments in *The Bad Beginning*; "For Beatrice—I cherished, you perished,/The world's been nightmarished," he mourns in *The End*.[55] As Dante's immortal love for Beatrice carries him through to the light of Paradise, Handler's Snicket likewise sees his deceased Beatrice as the lodestar of his life, yet in losing her, he merely becomes mired in stasis, narrating the tragic events that befall the protagonists of the series, the young orphans Violet, Klaus, and Sunny Baudelaire. Handler's novels are saturated with allusions to canonical literature, many of which appear little more than random asides to adult readers of children's novels, yet the allusions to Dante's Beatrice imbue these already dark tales with a deeper sense of melancholic and irrecoverable angst, which, while alien to Dante's Beatrice and her successful guidance of Dante as a lost soul in the *Divine Comedy*, nonetheless seems true, if exaggeratedly so, to Dante's sense of the pain of living without love.

This sampling of medieval and post-medieval versions of and responses to Dante and his work in high, popular, and even children's culture shows a distinct pattern. Because Dante himself is quickly detached from the specifics of his medieval context, becoming a figure of timeless genius who speaks across generations, he increasingly comes to stand for everyone, and the *Divine Comedy* becomes a metaphor for any kind of morality, whether it is the fairly neutral "I'd better watch what I do" sentiment concluding the Birk and Sanders film, or the morality of the loyalty quest of the Electronic Arts *Dante's Inferno* videogame. Hell may not be "other people," as Jean-Paul Sartre suggested,[56] but it is a place for other people, history's villains like Hitler, Jimmy Swaggart, Mussolini, or Dick Cheney, or more personal ones like "Mr. Argenti, my old swim coach." This contemporary view of Dante and his oeuvre both expands and limits; while the message of Birk and Sanders' film suggests that anyone in the modern world can relate to and learn from the *Inferno*—all of us jeans-and-hoodie wearing slackers who illegally download Metallica—it also takes away the specificity of Dante's conception of the divine plan, "l'amor che move il sole e l'altre stelle" ("the Love that moves the sun and the other stars"), which reduces the *Divine Comedy*'s complex philosophy to a simple behavioral model.[57]

In rendering Dante into a naked icon, artists and creators from both high and popular culture resignify his cultural meaning to fit their unique agendas, but then, so too did Dante himself. In refashioning his life and love, his political struggles and his intellectual daring, into literary fare, he stripped himself of some meanings and built others to fit into his narrative design. Consequently, these naked icons of Dante are not so much to be bewailed as bastardized visions of his literary greatness but as necessary interventions into the past to create in the present. As with all other iconic representations of the Middle Ages, from Chaucer cookies to Disney's castles, the medieval is bleached in favor of the modern, but what is reconceived in the process offers intriguing insights into the longevity and adaptability of the medieval past: from naked icons spring endless permutations of the medieval of today.

Notes

1 George Eliot, *Middlemarch* (1872; Oxford: Oxford University Press, 1998), 23.
2 Chastity belts offer a particularly interesting case study in medievalism; see Albrecht Classen, *The Medieval Chastity Belt: A Myth-Making Process* (New York: Palgrave Macmillan, 2007).
3 Vivian Sobchack, "The Insistent Fringe: Moving Images and Historical Consciousness," *History and Theory* 36.4 (1997): 4–20.
4 Klaus Rieser, "Icons as a Discursive Practice," *U.S. Icons and Iconicity*, ed. Walter Holbling, Klaus Rieser, and Susanne Rieser (Vienna: Austrian Association for American Studies, 2006), 7–16, at 8.
5 Konstantinos Blatanis, *Popular Culture Icons in Contemporary American Drama* (Cranbury, NJ: Associated University Presses, 2003), 11.
6 See Chaucer's Wines, online, for the full range of mead selections; available: www.chaucerswine.com/Home.asp, accessed 24 January 2012. Finding Chaucer's Shortbread Rounds requires a visit to the Kent Cheese Company, which also makes Chaucer's Choice cheese.
7 Giovanni Boccaccio, "Accessus," *Boccaccio's Expositions on Dante's* Comedy, ed. and trans. Michael Papio (Toronto: University of Toronto Press, 2009), 39–52, at 43.
8 Giovanni Boccaccio, "Accessus," 43–44.
9 Giovanni Boccaccio, "Accessus," 45.
10 Giovanni Boccaccio, "Accessus," 45.
11 T. S. Eliot, "Dante," *Selected Essays* (1932; New York: Harcourt, Brace, 1950), 199–327, at 225.
12 T. S. Eliot, "What Dante Means to Me," *To Criticize the Critic* (New York: Farrar, Straus, & Giroux, 1965), 125–35, at 134.
13 Nick Havely, "Introduction: Dante's Afterlife, 1321–1997," *Dante's Modern Afterlife*, ed. Nick Havely (London: Macmillan, 1998), 1–14, at 3. Additional studies of Dante's influence on subsequent writers include Steve Ellis, *Dante and English Poetry: Shelley to T. S. Eliot* (Cambridge: Cambridge University Press, 1983); Stuart McDougal,

Dante among the Moderns (Chapel Hill: University of North Carolina Press, 1985); Valeria Tinkler-Villani, *Visions of Dante in English Poetry: Translations of the* Commedia *from Jonathan Richardson to William Blake* (Amsterdam: Rodopi, 1989); and Antonella Braida, *Dante and the Romantics* (Basingstoke: Palgrave Macmillan, 2004).

14 Nick Havely, "Introduction: Dante's Afterlife," 3.

15 Percy Bysshe Shelley, "A Defense of Poetry," *Shelley's Critical Prose*, ed. Bruce McElderry (Lincoln: University of Nebraska Press, 1967), 3–40, at 25.

16 Albert S. Roe, *Blake's Illustrations to the* Divine Comedy (1953; Westport, CT: Greenwood, 1977).

17 Dante Alighieri, "The Letter to Can Grande (Epistolam X ad Canem Grandem della Scala)," *Literary Criticism of Dante Alighieri*, ed. and trans. Robert S. Haller (Lincoln: University of Nebraska Press, 1973), 95–111, at 95.

18 Quotations from and translations of the *Divine Comedy* are taken from Dante Alighieri, *The Divine Comedy*, trans. Mark Musa (Bloomington: Indiana University Press, 1996–2004); this passage is taken from *Inferno* 1.1. We chose this translation for its readability and its fidelity to Dante's original. While poetic, Musa's translation takes fewer liberties than some of his more famous colleagues, from Longfellow to Ciardi; on the other hand, Musa's attempt to create a natural English form by using iambic pentameter reflects a medievalist impulse in itself. Musa makes the poem fluid to English readers the way the Italian *terza rima* is for Italian readers, but this transformation filters the poem through Shakespearian poetics. Musa comments that "a translator should make a good lover," and adds, "Perhaps it must always be the voice of Dante's translator that we hear ... , but he should have listened most carefully to Dante's voice before he lets us hear his own" ("Translator's Note: On Being a Good Lover," in Dante Alighieri, *The Divine Comedy, Vol. 1: Inferno*, trans. Mark Musa [New York: Penguin, 2003], 57–64, at 57). Given this consciousness of his project, Musa appears to feel responsible for replicating as much of Dante's language and the experience of reading it as possible.

19 Dante and Musa, *Purgatory*, 1.94–95.

20 Dante and Musa, *Purgatory*, 1.128–29.

21 Dante and Musa, *Purgatory*, 11.94–96.

22 Images of Dante, as depicted by various artists, are readily available online. For Giotto's image of Dante, see Andrew Martindale and Edi Baccheschi, ed., *The Complete Paintings of Giotto* (New York: Abrams, 1966), 122.

23 Giovanni Boccaccio, "Accessus," 44.

24 A full-color reproduction of Domenico's portrait of Dante is available in Hein-Thomas Schulze Altcappenberg, *Sandro Botticelli: The Drawings of Dante's* Divine Comedy (London: Royal Academy of Arts, 2000), 21.

25 For the illustrations of Sandro Botticelli (1445–1510), see Hein-Thomas Schulze Altcappenberg, *Sandro Botticelli: The Drawings of Dante's* Divine Comedy. Luca Signorelli (1499–1502) painted a fresco of Dante with scenes from the *Divine Comedy* for the Cappella di San Brizio, in the Duomo, Orvieto; see Creighton Gilbert, *How Fra Angelico and Signorelli Saw the End of the World* (University Park: Pennsylvania State University Press, 2003), esp. 53–54.

26 Francesca Salvadori, ed., *John Flaxman: The Illustrations for Dante's* Divine Comedy (Milan: Royal Academy of Arts, 2004).

27 For Doré's illustrations, see Eugene Paul Nassar, *Illustrations to Dante's* Inferno (Rutherford: Fairleigh Dickinson University Press, 1994). Nassar's study includes numerous artists not addressed in this brief survey of Dante's iconicity in the visual arts, such as Yan Dargent, Luigi Ademolli, Federico Zuccaro, Francesco Scaramuzza, Joseph Anton Koch, and Ebba Holm, among numerous others.

28 Henry Holiday's "Dante and Beatrice" is held at the Walker Art Gallery in Liverpool and is reproduced in Christopher Wood, *The Pre-Raphaelites* (London: Seven Dials, 1981), 128.

29 Italy's tendency to treat Dante as a Renaissance figure reveals the flimsy borders dividing the Middle Ages, the Renaissance, and medievalism. Dating the Renaissance from Giotto is effective in art but not literature; it is hard to argue, for instance, that Boccaccio (1313–75), who follows Dante by several years, is not a medieval writer.

30 Wolfgang Everling, *Dante Alighieri's* Divina Commedia *Illustrated by Salvador Dalí* (Hamburg: Verlag Dante, 2003).

31 "To Hell and Back," necaonline.com, accessed 30 November 2011.

32 "NECA Takes You to Hell and Back with New *Dante's Inferno* Collectible Figure," youbentmywookie.com, accessed 30 November 2011.

33 "NECA Takes You to Hell and Back."

34 Many thanks to Kevin Stevens, who constructed an extensive walk-through of the game that indicated its many features, both those with antecedents in Dante's poem and those wholly fabricated. While some demons, like Minos, are similar to Dante's descriptions, many of the monsters of Hell bear more resemblance to creatures from science-fiction horror movies than to those from medieval narratives.

35 "NECA Takes You to Hell and Back."

36 Dante and Musa, *Inferno*, 1.1.

37 Sandow Birk and Marcus Sanders, *Dante's Inferno* (San Francisco: Chronicle, 2004), 1.1–3. See also their *Dante's Purgatorio* (San Francisco: Chronicle, 2005) and *Dante's Paradiso* (San Francisco: Chronicle, 2005).

38 Dante and Musa, *Inferno*, 2.37–42.

39 Birk and Sanders, *Dante's Inferno*, 2.37–42.

40 Birk and Sanders, *Dante's Inferno*, 27.

41 *Dante's Inferno,* dir. Sean Meredith, perf. Dermot Mulroney and James Cromwell (Dante Films, 2007).

42 Sean Meredith, "Film Synopsis," www.dantefilm.com/about.html, accessed 27 November 2011.

43 Dante and Musa, *Purgatory*, 33.143–45.

44 Matthew Pearl, "A Conversation with the Author," *The Dante Club* (New York: Random House, 2004), 375–78, at 376.

45 Cosetta Gaudenzi, "Dante's Introduction to the United States as Investigated in Matthew Pearl's *The Dante Club*," *Italian Culture* 26 (2008): 85–103, at 86.

46 Cosetta Gaudenzi, "Dante's Introduction," 86.

47 Matthew Pearl, "A Conversation with the Author," 376.

48 Nick Tosches, *In the Hand of Dante* (Boston: Back Bay, 2002), 136.

49 Nick Tosches, *In the Hand of Dante*, 371.

50 Dante and Musa, *Paradise*, 1.4–12.

51 Nick Tosches, *In the Hand of Dante*, 25.

52 Ezra Pound, "Notes for Canto CXX," *Drafts and Fragments of Cantos CX–CXVII* (New York: New Directions, 1959), qtd. in Tosches, *In the Hand of Dante*, 26.

53 Dante and Musa, *Purgatory*, 13.133–38.

54 Nick Tosches, *In the Hand of Dante*, 37.

55 Daniel Handler (as Lemony Snicket), *A Series of Unfortunate Events: The Bad Beginning* (New York: HarperCollins, 1999) and *The End* (New York: HarperCollins, 2006), unnumbered dedication pages of the respective novels.

56 In Sartre's words, "L'enfer, c'est les autres," in *No Exit and Three Other Plays* (New York: Vintage, 1955), 47.

57 Dante and Musa, *Paradise*, 33.145.

3 Literary Medievalisms
Inventing Inspirations

In his "Meditation 17," John Donne famously declares, "No man is an *Iland*, intire of its selfe; every man is a peece of the *Continent*, a part of the *maine*,"[1] and these words convey his belief in the interconnectedness of all humanity and the undesirability of isolating oneself from human fellowship. His insights capture an important truth of literary influence as well: writers cannot isolate themselves from the languages, literatures, and previous authors whom they have learned and loved, assimilated and incorporated, resisted and renounced. It is inconceivable that an author could be wholly free from external influence; to create *ex nihilo* is an impossibility proven simply by the fact that others have come before. Countless studies of great writers and their literature explore how various factors—including previous authors, literary traditions, historical events, and sociological milieus—influenced them while composing their works, thereby proving the truth of Donne's words beyond the realm of interpersonal metaphysics to that of literary creation as well.

Among modern theories of literary influence, the ideas of T. S. Eliot and Harold Bloom stand preeminent. Eliot argues in his "Tradition and the Individual Talent" that authors must be assessed in relation to the past: "No poet, no artist, has his complete meaning alone. His significance, his appreciation is the appreciation of his relation to the dead poets and artists. You cannot value him alone; you must set him, for contrast and comparison, among the dead."[2] Yesteryear's authors provide the necessary ballast to assess the accomplishments of their descendants, and Eliot builds upon this foundation to argue that artists must evacuate themselves of themselves to better accommodate previous traditions: "What happens is a continual surrender of [the artist] as he is at the moment to something which is more valuable. The progress of an artist is a continual self-sacrifice, a continual extinction of personality."[3] Immersed in the past as they create in the present, artists and authors experience a never-ending dialectical tension between their unalterable presence in the present and an illuminating and paradoxically liberating absence in the past.

In contrast to Eliot's proposition that writers must purge themselves of their present consciousness to access the past, Bloom sees literary influence as a source of anxiety, if not outright aggression. Writers must struggle to find fresh styles that will separate their works from those of past greats, and in so doing they confront and conquer their forebears. In *The Anxiety of Influence*, Bloom summarizes his argument that poetic influence necessitates perversions of previous traditions:

> Poetic Influence—when it involves two strong, authentic poets—always proceeds by a misreading of the prior poet, an act of creative correction that is actually and necessarily a misinterpretation. The history of fruitful poetic influence ... is a history of anxiety and self-saving caricature, of distortion, or perverse, willful revisionism without which modern poetry as such could not exist.[4]

Accepting traditions without confronting them, Bloom suggests, would result in aesthetic sterility, and so authors must determine innovative ways to speak: they must cast off the weight of previous traditions so that new ones may be born. It is a process of wrestling and renewal, with flashes of discord and insight illuminating the creation of new literatures.

To Bloom's dismay, many critics have misconstrued his ideas concerning poetic anxiety to argue for Oedipal readings of literary influence, in which the "son" (a modern writer) metaphorically kills his "father" (canonical writers and previous traditions) to assert his unique identity as an artist. In response, Bloom declared, "I never meant by 'the anxiety of influence' a Freudian Oedipal rivalry, despite a rhetorical flourish or two in this book."[5] Such a misreading of Bloom nonetheless offers a complementary model of understanding poetic influence, for surely even the cockiest of today's authors must ponder the challenge of writing in the shadow of Chaucer, Shakespeare, Milton, Wordsworth, Austen, and Woolf. In attempting to join their ranks, who would not feel intimidated by their majestic accomplishments? Whether through parody, pastiche, allusion, or intertextual play, contemporary writers embed past traditions in their writing, if not in an attempt to "kill" their forebears, at least in an effort to tame them so that their own unique achievements shine through according to their own artistic merits.

In a refreshing rejoinder to Eliot's, Bloom's, and Oedipal models of poetic influence, based as they are on comparison and confrontation, Stephen Guy-Bray sees relationships between poets as potentially amorous, and he challenges assumptions of conflict foregrounded in the creative process: "there is no reason to think that a poet's engagement with literary tradition must be an unpleasant duty or a painful task." In his analysis of the poetic relationships between various authors, including those of Geoffrey Chaucer and Edmund Spenser, Walt Whitman and Hart Crane, and, appropriately enough, T. S. Eliot and Harold Bloom, he observes the "long tradition among poets of presenting their predecessors and contemporaries as inspiring love as well as poetry" and investigates how "this sort of writing positions the two poets as a male couple."[6] Surely writers may be inspired by the past as much as they may feel overwhelmed by it, and they are as likely to feel affectionate gratitude for literary masterpieces that spurred them to write as they are to feel anxiety, emptiness, or aggression. Writing is in many ways a naked act, an opening of the self to the world, and writers may expose themselves with affection, rather than aggression, as they interact with the past to create in the present.

Each of these theories concerning the ways in which authors grapple with the past bears merit, and perhaps they are most usefully thought of as uniting in a host of mirrorings and refractions that may then describe a particular writer's relationship to his or her forebears. Authors could simultaneously construe their relationships to the past as an erotic misprision, or as an anxious grappling with a living history, or as an Oedipal trauma with a beloved (rather than feared) father, or any other permutation of the ways in which one can view the past and those who have come before. In sum, the potential interlacings of these various theories point to the ways in which authors must invent both past authors and the past itself as they rewrite their influences into unique forms, and so they must also retrospectively attune their unique agendas for their contemporary audience. Quite simply, no model of literary influence can delineate precisely the ways in which authors voice their narratives to contrast with and/or to complement those of the past. But as long as time remains linear, writers must tackle both the burdens and the pleasures of history, and in so doing, they invent the past as they need it to be. If one were to consider, for example, Chaucer's influence on such subsequent canonical authors as Shakespeare, Milton, Wordsworth, and Eliot (both George and T. S.), it would quickly become apparent that no single model of poetic influence could successfully decipher the complex web of influence and inspiration between them.

As authors invent the necessary inspirations from past authors and aesthetic traditions to write new literature, those who rewrite the Middle Ages concomitantly invent new Middle Ages for their fictions as well. In this regard, literary medievalism bears many branches: that of canonical authors whose fictions and treatises shaped the course of western literature, including Boethius, Chrétien de Troyes, Marie de France, Geoffrey Chaucer, Dante Alighieri, Giovanni Boccaccio, Christine de Pizan, and Thomas Malory; that of literary masterpieces that established foundational patterns, plotlines, and themes, including *The Consolation of Philosophy*, *Lancelot (Le Chevalier de la charrete)*, "Lanval," the *Canterbury Tales*, the *Divine Comedy*, *The Decameron*, *The Book of the City of Ladies*, and *Morte D'Arthur*; that of literary traditions and genres that shaped the expected parameters of various narratives, including dream visions, allegories, lyrics, epics, fabliaux, and romances; and that of social, religious, and theological beliefs that promise to guide readers to spiritual truths, including chivalry, Christianity, and crusading. The Middle Ages, a *tabula rasa* always inviting new rewritings and fresh erasures, inspires numerous authors due to its malleability and protean adaptability for a wide range of narrative and poetic circumstances.

The scope of literary medievalisms ranges extensively, and it is beyond the purview of this chapter to map out the multiple trajectories drawn by the many authors who have animated medieval traditions in subsequent literatures of subsequent centuries. Nonetheless, authors of certain periods sometimes coalesce around specific, if idiosyncratic, visions of the Middle Ages and its authors. In the Renaissance, writers such as Edmund Spenser and Shakespeare exhibit a sense of idyllic nostalgia for the Middle Ages, positing it as a time of innocence and poetic virtuosity, while diverging in their view of medieval history's role in the present day. In the opening lines of Spenser's *Faerie Queen*, the narrator breaks from the classical pastoral tradition of shepherds singing for their beloveds to undertake an epic poem, one that is grounded in the medieval genre of courtly romance and its tales of knights' daring chivalry on behalf of their ladies:

> Lo I the man, whose Muse whilome did maske,
> As time her taught in lowly Shepheards weeds,
> Am now enforst a far vnfitter taske,
> For trumpetes sterne to chaunge mine Oaten reeds,
> And sing of Knights and Ladies gentle deeds;
> Whose prayses hauing slept in silence long,
> Me, all too meane, the sacred Muse areeds
> To blazon broad emongst her learned throng:
> Fierce warres and faithfull loues shall moralize my song.[7]

With these words Spenser's narrator elevates the romances of his medieval English predecessors to the status of epic, traditionally recognized as the highest of poetic forms. Aligning his work with romances of England's legendary King Arthur, Spenser creates a prototypically English medievalism through his story of the king questing for Gloriana's love. In contrast, Shakespeare's medievalism primarily addresses true historical figures, as is apparent in such history plays as *King John*, *Richard II*, *Henry IV Part I*, *Henry IV Part II*, *Henry V*, and *Richard III*. Shakespeare, however, writes history for its dramatic effect rather than with any deep concern for historical verisimilitude, and so he frequently alters historical accounts to increase the dramatic appeal of his source material. Donald Watson assesses the meaning of history for the Elizabethan stage and contends, "The Elizabethans themselves never doubted that all history is contemporary history: the value of history exists in its practical utility as a teacher of religious, ethical, and administrative lessons."[8] Furthermore, because Shakespeare's plays are continually restaged in the present, such adaptations of history resonate beyond Shakespeare's initial productions to any contemporary staging, as Ton Hoenselaars notes: "As Shakespeare's histories are appropriated, they come to mediate between medieval past and contemporary politics ... thus writing modern history both in Britain and abroad."[9]

Although Spenser and Shakespeare employ the medievalisms of romance and history divergently, the poets unite in extolling Chaucer as the preeminent poet of the Middle Ages. In his *Shepheardes Calendar*, Spenser praises his forebear in the allegorical form of Tityrus:

> The God of shepheardes *Tityrus* is dead,
> Who taught me homely, as I can, to make [compose poetry].

> He, whilst he lived, was the soveraigne head
> Of shepheards all, that bene with love ytake.[10]

Spenser invents a vision of Chaucer as a pastoral poet with these lines, despite the fact that Chaucer's literature—the rowdy ribaldry of the *Canterbury Tales*, the epic romance of *Troilus and Criseyde*—does not evince an overarching pastoral sensibility. Shakespeare likewise lauds Chaucer for his poetic genius in the Prologue of *The Two Noble Kinsmen* (which he co-wrote with John Fletcher). The play is based on Chaucer's *Knight's Tale*, which also inspired the frame narrative of Shakespeare's *A Midsummer Night's Dream*, and Shakespeare and Fletcher attribute an international reputation to their English forebear:

> We pray our play may be so; for I am sure
> It has a noble breeder and a pure,
> A learned, and a poet never went
> More famous yet 'twixt Po and silver Trent.
> Chaucer (of all admir'd) the story gives;
> There constant to eternity it lives.[11]

Both Spenser and Shakespeare invent Chaucer as an inspirational figure for their writing: Spenser in the formulation of a pastoral Chaucer, Shakespeare in the creation of a Chaucer heralded as an international genius. Neither image is based on accurately representing Chaucer as an historical figure or as a poet of the fourteenth century; rather, the Chaucers that Spenser and Shakespeare respectively create suit their rhetorical purposes and strengthen their membership in the English literary pantheon through their reverent citations of the man often deemed its father figure.

Considering Chaucer as Shakespeare's literary father may be insufficient to understand Chaucer's, and as a result, the past's meaning for Shakespeare. As E. Talbot Donaldson points out, Chaucer's work offers not just subject matter but also "a kind of substructure," or even an "infrastructure," in which the earlier poet provides, if not a foundation, then "some of the important ways and means by which he was enabled to build as he did."[12] Donaldson notes a surprising lack of verbal echoes between the two authors, yet his exploration of Shakespeare's debt to Chaucer recognizes a series of connections that go beyond the appropriations of stories, whether historical or literary, and instead creates a legacy evident primarily in a shared sense of tone and treatment of narrative. To wit, in Shakespeare's various replayings of the "Pyramus and Thisbe" story from Ovid (in *Romeo and Juliet* and *A Midsummer Night's Dream*, both written circa 1595), Donaldson suggests that his recognition both of the absurdity of the recognition scene and the dangers of giving in to that absurdity grow from the playwright's understanding of Chaucer's staging of a similar scene in *Troilus and Criseyde*: "If Shakespeare learned anything from Chaucer about melodrama," Donaldson acknowledges, "it was to curb its rhetoric so that it does not become posturing." Such a realization allowed Shakespeare to modulate tone and rhetoric, such that "no perception of absurdity is, of course, permitted in the deaths of Romeo and Juliet," despite the play's structural parallels to Ovid's and Chaucer's handling of similar material.[13] Donaldson also credits Chaucer for Shakespeare's understanding of the "irresponsibility of romantic love," which "leads [his characters] to speculate on and illustrate love's obsessiveness and its randomness: how quickly lovers surrender themselves to it," and "how haphazard the process of love is."[14] In seeing the influence of Chaucer on Shakespeare's understanding of love, war, comedy, rhetoric, and parody, it is clear that Chaucer's meaning as literary father of Shakespeare goes well beyond such straightforward issues as what to write about and how to write about it. Chaucer does not constitute a source parallel to Holinshed's *Chronicles* for Shakespeare, but rather a source of how fiction and genres function. Shakespeare's medievalism, therefore, appears not so much in how he talks about the kings under whom Chaucer wrote, but in how he writes about pressing subjects that jointly interested both him and his forebear.

Shakespeare found Chaucer's literature inspiring, yet there is little sense that he found in the medieval past a paradigm for his sense of personal identity; in contrast, the Cavalier poets of the seventeenth century, including Richard Lovelace, Robert Herrick, and Sir John Suckling, styled themselves as modern reincarnations of medieval chivalric ideals. These poets celebrated a vision of courtly life starkly distinct from the Puritans against whom they fought the English Civil Wars to defend King Charles I, and, in so doing, they invented contemporary identities for themselves through the medieval past. Poems such as Lovelace's "To Lucasta, Going to the Wars" and "To Althea, from Prison" affirm the inherent nobility of serving the king, and Herrick's "Delight in Disorder" and "Corinna's Going A-Maying" and Suckling's "A Ballad upon a Wedding" and "Out upon It!" express a *carpe diem* sensibility of randy and ready sensuality. In regard to its medievalism, the cavalier ideal harkens back to medieval social structures in which dutiful courtiers serve their king with unwavering loyalty while also striving to please their beloveds. As Earl Miner observes, "Cavalier social values are those of an aristocracy and gentry that two centuries before might have struggled against the throne but that now sought to protect the King for all his faults ... against his enemies, and to preserve crown, mitre, estates, and what was often termed 'our liberties.'" Thus, despite the lasciviousness and droll sensuality of many Cavalier lyrics, the poets look to past cultural mores to defend their current practices, as Miner affirms: "That conception of the good life that is central to Cavalier poetry is in one sense wholly traditional."[15] The Cavaliers' debt to the Middle Ages is slight in terms of specifically literary creation, yet critical to their self-fashioning as courtiers, which again points to the amorphousness of literary influence in determining how subsequent authors see themselves in relation to historical eras prior to their own.

As the preceding examples of Renaissance and seventeenth-century poetry indicate, it is difficult to imagine how authors could avoid employing medievalisms in their writing to some degree, given the relative proximity of the historical periods and the continuing intellectual influence of the Middle Ages. Although the Renaissance was envisioned as a break with the medieval past, such a break could not dissever the present from the past, especially in regard to pedagogical practices that focused heavily on Latin writers and that held sway throughout both periods. As such, the so-called break between the Middle Ages and the Renaissance may be seen as more an anxiety about the past's influence than a real severance from this past. Within this pedagogical milieu, even authors frequently viewed as unsympathetic to medieval values and aesthetics are steeped in medieval traditions. Due to his Puritanism, John Milton is often viewed as anti-medieval in his religious sensibilities, but, as John Mulryan explores, Milton's literature, including his masterpiece *Paradise Lost*, bounteously employs medieval themes and motifs:

> What possible sympathy could [Milton] the arch-Puritan reformer, the enemy of schoolmen and episcopacy, of all manner of hierarchy and priesthood, of censorship and papal power, have with the Middle Ages? This roll call of anti-medieval epithets applied to Milton may suggest that scholars are so learned in this corner of Milton's imagination that they have forgotten an obvious truth about Milton, that he was intimately acquainted with almost all of the learning available during his time, including the classical, the medieval, and the modern.[16]

From his anti-monasticism to his iconography, from his readings of Chaucer and *Roman de la Rose* to his sense of history's meaning, Milton saturates his literature with medievalisms. Highly conservative in many of his positions yet strikingly unorthodox in others (such as in his defense of divorce), Milton ambivalently rewrites in *Paradise Lost* the "advent'rous song" of Adam and Eve's fall through a lens both medieval and resolutely anti-medieval. Certainly the numerous echoes of Dante throughout *Paradise Lost* point to Milton's interest in his predecessor's treatment of spiritual truth within a cosmic vision of narrative, one that his own epic addresses with no less a sense of religious conviction, if with diverging views of dogma.[17]

The late eighteenth century witnessed a striking revival of interest in the Middle Ages, and a striking shift in the meaning of the Middle Ages, due to the popularity of gothic novels. Although poetic and prose traditions are often seen as at odds with each other and were constituted differently in the eighteenth century, the advent of the gothic is apparent in the fascinations of poets like Thomas Gray, who are often considered to be so much of their time that they are cut off from their relationships to the past. In his poem "The Bard," Gray imagines a Welsh poet addressing Edward I, conqueror of his lands and people; his story draws from the legend that Edward ordered the death of all Welsh bards in 1283. This poem was printed by Horace Walpole, author of such gothic fictions as *The Castle of Otranto* (1764) and *The Mysterious Mother* (1768), at his gothic-revival home, Strawberry Hill, in 1757, and so the connection between Gray's "The Bard" and the rise of this medieval fascination seems almost over-determined.[18] As a prophecy of the return of Welsh rulers and a revival of British poetry under Spencer, Shakespeare, and Milton, "The Bard" links contemporary with medieval concerns, echoing the kinds of connections made between pre-Anglo-Saxon and Norman history seen in Geoffrey of Monmouth and Gerald of Wales. The tendency to reach over a specific era to an imagined past both takes advantage of the Middle Ages as subject matter and also revives a medieval methodology of thinking about one's history in relationship to the present. Declaring, "No more our long-lost Arthur we bewail/All-hail, ye genuine kings, Britannia's issue, hail!" Gray engages a double medievalism, looking to the past to think through the meaning of that past and its repercussions in the present.[19]

The medieval influence on Gray can also be seen in his poems on Norse and Welsh subjects such as "The Descent of Odin" and "The Triumph of Odin," connected in part to his fascination with the fabricated Irish bard Ossian, whose "Fragments" the literary charlatan James McPherson claimed to have translated. In this fascinating case of a medieval poet invented virtually *ex nihilo*, McPherson published a series of works, mostly based on folk tales and other legends, that he claimed represented the work of the long-lost Gaelic poet Ossian. Although Samuel Johnson essentially called McPherson's bluff, many other famed authors in addition to Gray found Ossian intensely thrilling— Goethe found the pseudo-poet's work deeply moving, and, in *The Sorrows of Young Werther*, he portrays Werther reading selections aloud to Lotte, holding them up as some of the greatest poetry ever written. Many readers credited Ossian with all that was great about English poetry, seeing echoes of Homer, antecedents of Milton, and the true roots of a British heritage.[20] This poetic medievalism provided more than a way of casting the intersections of past and present history, and although Ossian was not the true origin of British literature, the fascination with him presaged the gothic revival and its literary achievements that bore fruit on their own merits. "Gothic poetry," Michael Alexander points out, "still shows as a minor byway. Yet it proved to be enchanted ground," for poems and stories of mystery and horror have proven to be resilient fantasies of the Middle Ages. As in many such instances, literary medievalisms need not be accurate, as problematic a term as this may be for assessing an author's relationship to the past, as they must be fertile.[21]

Although he recognized the Ossian poems as fabrications, Horace Walpole admired them, and fabrications of this kind were essential to the genre he created: at the heart of *The Castle of Otranto* lies a fabricated manuscript, found in the library of an ancient (read, medieval) family. Walpole's novel unleashed a wave of such pseudo-medieval narratives of intrigue, horror, and suspense, many of which are set in a vaguely recognizable yet foreboding medieval past, one populated with dank castles, fetid dungeons, and cursed or morally opprobrious nobles. *The Castle of Otranto* itself blends these medieval themes with, in Michael Alexander's estimation, an "eclectic medley of elements supposedly found in medieval romances ... it is a hybrid of various genres."[22] William Warburton, who edited Alexander Pope's works, describes *The Castle of Otranto* as set "in Gothic chivalry," such that it catalyzes "the full purpose of the *ancient Tragedy*, that is, *to purge the passions by pity and terror*."[23] "Gothic chivalry" conflates distinct and incongruous medieval concepts, combining the architectural style of medieval cathedrals with the refined manners and social practices of courtiers. Other novels in the eighteenth-century gothic tradition—including Matthew Lewis's *The Monk* and *The Castle Spectre*, and Ann Radcliffe's *The Mysteries of Udolpho* and *The Italian*—are medieval only in a very loose sense, primarily from an attenuated vision of the genre of medieval romance and their settings in medieval architecture of castles and gothic cathedrals.[24] Yet the entire gothic impulse, poetic and novelistic, shows medievalism as an effective method of literary exploration in the face of the decline in prestige of neoclassical notions of literary perfection and social control. As with the Pre-Raphaelites in the nineteenth century, writers of the gothic revival found in their fictional Middle Ages an escape from the rigidities of eighteenth-century classical ambition and public correctness.

For Romantic poets such as William Wordsworth, William Blake, Samuel Taylor Coleridge, Percy Bysshe Shelley, Lord Byron, and John Keats, the Middle Ages constituted a time of innocence without artifice, but they also acknowledged the artistic genius of their predecessors. Wordsworth, for instance, praised Chaucer's genius and its influence on his work: "When I began to give myself up to the profession of a poet for life, I was impressed with the conviction, that there were four English poets whom I must have continually before me as examples—Chaucer, Shakespeare, Spenser, and Milton. These I must study, and equal if I could; and I need not think of the rest."[25] Wordsworth is primarily remembered for his evocative celebrations of nature and childhood, as well as for his *Prelude*, which, as its subtitle affirms, considers the "Growth of a Poet's Mind," but he also translated several of Chaucer's poems, including the *Prioress's Tale*, the *Manciple's Tale*, and excerpts from *Troilus and Criseyde*. Beyond such affinities with past writers, Romantic poets imbued many of their works with medieval models of poetic personae: Elizabeth Fay identifies a form of "radical troubadourism" in the Romantic era, discerning in the literature of Coleridge, Keats, and Shelley a "poetic posture that associates itself with the radical posture of the medieval troubadour who pits himself against the lord-knight figure in an essentially political act by assailing, both emotionally and sexually, the lord-patron's lady."[26] The medieval persona of the troubadour is inextricably interlaced with subsequent models of poetic self-presentation, and although Romantic poets are typically referred to as such for their view of nature, medieval troubadours model a complementary image of the self as lover that permeates the artistic achievements of their Romantic descendants.

Within this tradition, Porphyro's stealing off with Madeline in Keats's "The Eve of St. Agnes" exemplifies the allure of the troubadour persona. Keats's Middle Ages is a complex place, clearly a Romantic reconstruction balanced between the static and cold world represented by the beadsman and the colorful, lively world of love and desire. The past is represented by the figures on the chapel:

> Along the chapel aisle by slow degrees:
> The sculptur'd dead, on each side, seem to freeze,
> Emprison'd in black, purgatorial rails:
> Knights, ladies, praying in dumb orat'ries,
> He passeth by; and his weak spirit fails
> To think how they may ache in icy hoods and mails.[27]

The constant reminder of the ancient, cold beadsman constructs the Middle Ages as a past, even as the narrative of the poem brings it into the present, yet this tension remains as the action moves to the poem's main story, and readers are reminded that the "argent revelry" is "haunting fairily/The brain, new-stuffed, in youth, with triumphs gay/Of old romance."[28] The love story at the poem's center is this "old romance," and, ultimately, it becomes as much a part of the past as the stone knights and ladies in the chapel, as Keats concludes, "And they are gone: ay, ages long ago/These lovers fled away into the storm."[29] Furthermore, "The Eve of St. Agnes" is hardly Keats's only visit to the Middle Ages; in the companion "The Eve of St. Mark," "A Dream, After Reading Dante's Episode of Paolo and Francesca," and "Written on a Blank Space at the End of Chaucer's Tale of *The Flowre and the Lefe*," he returns to the past, a place both fruitful and sterile. Chaucer and Dante may inspire Keats, but they also leave him with a similar sense of floating "about that melancholy storm."[30] Indeed Keats's persistent interest in the Middle Ages seems an engagement cast in cold and death, and in "La Belle Dame sans Merci," the knight sees "pale kings and princes too,/Pale warriors, death-pale were they all."[31] The medieval period, for Keats, is itself a kind of Belle Dame sans Merci: seductive, desirable, and captivating but ultimately dead, a place of seeming warmth and music and sweetness, but ultimately one where "the sedge is withered from the lake,/And no birds sing."[32]

This tension between poetic inspiration and a potentially sterile past is upturned by Walter Scott, who found only fruit in his imagined Middle Ages. His investigation of the period began in poetry, with *The Lay of the Last Minstrel*, *Marmion*, and *The Lady of the Lake*, all of which were more widely popular than the efforts of his Romantic colleagues. These drew their subject matter from medieval romance, and much of their metrical form from Chaucer.[33] With his shift to prose, Scott brought his vision of the Middle Ages to a wider and more ardent audience. In so doing, he created a "new romance of British national identities," which "celebrates past and present and puts them into a new relation."[34] Calling Scott's medievalism one that invokes "the fun of dressing up and make-believe," Michael Alexander notes that Scott's "message is that the spirit of chivalry need not die."[35] Indeed, the role of Sir Walter Scott in perpetuating literary medievalisms during the Romantic era cannot be underestimated, for not only did he revive interest in medieval romances, his romances themselves became "medieval" models for subsequent writers. In such novels as *Ivanhoe* and *Quentin Durward*, Scott reinvented the Middle Ages for his contemporary readers, and in so doing, he reinscribed such literary and cultural stereotypes from western accounts of the Crusades as the virtuous knight, the beautiful beloved, and the treacherous Saracen. These are not just cultural artifacts, but also exempla; as Michael Alexander observes, from Scott forward, the "Medieval Revival was always interested in how people should live now in the present as well as in how people had lived in the past."[36] As such, the "past" becomes more an inclusive fiction than a specific history. Jerome Mitchell extensively documents Scott's indebtedness to medieval sources,[37] but it is ironic that Scott's novels defined the Middle Ages for the nineteenth-century cultural imaginary, because so many of his novels are set in a post-medieval period: the events of *Guy Mannering* occur in the 1760s through 1780s; *Rob Roy* takes place in the years prior to a 1715 uprising in Scotland; and *The Pirate* unfolds during the advent of the eighteenth century. In Scott's medievalism, as in the pseudo-medievalism of gothic novels, the allure of the Middle Ages is divorced from history yet organically linked to a pre-modern sensibility that can only be denoted through the amorphous boundaries of the Middle Ages.

The Industrial Revolution radically transformed British and American society during the Victorian era, and many authors and artists turned to the Middle Ages as an antidote against the pressures of modernity in celebration of a simpler time of simpler technologies: crafts instead of industries, artisans instead of factory workers. Alfred, Lord Tennyson's paean to the Middle Ages, *The Idylls of the King*, takes as its subject the matter of the Arthurian legend, imbuing these medieval tales with a sense of melancholic regret for their inevitable passing. The Victorian era is rightly acclaimed as the apex of the British novel tradition, and although the medievalism of such authors as Jane Austen, Charlotte Brontë, Charles Dickens, Wilkie Collins, Anthony Trollope, and George Eliot is often muted, it nonetheless appears in telling moments of characterization, setting, or plot. Austen's *Northanger Abbey* parodies the gothic novels popular in her day, which were themselves medievalist ventures. As Judith Johnston explains in her discussion of George Eliot's medievalism,

> In sociological terms, the interest in the Middle Ages is a response to the transition from a medieval to a "modern" world. The Victorians believed a similar transition was occurring in their own time, rapidly emerging into a new scientific and industrial energy that had its effect on every strand of life, but particularly upon religion and the arts. By the 1870s Eliot was writing from the centre of this new and modern British world.[38]

As Johnston explores in regard to Eliot's oeuvre, *Middlemarch* employs tropes of medieval hagiography, allegory, and exemplum, and *Daniel Deronda*, those of chivalric quests and Arthurian legends. Also, canonical authors of the Middle Ages influenced their Victorian descendants such as Dickens, who found inspiration in Chaucer and Dante.[39] If many of these Victorian novelists are not as committed and idealistic in their medievalism as Tennyson, they nonetheless perpetuate the importance of invented medievalisms in literature by recognizing the Middle Ages's duality as a past unto itself and as a past increasingly reinvented by their gothic predecessors and other authors.

If the preceding paragraphs unintentionally suggest that medieval authors and medievalisms have been enthusiastically embraced as they are reformulated into new literatures, the great American humorist and novelist Mark Twain refutes such a simplified acceptance of the period. More particularly, Twain's invective focuses on Walter Scott's medievalism and the ways in which his romances perpetuated medieval modes of thought in the U.S. South of the 1800s. In his *Life on the Mississippi* (1883), Twain excoriates Scott's novels for their re-creations of the Middle Ages, which he believes to be staunching cultural progress in the South:

> Then comes Sir Walter Scott with his enchantments, and by his single might checks this wave of progress, and even turns it back; sets the world in love with dreams and phantoms; with decayed and swinish forms of religion; with decayed and degraded systems of government; with the sillinesses and emptinesses, sham grandeurs, sham gauds, and sham chivalries of a brainless and worthless long-vanished society. He did measureless harm; more real and lasting harm, perhaps, than any other individual that ever wrote. Most of the world has now outlived [a] good part of these harms, though by no means all of them; but in our South they flourish pretty forcefully still. ... There, the genuine and wholesome civilization of the nineteenth century is curiously confused and commingled with the Walter Scott Middle-Age sham civilization, and so you have practical, common-sense, progressive ideas, and progressive works, mixed up with the duel, the inflated speech, and the jejune romanticism of an absurd past that is dead, and out of charity ought to be buried. But for the Sir Walter disease, the character of the Southerner ... would be wholly modern, in place of modern and mediaeval mixed, and the South would be fully a generation further advanced than it is.[40]

Describing the Middle Ages as "brainless and worthless" certainly indicates Twain's contempt for the period, but how seriously can one take his words, given his own interest in the Middle Ages? Several of his works, including *A Connecticut Yankee in King Arthur's Court* and *The Personal Recollections of Joan of Arc*, are set in the medieval period, and even such lesser works as "A Medieval Romance," which satirizes the romance tradition, seem to do so with affection rather than with contempt. At the conclusion of *Connecticut Yankee*, protagonist Hank Morgan, who mercilessly derided the manners and mores of the Middle Ages throughout the novel, regrets his inability to return to this past, which adumbrates the desirability of a past that Twain mercilessly derides in other circumstances.

Twain's efforts to free American literature from medieval influences met with little success. Many of his predecessors in the U.S. South, including William Gilmore Simms, John Pendleton Kennedy, William Caruthers, and Nathaniel Beverly Tucker, wrote novels celebrating chivalry and other medieval values in a style reminiscent of Walter Scott, and many of his literary descendants also imbue their works with medieval and romance themes. Montserrat Ginés suggests that the history of the U.S. South attuned it to the appeal of Miguel de Cervantes's mad romancer Don Quixote, whose influence she identifies in the works of Mark Twain, James Branch Cabell, William Faulkner, Eudora Welty, and Walker Percy: "Within the context of American society as a whole, historical, economic, and social factors shaped the culture of the South, giving it a distinct character, and these factors provided extraliterary underpinnings sensitive to the Quixote spirit."[41] Likewise, the gothic elements of southern literature, notable in the works of such luminaries as William Faulkner, Truman Capote, Tennessee Williams, Carson McCullers, and Flannery O'Connor, again offer a doubled and doubly refracted medievalism, both of medieval traditions and of gothic reimaginings of the Middle Ages in subsequent centuries. Anthony Di Renzo sees in Flannery O'Connor's writings echoes of the medieval carnivalesque and grotesque, from riotous festivals such as the Feast of Asses on New Year's Day to gargoyles perched outside cathedrals; he argues that "the outlandish caricatures that decorate the façade of her fiction mock our pretensions but glorify our incorrigibleness. Her art sarcastically celebrates humanity's polymorphous perversity."[42] For these authors, latent medievalism and the darkness of the gothic tradition imbue their fictions with the appropriate atmosphere and philosophical tenor to consider the condition of the South and the cultural weight of losing the Civil War, a conflict fought to defend the indefensible practice of slavery.[43]

Medievalism in American literature is not the exclusive provenance of the South, and Kim Moreland traces medieval themes in the works of such modern American authors as F. Scott Fitzgerald and Ernest Hemingway. Within an American ideology that celebrates capitalism, industry, and the individual, medieval values might appear antithetical, and Moreland readily admits that medievalism clashes with American mores: "The medievalist impulse clearly runs counter to the major American cultural tradition at every point. Medievalism is feudal and aristocratic rather than capitalistic and democratic, Roman Catholic rather than Puritan, European rather than nationalist American, and regressive rather than progressive."[44] One could quibble with many of Moreland's assessments, but perhaps the most important distinction to make would be that she blends cultural structures of the Middle Ages with those of medievalism. The Middle Ages was indeed feudal, aristocratic, Roman Catholic, European, and, one could argue, regressive; medievalism, on the other hand, need share none of these characteristics, and many American narratives of medievalism combine a medieval setting with a quintessentially American, Horatio Alger-inspired narrative of rags to riches (such as the films *First Knight* [dir. Jerry Zucker, 1995] and *A Knight's Tale* [dir. Brian Helgeland, 2001]).

Such tales are not medieval in their origins, yet they are nonetheless strikingly successful examples of the ways in which the Middle Ages can be re-appropriated to suit American tastes.

This brief survey of medieval influences in the British and American literary record can in no measure circumscribe the truly international scope of this phenomenon. Most apparently, medieval influences flourished in other literatures of western Europe, including but not limited to those of Spain, France, Italy, and Germany. Furthermore, the reach of medievalism into nations associated with the British Commonwealth, including Australia, New Zealand, Canada, South Africa, and India, testifies to its ready adaptability to a range of cultural discourses. As Stephanie Trigg observes of Australian medievalisms, "Lacking a medieval past of their own, Australians have constructed an elaborate network of links to such a past, whether that past is idealized or the subject of critique, and whether those links are material, institutional, or imaginative."[45] Again, we see the necessity of invention: with the arrival of British convicts in Australia beginning in the late 1700s, the land (despite its indigenous peoples) appeared to lack the necessary history—the necessary medieval history—for certain types of artistic creation, and thus it was fabricated with nods, but not subservience, to the history of the Commonwealth.

Also, although this chapter focuses on the varying influence of medievalisms on the Anglo-American tradition, it would be remiss not to mention that medievalisms are truly international in their scope. The colonial regimes of Europe spread the legend and literature of the Middle Ages across the globe, and thus medievalisms emerge in the literatures of South and Central America, Africa, and Asia. Such an intermingling of indigenous and European traditions results in shifting views of the medieval past, as Simon Gikandi cautions: "For medievalism and medieval studies to be rethought from the vantage of decolonization, they need to be liberated from the baggage of barbarism—and the dangers associated with it—imposed on Africa by the agents of European modernization."[46] Gikandi admonishes his readers to engage critically with the Middle Ages and its complicity in current debates on postcolonialism and globalism, a strikingly necessary intervention into how medievalisms are formulated in the present day. For the greatest threat of medievalisms is their aura of fantasy, their magical patina that rewrites a troubling past into a rousing history. Hamid Bahri and Francesca Canadé Sautman likewise state, "No doubt, extolling the beauties of the past—especially those of the 'medieval' past—can be dangerous, but postcolonial theory encourages us to see that past as well as the present outside of the ironclad model of a Western-centered grand narrative."[47] Doing so, however, requires a double, if not a triple, parallax of vision: of the medieval past, of the present, and of the fantasies that create and re-create both temporalities to situate the rhetorical exigencies of the ideological superstructure at hand.

Continually reconceived, continually reimagined: the Middle Ages is invented anew in each telling, and the foundational aspect of the era in subsequent literatures is its malleability to the purposes of the author rewriting the past to

write in the present. One cannot dissect influences with the precision of a sur-
geon, no matter the theoretical models offered for this task. As Donald Howard
so elegantly summarizes, "Literary influence and literary tradition seem to
operate by their own logic, and we sense this operation in a poem or a poet but
cannot state its rules, cannot be sure there *are* rules."[48] But to consider the ways
in which descendant writers invent and reinvent the Middle Ages and its
authors is to be struck by the singular and ever renewable appeal of these
so-called Dark Ages, so malleable as to be the site of pastoral pleasures and of
gothic terrors, or of numerous other values and tropes. As Eliot's, Bloom's, and
Guy-Bray's theories of poetic influence implicitly demonstrate in their contrasts
and convergences, literary influences spin in unwieldy and overlapping arcs, yet
the one constant is the creator who must make the past mean something new in
the present, if his or her work is to succeed in speaking to the people of this
present, and possibly to those of the future as well.

Notes

 1 John Donne, "Meditation XVII" from *Devotions upon Emergent Occasions*, *The
   Complete Poetry and Selected Poems of John Donne*, ed. Charles Coffin (New York:
   Modern Library, 1952), 440–41, at 441.
 2 T. S. Eliot, "Tradition and the Individual Talent," *The Sacred Wood: Essays on
   Poetry and Criticism* (1920; London: Methuen, 1967), 47–59, at 49.
 3 T. S. Eliot, "Tradition and the Individual Talent," 52–53.
 4 Harold Bloom, *The Anxiety of Influence: A Theory of Poetry*, 2nd ed. (New York:
   Oxford University Press, 1997), 30.
 5 Harold Bloom, *The Anxiety of Influence*, xxii.
 6 Stephen Guy-Bray, *Loving in Verse: Poetic Influence as Erotic* (Toronto: University
   of Toronto Press, 2006), 106, xii. It should be noted that Guy-Bray's study focuses on
   male–male relationships, such as those among Virgil, Statius, and Dante, and
   between Chaucer and Spenser, but there is no reason to believe such poetic erotics
   could not be in play in poetic relationships between men and women or between
   women and women.
 7 Edmund Spenser, *The Faerie Queene*, ed. Thomas Roche (London: Penguin, 1987),
   1.1–9. Studies of Spenser's medievalism include David Summers, *Spenser's Arthur:
   The British Arthurian Tradition and the* Faerie Queen (Lanham: University Press of
   America, 1997); Paul Rovang, *Refashioning "Knights and Ladies Gentle Deeds": The
   Intertextuality of Spenser's* Faerie Queene *and Malory's* Morte D'Arthur (Madison:
   Fairleigh Dickinson University Press, 1996); and Andrew King, The Faerie Queene
   and Middle English Romance: The Matter of Just Memory (Oxford: Clarendon,
   2000).
 8 Donald Watson, *Shakespeare's Early History Plays: Politics at Play on the Elizabethan
   Stage* (Athens: University of Georgia Press, 1990), 11.
 9 Ton Hoenselaars, ed., *Shakespeare's History Plays: Performance, Translation, and
   Adaptation in Britain and Abroad* (Cambridge: Cambridge University Press, 2004), 39.
10 Edmund Spenser, *The Shepheardes Calendar*, *The Yale Edition of the Shorter Poems
   of Edmund Spenser*, ed. William Oram, et al. (New Haven: Yale University Press,
   1989), 1–213, at 112, lines 81–84 of "June."
11 William Shakespeare and John Fletcher, *The Two Noble Kinsmen*, *The Riverside
   Shakespeare*, ed. Blakemore Evans (Boston: Houghton Mifflin, 1997), 1689–1731, at
   1692, lines 9–14.

12 E. Talbot Donaldson *The Swan at the Well: Shakespeare Reading Chaucer* (New Haven: Yale University Press, 1985), 5.

13 E. Talbot Donaldson, *The Swan at the Well*, 26.

14 E. Talbot Donaldson, *The Swan at the Well*, 30.

15 Earl Miner, *The Cavalier Mode from Jonson to Cotton* (Princeton: Princeton University Press, 1971), 43, 309.

16 John Mulryan, "Introduction," *Milton and the Middle Ages*, ed. John Mulryan (Lewisburg: Bucknell University Press, 1982), 11–16, at 11.

17 Studies of Milton's debts to Dante include Irene Samuel, *Dante and Milton: The Commedia and Paradise Lost* (Ithaca: Cornell University Press, 1966); John Demaray, *Cosmos and Epic Representation: Dante, Spenser, Milton, and the Transformation of Renaissance Heroic Poetry* (Pittsburgh: Duquesne University Press, 1991); and Robert Hollander, "Milton's Elusive Response to Dante's *Comedy*," *Milton Quarterly* 45.1 (2011): 1–24.

18 Michael Alexander, *Medievalism: The Middle Ages in Modern England* (New Haven: Yale University Press, 2007), 1.

19 Thomas Gray, "The Bard: A Pindaric Ode," *The Works of Thomas Gray*, ed. William Mason (London: J. F. Dove, 1927), 386, at 3.1.13–14.

20 For a further discussion of the fascination with Ossian, see Michael Alexander, *Medievalism*, 3–4.

21 Michael Alexander, *Medievalism*, 8.

22 Michael Alexander, *Medievalism*, 5.

23 William Warburton, *The Works of Alexander Pope*, qtd. in Peter Sabor, *Medieval Revival and the Gothic*, *The Cambridge History of Literary Criticism*, Vol. 4: *The Eighteenth Century*, ed. H. B. Nisbet and Claude Rawson (Cambridge: Cambridge University Press, 1997), 470–88, at 481.

24 For a study of gothic influences in architecture, see Chris Brooks, *The Gothic Revival* (London: Phaidon, 1999).

25 William Wordsworth, *Translations of Chaucer and Virgil*, ed. Bruce Graver (Ithaca: Cornell University Press, 1998), 3.

26 Elizabeth Fay, *Romantic Medievalism: History and the Romantic Literary Ideal* (Basingstoke: Palgrave Macmillan, 2002), 7–8.

27 John Keats, "The Eve of St. Agnes," *The Complete Poems*, ed. John Barnard (New York: Penguin, 1973), 312–24, at 312, lines 13–18

28 John Keats, "The Eve of St. Agnes," 313, lines 39–41.

29 John Keats, "The Eve of St. Agnes," 323, lines 370–71.

30 John Keats, "A Dream, after Reading Dante's Episode of Paolo and Francesca," *The Complete Poems*, 334, line 14.

31 John Keats, "La Belle Dame sans Merci: A Ballad." *The Complete Poems*, 334–36, at 335, lines 37–38.

32 John Keats, "La Belle Dame sans Merci," 336, at lines 47–48.

33 For a discussion of Scott's specific use of Chaucer, see Michael Alexander, *Medievalism*, 40–43.

34 Michael Alexander, *Medievalism*, 49.

35 Michael Alexander, *Medievalism*, 49.

36 Michael Alexander, *Medievalism*, 64.

37 Jerome Mitchell, *Scott, Chaucer, and Medieval Romance: A Study in Sir Walter Scott's Indebtedness to the Literature of the Middle Ages* (Lexington: University Press of Kentucky, 1987), esp. 12–32.

38 Judith Johnston, *George Eliot and the Discourses of Medievalism* (Turnhout, Belgium: Brepols, 2006), 4.

39 Dickens's familiarity with Chaucer is documented in such studies as Lawrence Besserman, "Chaucer and Dickens Use Luke 23.24," *Chaucer Review* 41.1 (2006): 99–104, and F. T. Flahiff, "'Mysteriously come together':

Dickens, Chaucer, and *Little Dorrit*," *University of Toronto Quarterly* 61.2 (1991–92): 250–68.

40 Mark Twain, *Life on the Mississippi*, The Oxford Mark Twain, series ed. Shelley Fisher Fishkin (1883; New York: Oxford University Press, 1996), 467.

41 Montserrat Ginés, *The Southern Inheritors of Don Quixote* (Baton Rouge: Louisiana State University Press, 2000), 3.

42 Anthony Di Renzo, *American Gargoyles: Flannery O'Connor and the Medieval Grotesque* (Carbondale: Southern Illinois University Press, 1993), 215–16

43 For a study of the gendered repercussions of medieval ideals of chivalry and masculinity in southern literature, see Tison Pugh, *Queer Chivalry: Medievalism and the Myth of White Masculinity in Southern Literature* (Baton Rouge: Louisiana State University Press, 2013).

44 Kim Moreland, *The Medievalist Impulse in American Literature: Twain, Adams, Fitzgerald, and Hemingway* (Charlottesville: University Press of Virginia, 1996).

45 Stephanie Trigg, "Introduction: Medieval and Gothic Australia," *Medievalism and the Gothic in Australian Culture*, ed. Stephanie Trigg (Turnhout, Belgium: Brepols, 2005), xi–xxiii, at xxiii.

46 Simon Gikandi, "Africa and the Signs of Medievalism," *Medievalisms in the Postcolonial World: The Idea of "the Middle Ages" Outside Europe*, ed. Kathleen Davis and Nadia Altschul (Baltimore: Johns Hopkins University Press, 2009), 369–82, at 371.

47 Hamid Bahri and Francesca Canadé Sautman, "Crossing History, Dis-Orienting the Orient: Amin Maalouf's Uses of the 'Medieval,'" *Medievalisms in the Postcolonial World* 174–205, at 175.

48 Donald Howard, "Flying through Space: Chaucer and Milton," *Milton and the Line of Vision*, ed. Joseph Wittreich (Madison: University of Wisconsin Press, 1975), 3–23, at 21.

4 "Medieval" Literature for Children and Young Adults
Fantasies of Innocence

Medievalism in children's and Young Adult (YA) literature teaches young readers about the past, as it domesticates that past in order to explore the present.[1] The emergence of "medieval" literature for children testifies to both a fascination with and a misunderstanding of the period as an innocent and magical time, a misprision that extends to children themselves in the pre-Freudian yet persistent vision of children and childhood as emblematic of innocence.[2] As John Ganim argues of medievalism and its production of innocence in the present, "Filtered through the lens of Tolkien, Disney, various theme restaurants, commercially produced 'fairs,' and even Las Vegas ... popular medievalism has acquired the function of licensing innocence."[3] Within the realm of children's literature, for example, Howard Pyle's *The Merry Adventures of Robin Hood* and Sidney Lanier's *The Boy's King Arthur* tell medieval stories but remove the darker, more troubling elements from them, creating a somewhat cartoonish world; in complementary contrast, J. R. R. Tolkien, Lloyd Alexander, and Susan Cooper create medieval worlds in which far more complex problems and relationships can be resolved yet nonetheless retain an aura of fantasy. Recent "medieval" children's and YA literature, such as Judson Roberts's *Strongbow Saga* and Karen Cushman's *Catherine, Called Birdy*, use the Middle Ages simultaneously to defamiliarize the setting and to examine contemporary problems. Throughout these vastly disparate works registers the figure of the child, one who must be protected from the Middle Ages while simultaneously being exposed to it.

In all "medieval" children's and YA literature, neither the Middle Ages nor the Child exists. Jacqueline Rose argues in her classic study of children's literature, *The Case of Peter Pan, or the Impossibility of Children's Fiction*, that authors fabricate the children for whom they write their fictions:

> There is no child behind the category "children's fiction" other than the one which the category itself sets in place, the one which it needs to believe is there for its own purposes. These purposes are often perverse and mostly dishonest, not willfully, but of necessity, given that addressing the child must touch on all of these difficulties, none of which dares speak.[4]

As authors of children's literature construct the children necessary for their fictions, both in terms of the readers of the texts and any children depicted therein, so too must authors of "medieval" children's literature create the Middle Ages that they need for their narratives to unfold: an Edenic era of innocence, or a time of courtly intrigue, or a fantasy of dungeons and dragons, or any combination or extension thereof, for the purpose of rewriting the past in the present. These multiple, contradictory, and illusory Middle Ages, like the child whom Rose theorizes, are often "perverse and mostly dishonest," yet such dishonesty need not be lamented as much as explored for the contradictions and contrasts between yesterday and today that mutually constitute the child and the past.

Perhaps what is most striking about the tendency of post-medieval authors to mine the Middle Ages for children's fictions is a vision of the past, in its history and its literature, as reflective of or particularly appropriate to young people's experience. Given the various wars, plagues, and sundry unpleasantnesses of the Middle Ages, and given its vision in the popular imagination as the Dark Ages, its suitability as a setting for children's fictions and children's moral lessons is anomalous. Such a tendency to bowdlerize the past is evident in Lady Charlotte Guest's 1838 translation of the *Mabinogion*, which she dedicates to her young sons:

> My dear children,—Infants as you yet are, I feel that I cannot dedicate more fitly than to you these venerable relics of ancient lore, and I do so in the hope of inciting you to cultivate the literature of "Gwyllt Walia," in whose beautiful language you are being initiated, and amongst whose free mountains you were born. May you become early imbued with the chivalric and exalted sense of honor, and the fervent patriotism for which its sons have ever been celebrated.[5]

As many readers of her translation have noted, Guest cleansed her source text of its more troubling elements, softening scenes of sexuality and violence to make them appropriate for young readers. Erica Obey suggests Guest misperceived an etymological correlation between the eponymous word *mabinogi* and the Welsh word *mab*, which means *boy*, an error that led her to recast these legends as fodder for children's entertainment and enlightenment.[6] Regardless of this possible semantic slip, Guest perceived the *Mabinogion* as relevant to children's experience, extolling her young boys to learn from the chivalric values of this past and thus casting the Middle Ages as a locus of children's fantasies. While Guest and many other authors of medieval juvenilia clearly operate at the level of fantasy, whereby the past is domesticated and reinvented, there is an element of truth to their assumptions: a great deal of medieval literature focuses on the quest of the *juvens*, or youth, whose adventures symbolize the passage of childhood to adult responsibility. These narratives, like their modern progeny, sanitize the filth and plague often associated with the medieval period from their pages, thus creating a fantasy of the Middle

Ages that continues apace today. There is nevertheless a great deal of violence and conflict present in them, the former of which contemporary authors generally lighten for the modern reader, the latter of which is used for multiple purposes in generating plots and tension.

In this regard, "medieval" children's literature, like much of children's literature as a whole, often divulges moral lessons, and such didacticism influences the perceptions and portrayals of the Middle Ages within these narratives, although whether literary didacticism is a particularly medieval quality is a debatable point. Judith Hillman observes the didactic nature of much early children's literature that sought to inculcate religious values: "Didacticism prevailed ... and most material written and published for children had as its primary purpose the instruction of young souls so that they would be worthy to die."[7] The intersection of didacticism and the Middle Ages is evident in the chivalric focus in numerous texts of the genre, including Sidney Lanier's *The Boy's King Arthur* and its companion texts, *The Boy's Froissart*, *The Boy's Mabinogion*, and *The Boy's Percy*. In his Introduction to *The Boy's King Arthur*, which he sees as a chivalric primer, Lanier exhorts boys to emulate the chivalric models of the medieval past: "Into the fine fellowship then, of lordly Sir Lancelot, of generous Sir Tristram, of stainless Sir Galahad, of gentle Sir Percival, of meek Sir Gareth of Orkney ... I commit you." He then aligns his hortatory purpose with that of his literary forebear William Caxton, ascribing to himself "feelings so like those with which Caxton closes his prologue" that he quotes at length Caxton's introduction to Thomas Malory's *Morte D'Arthur*:

> And for to passe the tyme, this book shal be plesaunte to rede in, but for to gyve fayth and byleve that al is trewe that is contained herin, ye be at your lyberte; but al is wryton for our doctryne, [and this book is therefore sent forth] to the entente that noblemen may see and lerne the noble actes of chyvalrye, the jentyl and vertuous dedes, that somme knyghtes used in tho days, by whyche they came to honour, and how they that were vycious were punysshed, and often put to shame and rebuke, humbly bysechyng al noble lordes and ladyes ... that they take the good and honest actes in their remembraunce, and to folowe the same.[8]

Despite the roughly four-hundred years between the publication of their respective works, Caxton and Lanier agree on the pedagogical merit inherent in chivalry: it is a social structure intrinsically instructive, as readers are encouraged to emulate the actions of Arthurian knights to enact in the present the moral virtues of yesteryear. Whereas Caxton sees "noble actes of chyvalrye" as instructive for "noble lords and ladyes," Lanier depicts chivalry as a foundational value for its potential to elevate boys into manhood.

So too does Madalen Edgar's *The Boy's Froissart* rewrite adult history into a child's didactic lesson, as its opening citation of Froissart establishes. In Edgar's translation of Froissart's words, the Introduction proclaims, "To the intent that the honourable and noble adventures of feats of arms, done and achieved by the wars of France and England, should notably be enregistered and put in perpetual memory, whereby the trewe and hardy may have ensample to encourage them in their well-doing, I, Sir John Froissart, will treat and record an history of great lousage and praise."[9] In this passage, Froissart's words address the "trewe and hardy" rather than a particular age group, and so they are particularly suitable to adapt for young boys who are presumed to be already "trewe and hardy" as they grow further into manhood. Likewise, in the Preface to his *Boy's Froissart*, Lanier outlines the ways in which reading medieval history builds masculinity:

> Perhaps no boy will deny that to find the world still reading a book which was written five hundred years ago is a very wonderful business. For the world grows,—faster than a boy; and when you remember how it is only ten years since you were reading Jack the Giant-killer, and how you are *infinitely* beyond all that *now*,—you know,—you readily see that it must be a very manful man indeed who can make a book so strong and so all-time like as to go on giving delight through the ages, spite of prodigious revolutions in customs, in governments, and in ideas.[10]

In these *Boy's* texts, literature and history originally composed for medieval adults is rewritten for post-medieval children, ostensibly to model exemplary stories of the past, but also to diminish the past: what was once the realm of men is now colonized by boys as a period of innocent and ennobling play. Lanier's argument also tacitly establishes a hierarchy among texts: young boys read fairy tales like "Jack the Giant-killer," but older boys—those who aspire to becoming "manful men"—read abridged versions of medieval history. But then why not read medieval history itself? The very creation of these *Boy's* texts indicates that the Middle Ages should be an inappropriate period for children, for it must be stripped of its offensive medievalness before it can be repackaged as wholesomely medieval.

Such authorial posturings reimagine the Middle Ages as a site for children's play and modern didacticism, and within Guest's, Lanier's, and Edgar's dedications and introductions to audiences of boys, the stories and history of the past are conscripted to the service of post-medieval children. Of course, post-medieval appropriations of the Middle Ages as a source for children's literature need not only rely on medieval history and literature for this purpose, because post-medieval re-creations of the Middle Ages, such as those of Sir Walter Scott's Waverley novels, likewise provide substantial fodder for children's medievalisms. Medievalism is an unwieldy agglomeration of fact and fiction from yesterday and today, and it accumulates within its folds post-medieval reconstructions of the Middle Ages as readily and as freely as it does the Middle Ages itself. Thomas Nelson Page's *Two Little Confederates* models such an incorporation of post-medieval medievalisms into its fictions. This novel, long considered a classic of southern children's literature, though troublesomely so due to its racial politics, turns to the medieval past, as mediated through Scott's novels, for representations of proper masculine virtue. Young protagonists Frank and Willy learn honor in their Civil War present by emulating the heroes of long-ago who were then rewritten by Scott: "It was thought an honor to furnish food to the soldiers. Every soldier was to the boys a hero, and each young officer might rival Ivanhoe or Coeur de Lion."[11] Scott's *Ivanhoe* showcases its eponymous hero and Richard the Lionhearted as models of proper masculinity, and Page appropriates Scott's medievalisms for the purpose of depicting the chivalric heroism of his young protagonists. Readers later see Frank and Willy enjoying another of Scott's romances: "One evening, the boys had just teased their Cousin Belle into reading them their nightly portion of *The Talisman*, as they sat before a bright lightwood fire."[12] As Frank and Willy grow into manhood following their exposure to medieval heroes and southern soldiers, other characters establish the young protagonists as paragons of virtue for others to emulate: "'Yes'm, they's got 'em, sho' 'nough. They's the beatenes' boys!'" avows old Balla after the young protagonists succeed in capturing some hogs.[13] *Two Little Confederates* trumpets its ideological view of southern masculinity as filtered through Scott's chivalric medievalism, and Frank and Willy prosper as protagonists because they successfully incarnate these medieval values in their daily lives, despite the fact that their chivalry is doubly removed from the Middle Ages due to Walter Scott's position as intermediary.

These brief examples of nineteenth- and early-twentieth-century "medieval" children's literature, despite their many differences, agree that chivalry guides boys into proper manhood, and this congruency highlights the ways that chivalry contributes to the ideological perpetuation of antiquated values in later years. Kim Moreland argues that the "contemporary evocation of medieval chivalry and courtly love in particular came to function as a standard against which modern American life was judged and found wanting" in the nineteenth and twentieth centuries,[14] and thus myths of chivalry infuse children's literature as a defining principle of its culture. Literary examples establish chivalric paradigms for young readers to emulate, thereby inculcating medieval values in the present through modern texts' rewriting of the past.

Among more recent examples of children's medievalisms, J. R. R. Tolkien's *Lord of the Rings* may be the best-known work of literature for young adults set in the Middle Ages, and it increasingly finds itself in extensive company. From classic series like Lloyd Alexander's *Chronicles of Prydain* and Susan Cooper's *The Dark Is Rising*, to contemporary examples such as Judson Roberts's *Strongbow Saga* and Anne Eliot Crompton's *Gawain and Lady Green*, the Middle Ages is a popular venue for the exploration of adolescent life and experience, although unlike the material for children explored above, it offers a greater balance of possible gender roles. Some, like Karen Cushman's *Catherine, Called Birdy* and Elizabeth Janet Gray's *Adam of the Road*, are Newbury Award winners, while others receive less acclaim. Many draw heavily from medieval sources: Lloyd Alexander's series incorporates stories and themes from the *Mabinogion* while engaging in some of the same sanitizing that

Charlotte Guest undertakes in her translation; T. H. White's *Once and Future King* offers a retelling of the Arthurian legend, heavily influenced by world politics and wars; and Anne Eliot Crompton reworks *Sir Gawain and the Green Knight* from a feminist point of view. Many and diverse retellings of King Arthur and Robin Hood populate this genre as well, too numerous too list, but including their famed incarnations as Disney films: *The Sword in the Stone* (1963) and *Robin Hood* (1973). These authors follow Tolkien, who drew inspiration, detail, and even language from the medieval sources of his own scholarship, although their relationship to these stories and their sense of responsibility to their source material varies. Other authors tell stories more inspired by medieval history, locating their narratives at particular points or locations, such as the Crusades, while still others choose quasi-medieval, magical settings that often draw from a medieval fantasy created by a strange nexus of Victorian medievalism, Medieval and Renaissance Fairs, and "medieval" movies.

Although any substantial body of material resists classification, it is possible to suggest a primary division of categories for "medieval" children's literature: the realistic and the fantastic. Much "medieval" literature for young readers follows the assumptions of medieval romance, in which liminal spaces open up the possibility of magic, of rules and expectations turned upside down; on the other hand, a sizeable body applies the standards of the realist novel, attempting to set the story in a detailed and lifelike (if not authentic) past, whose characters inhabit a world where their feet remain firmly on the ground. (Other works attempt to combine these two impulses, such as Kathryn Lasky's *Hawksmaid: The Untold Story of Robin Hood and Maid Marian*, which references privies and middens, while people turn into birds.) Yet in all of these texts, the Middle Ages exists as a potent fantasy, whether of a simpler time of clearer values; a violent, dangerous era of tribal conflict and familial strife; or a place of potential, where the lack of central authority and traditional restraints on adolescent life, such as parents and schools, permits various types of exploration. These can, of course, be more or less effective, but the savagery of Halfdan's Viking world in the *Strongbow Saga*, or the somewhat simple and gentle manor house in *Catherine, Called Birdy* are no more authentically medieval than the magical realms of T. A. Barron's Merlin books or of Stephanie Spinner's *Damosel*. Catherine Brown points out that "the past can feel like a place as much as it does a time—a foreign place, outside the doors of the familiar, beyond the gate and the gatekeepers of the now," and from this perspective the Middle Ages is "especially beyond the pale."[15] While "medieval" children's literature makes this difference apparent, often stressing the ways in which the details of life are inherently unlike our own, the question also arises of what makes the Middle Ages such an appealing setting for children's and YA literature. (There is not, for instance, an equivalent body of children's fiction set in the eighteenth century.) "There is no question," Brown says, "that the Middle Ages is an other, perhaps even a foreign place, someplace ... beyond our own doors. What are we doing when we go there? What happens to 'here' and 'there' when we go? The question isn't whether medieval people did things differently than we do now; the question is what we as putative nonmedievals are going to do with the difference."[16] For children's and YA literature set in the Middle Ages, a similar question thus arises: what are children and adolescents to do with the Middle Ages?

In these novels, the medieval past, however it is constructed or defined, is a kind of other, whose differences we putative non-medievals must engage. Yet it is also easy to see that the stories told about the period are not just modern translations of classic medieval stories, along the lines of Lanier's *Boy's* texts. Following the conventions of adolescent literature, these novels offer engaging protagonists attempting to find themselves in the confusion of the world around them, seeking their own voices and visions, often in opposition to the structures and assumptions of their societies in texts that draw heavily on the expectations of the *bildungsroman* (although this genre, of course, has origins in medieval quest romance). Thus Catherine, in Cushman's *Catherine, Called Birdy*, attempts to discover her identity and her personal strengths while railing against an arranged marriage to an older, brutish man whom her parents have chosen for her, and Jane, in Cushman's *The Midwife's Apprentice*, aspires to rise above the serfdom into which she has been born. Judson Roberts's Halfdan in the *Strongbow Saga* attempts to find true brotherhood, to reclaim his heritage, and, by gaining experience as a Viking warrior, to triumph over those who would oppose him. If these themes are not revolutionary in perspective—medieval authors depict female protagonists resisting love and marriage in texts including the life of *St. Christina of Markyate* and Chaucer's *Knight's Tale*, *Man of Law's Tale*, *Second Nun's Tale*, and *Troilus and Criseyde*, and nearly every Icelandic Saga tells a story similar to the one Roberts constructs—many of the reactions, sentiments, and expressions of the characters are decidedly more contemporary. Thus the issue arises of whether "medieval" children's and YA literature should attempt to replicate the Middle Ages as a distant and somewhat inaccessible past, or whether it should attempt to replicate the qualities of medieval literature—historically accurate language, challenges, clothing, as well as the romance's particular relationships to anachronism and fantasy—that a young medieval person would experience reading (or hearing) the literature of his or her time.

Rebecca Barnhouse, author of *Recasting the Past: The Middle Ages in Young Adult Literature*, suggests that the success or failure of adolescent fiction set in the Middle Ages rests on a single criterion—the text's authenticity. "Novelists," she declares, "must not only get the facts right, they must also present *all* of their characters as authentically medieval, reacting to people and events around them with authentically medieval sensibilities."[17] This perceived need for historical accuracy leads her to strong judgments: works such as Gray's *Adam of the Road* and Cushman's *Catherine, Called Birdy*, for instance, get higher marks than classics like T. H. White's *Sword in the Stone* because, in Barnhouse's view, they present medieval life as raw and real, and for the most part, they do not depict their characters engaging in anything that might be deemed a contemporary problem.

In condemning Berit Haahr's *The Minstrel's Tale*, Barnhouse calls it "even further removed from history" than many of the other works she does not approve of, and continues,

> ostensibly set around the year 1330, this slight novel owes more to "Ye Olde Renaissance Fayres" than it does to the Middle Ages. Thirteen-year-old Lady Judith cuts her hair, dons boy's clothes, and runs away to avoid marriage to a much older man, "the repulsive Lord Norbert." She befriends a peregrine falcon who defends her as she journeys the two hundred miles to Eltham Palace, where she hopes to fulfill her dreams of being a musician by joining the King's Minstrels. Along the way, she staves off the advances of a young woman who, thinking she is a boy, wants to marry her. She also develops a modern social conscience, worrying about girls' lack of education and the treatment of serfs. She lengthens her journey by helping some beleaguered peasants bring in their harvest. In the happily-ever-after ending, Judith gets to be a musician *and* to marry the man she loves, with no consequences. She still gets to be rich, too.[18]

By focusing on what she finds ahistorical, Barnhouse overlooks the highly medieval elements of this story: Lady Judith's path echoes that of Yde in *Yde et Olive*, who dresses as a boy to escape marriage to her father and is then married to another woman (although Yde ultimately turns into a man, in a narrative twist Haahr does not replicate). Judith, in her musical career and successful marriage, also pays homage to Silence in the *Roman de Silence*, who passes as a male jongleur and is sexually accosted by her lusty queen, and to Nicolette, in *Aucassin et Nicolette*, who also becomes a musician and poses as a man so that she can return to Beaucaire to marry Aucassin. Only Haahr's peregrine falcon is something of a Disney-esque stretch, although various talking birds populate medieval narratives, such as Chaucer's peregrine falcon in the *Squire's Tale* and the talking eagles in the *Parliament of Fowls*, who debate love in highly courtly language. Judith's anxiety about women's education is not as anachronistic as Barnhouse would suggest: one need only read Christine de Pizan's *Livre de la Cité des Dames*, or return to the *Roman de Silence*, to see that medieval authors were quite aware of gender inequality and the values of education, if not expressing as much sympathy for peasants.

Furthermore, Barnhouse insists on an exclusionary view of the Middle Ages as a time of unvarnished prejudice, bigotry, and violence. One critique often expressed of "inauthentic" medieval narratives is that their characters evince tolerance, if not sympathy and compassion, for Saracens, and while a medieval audience would likely not share the ecumenical concerns of a modern audience, the "good Saracen" who converts to Christianity as the narrative unfolds is a common figure in medieval narratives. Consider, for instance, Floripas in the *Sir Ferumbras* romances, Orable/Guiborc in *Guillame d'Orange*, and Floris in the *Floris and Blancheflor* romances. The portrait of Saladin in Catherine Jinks's *Pagan's Crusade* is not, finally, so different from what we find in the *Richard, Coeur de Leon* romances. By definition, modern views of tolerance are absent from the Middle Ages, but it is nonetheless relatively common to find medieval voices recognizing a shared humanity with other peoples. Peter the Venerable is hardly a model of modern tolerance, yet he seeks to convert Muslims to Christianity by appealing to their shared humanity, irrespective of racial difference, in contemplating the Divine: "Is it not that which by the common consent of all races, according to the proper term in the respective language, is believed to be God, is called God?"[19] Likewise, the Jewish prayer "All the World Shall Come to Serve Thee" ("V'yehehtayo Kol L'avdechah"), which Rabbi Morris Silverman characterizes as "remarkable for its universalistic outlook," despite being written in the Middle Ages, a time he calls "marked largely by intolerance, prejudice, and violence," illustrates an ecumenical view of unified belief.[20] It is hard to argue, as Barnhouse does, that YA literature should exclusively show medieval characters as intolerant, unlikeable, and violent xenophobes. Although Barnhouse praises Michael Cadmun's *Book of the Lion* because the character Edmund expresses repugnant moral sensibilities, this literary strategy might not be an effective way to excite readers about the book and its characters. One might as well read histories of racism and xenophobia, if one wants only the cold realism of cultural prejudice.

Barnhouse also takes issue with Cushman for Birdy's and her friend Perkin's attitudes toward literacy and reading, which she finds inauthentic, but she credits Cushman for depicting Birdy as anxious and skeptical about the Jews seeking refuge at the manor, expecting them to have horns and tails. Barnhouse is pleased that "Birdy does not think in any depth about the reasons the Jews are leaving England. Particularly, she doesn't question their persecution by Christians," while taking her to task because

> Perkin and Birdy value books as a means to gain knowledge. ... By this unintentional didacticism, the writer commits anachronisms instead of giving us the real Middle Ages. Thus, not only do they underestimate the cultural differences between medieval and modern society, they also underestimate their readers' ability to comprehend and learn from such differences, condescending therefore to both the past and the present.[21]

It is tempting to ask what, exactly, the "real Middle Ages" might be. In her assumptions, Barnhouse falls victim to an understanding of the function of the past—that the past must have an identifiable use and utility for the present—that Louise Fradenburg describes:

> Many versions of historicism have embraced, in one form or another, the belief that the differences between our "modernity" and the "alterity" of the Middle Ages are much more important than what they might be said to share; these differences have often become definitive for the purposes of

interpretation, even if a radical discontinuity between past and present is not explicitly asserted.[22]

In making the differences between "now" and "then" the center of her discussion, Barnhouse misses the ways in which contemporary fiction for adolescents that is set in the Middle Ages shares profoundly with its medieval literary counterparts. Indeed, one could well respond in such a debate with a relevant cliché: the more things change, the more things stay the same. This truism, despite its overuse, captures the continuing relevance of issues that define children's quest to understand their discombobulating world: relationships with peers and parents, questions of identity and community, and eternal concerns of purpose and life's meaning that predate the Middle Ages and continue long after its waning. This is not to argue against the striking variability between past and present, but merely to observe that great fictions tackle enduring questions, no matter their sociotemporal settings.

If we are to take Barnhouse at her word, most medieval authors also "condescended both to the past and present" and "underestimated their readers' abilities." While there are certainly medieval texts that offer a more literal picture of their times, much medieval fiction is either set in a past that, for all its emphasis on its pastness, remarkably resembles the present, and a past that engages problems contemporary to its authors' and readers' time. The world of Chaucer's *Troilus and Criseyde* would look far more contemporary to a fourteenth-century reader than it would to an ancient Trojan or Greek, and ancient Troy, for Chaucer, is a wonderfully appropriate setting for asking questions about the roles and functions of courtly love, the intersections of public and private life, and the cultural function of the romance genre; so, too, does Chaucer's *Knight's Tale* elucidate his contemporary world more than it does classical Athens. Even in ostensibly historical works, such as Geoffrey of Monmouth's *History of the Kings of Britain* or Gerald of Wales's *History and Topography of Ireland*, "history" does not attempt to create an accurate portrait but to tell a story in which the past leads, inexorably, to the present, even if that present is 1281. Otherwise, why depict dragons as responsible for a castle's architectural insecurity, or have werewolves wandering in the forests? Perhaps in its construction of a past that can speak to and incorporate the values of the present, children's and YA literature about the Middle Ages is at its most authentically medieval.

That said, authors of "medieval" children's literature often portray two distinct versions of the Middle Ages, in line with the overarching distinction between realist and fantasy fictions: the realist texts are often ripe with strong smells, dung, disease, and rot, whereas in the fantastic Middle Ages, the smells and dung are tempered with mystical beings and holy grails, while Ladies of the Lake turn into mists and use authentically medieval blacksmithing techniques to forge Excalibur.[23] While the former might replicate the ways a contemporary reader would likely experience a medieval street, this raw and real vision of the Middle Ages is no less a fantasy than the Holy Grail Middle Ages. If, as

Catherine Brown notes, "The Middle Ages were invented to be a foreign country," we can then read this foreignness of the period as a kind of liminality.[24] Such mystical worlds are familiar liminal spaces out of beloved medieval romances, and thus the "historical" Middle Ages becomes no less its own liminal space for contemporary adolescents, a past where the rules and expectations that govern contemporary life (as well as the technologies and structures that bind us to particular families and relationships) are undermined by a different, and sometimes looser, set of rules. In both fantasies, the adolescent individual's experience is governed by a freedom unavailable in the present; it's no wonder that Adam goes on the road and Birdy runs away. Drawing from the conventions of quest romance, that supreme locus of medieval fantasy, even the most "authentic" stories of the Middle Ages are ultimately offering a world very different from what medieval adolescents themselves experienced. And while it is certainly galling when Matty, in Lasky's *Hawksmaid*, is hidden in a potato hole—Lasky should have done her homework and hidden Matty among the turnips—the "realities" of her life (such as the extended description of the privy) are no more authentically medieval than the fantastic elements of the story that have her turning into a hawk (and then becoming Maid Marian, who seems to be a particular locus for medieval fantasies of female development).

To explore these competing fantasies further, let us look at two recent series that tell essentially the same story of a young orphan who is raised in an orphanage and becomes a squire to the Knights Templar, with complications and adventures ensuing. In Catherine Jinks's *Pagan's Crusade* series, which may be called the "authentic" one, the hero, Pagan Kidrouk, an Arab Christian in Jerusalem, is raised in a monastery where he learns to read, escapes its rigid rules, and apprentices himself to the Knights Templar to earn sufficient funds to pay off a gambling debt. Made squire to the austere and idealistic Lord Roland Roucy de Bram, he finds himself first at the Battle of Jerusalem, then in France during the Cathar Conflict, in a French monastery, and finally as the Archdeacon of Carcassone during the siege. In Michael Spradlin's *Youngest Templar* series, which employs more supernatural and fantasy elements, young Tristan is orphaned and raised in a monastery where he learns to read and becomes Squire to Lord Thomas Leux, idealistic Templar Knight, fighting at the battle of Acre. He is charged with carrying the Holy Grail back to England, with the help of Robard Hode (Robin Hood) and Maid Marian (who this time is a Saracen Hashashin called Maryam). Much adventure ensues as Tristan finds himself at the center of the Cathar Conflict. In the third volume, he returns to England, where he discovers the truth of his parentage—he is the illegitimate son of Henry II—and delivers the Grail to a safe place. The difference in the second story is that repeatedly, Tristan and his friends are miraculously saved by the Grail. Although Spradlin does not revel in mysticism as much as other YA authors, the series suggests a current of liminal possibility, of a magic operating just below the surface of the story's real world.[25]

For Jinks's Pagan, Jerusalem is a place of bad smells and revolting jokes. Confronted in the opening scene of *Pagan's Crusade* by the Standard-Bearer of the Templars, Pagan notes, "Rockhead smells rich and rare, like a well-matured piece of cheese. No baths for the Templars. Hot water is for girls and porridge and other soft, wet things," and when asked why he left the Jerusalem garrison, notes "It was the jokes, sir. In the guardroom ... I don't like leper jokes. Or dysentery jokes. Especially when I'm eating."[26] When Rockhead opens his mouth, Pagan sees "his jagged black fangs underneath. Fangs like the ruins of burned-out sentinel boxes."[27] While this detail might win Barnhouse's praise for its graphic nature, it is worth pointing out that someone who lived in the medieval period would be far less likely to notice the smells and ruined teeth of his compatriots, given the typical nature of such things, and while Pagan's revulsion at the unwashed French in *Pagan in Exile* shares something in common with the Saracen responses to Christian bathing habits in medieval encounter narratives, Jinks's dwelling on filth and decay creates its own fantastic vision of the Middle Ages. This earthy context allows Pagan a place for his highly sarcastic perceptions; however, it also shows Pagan to be deeply medieval. For all his exclamations like "Jesus Christ in cream-cheese sauce," Pagan is fundamentally religious. Although he runs away from his monastery and is ejected from a second one in *Pagan's Vows*, he operates on an underlying system of profound belief. Often highly irreverent, willing to criticize the institutional church, and able to coexist easily with the Cathars in Provence, he nonetheless remains fully Catholic and matures into the role of the Archdeacon of Carcassone and author of the *Vita* of Lord Roland, Templar Knight turned monk.

Jinks's medieval setting allows Pagan to find an alternative to his abandonment, as well as a place for his unique perspectives and skills. Both the *Pagan's Crusade* and *Youngest Templar* series are concerned with a problem one might call medieval and modern—the finding of identity and support outside the boundaries of the traditional family. For many adolescents, the search for identity is often about disconnecting from their families and striking out on their own, an experience for which quest romance is an effective metaphor, and for both Pagan and Tristan, the discovery of alternative systems of support is essential to their stories. At the end of *Orphan of Destiny*, the final book in the *Youngest Templar* series, Tristan is reunited with the Master of the Order. Sir Charles apologizes, saying "I'm sure he [Sir Thomas] regretted not being able to send help with you," and Tristan, looking at Robard and Maryam, responds, "It's all right, sire, ... I managed to find help on my own."[28] Here we recognize that more important than the actual discovery of familial identity are the friendships he has formed. At the end of each of the books in the *Pagan's Crusade* series, readers are reminded of the intense bond between Pagan and Lord Roland, who despite their striking differences, have come to rely on each other. At the end of the first book, in the face of Roland's anger at him for ransoming him from Saladin, Pagan says, "My lord, have some mercy. For God's sake, think of me. Don't you understand? You're all I have left."[29] In the second, a similar scene takes place: when Roland expresses his desire to leave the fighting life and enter a monastery, Pagan declares, "My Lord, I am safe and happy with you. ... Where you go, I'll go. ... If you become a monk, I can become a monk. Or at least a monastery servant."[30] When the two are compelled to separate at the end of the third book, Pagan calls Roland "my mother and father. My friend. My lord," and beseeches him among copious weeping, "Help me. Please help me to leave you."[31] In the fourth book, when Pagan is Archdeacon of Carcassone and Lord Roland dies, Pagan is nearly paralyzed with despair, and only the ministrations of Brother Isidore, his scribe, his own adopted orphan, can move him. In both *Pagan's Crusade* and *Youngest Templar*, the world of medieval relationships provides alternative communities to the family; in the monastery and the comitatus, both boys find themselves and their identities that are undefined at the start of their narratives. For both orphans, a sense of detachment is replaced by a sense of self within the context of the relationships and circumstances around them: how they forge loyalties and deal with conflicts personal and political, how they choose their friends, and how they uphold their values in the face of challenges.

What becomes clear from reading these stories is that the Middle Ages is an appropriate fantasy world in which to act out these modern—or perhaps timeless—issues. If Chrétien de Troyes would not use the same language to describe the events befalling his Arthurian heroes Yvain, Perceval, Erec, or Cligés, he nonetheless engages them in similar quests to discover their identities. Only after surviving a series of challenges, for instance, can Yvain transform from his position as the amorphous "Knight of the Lion" and reclaim himself, his place, and his wife; and Perceval's stunning ignorance of his family history, such that he does not even know his name for a large part of the narrative, establishes his quest for his identity as equally significant as his quest for the Holy Grail. In reading "medieval" literature for young adults, then, it is possible to see that while the material will not replace a rigorous history class, it can open up an authentically medieval experience. The same experience is true in reading medieval literature: the stories of Dante, Boccaccio, Chaucer, and other medieval writers open readers' eyes to literary medieval worlds, not historical ones, and thus they can be just as misleading about historical realities as children's literature, if one were to read them without critical attention to the interpretive demands of fiction and the vagaries of history.

Indeed, Barnhouse herself seems to have come to this realization: in her move from critic of "medieval" children's literature to author of this genre, it is apparent that authenticity at times necessitated too high an artistic price. In her *The Coming of the Dragon*, a YA version of the legend of Beowulf from the perspective of an adolescent Wiglaf, she shifts her source text and the historical details of her setting in numerous ways. Wiglaf, an orphan nicknamed Rune in her retelling, is the prototypical cowardly weakling who learns honor and valor serving King Beowulf in his battle against the dragon decimating their kingdom. Whereas *Beowulf* encodes the transition from paganism to Christianity with its Old Testament references to monotheism, *The Coming of the Dragon* includes prayers to Odin, Thor, and Freya. As Barnhouse affirms in the "Author's Note" concluding her text, her decision in this regard undoes the promise of an authentic Middle Ages: "The *Beowulf* poet doesn't specify what gods and god-desses his characters worshiped, just that they were heathens, so I have drawn on what we know about Norse religion to invent cultural references for my characters. The result is no more historical than the poem *Beowulf* is."[32] Of course, *Beowulf* is embedded in history, but a pseudo-history necessary for the poet's reconstitution of a pagan past merging with an increasingly Christian present. And so too Barnhouse's *The Coming of the Dragon* grapples with an old tale that muses on eternal themes, even if Wiglaf is not an adolescent rising to manhood in her source text. In contrast to *Beowulf*'s elegiac conclusion, her retelling ends happily as Wiglaf heals blood feuds, quells a rebellion against his rule, and prepares to marry a peace weaver who just happens to be "beautiful, like a queen from the legends. He stared at her face, letting his eyes linger on her dark brows, her straight nose, her slightly parted lips."[33] Such a pat ending rejects the elegiac and foreboding tone of *Beowulf* in favor of a happy-ever-after fantasy, but such rewritings, as drastic as they are, advance Barnhouse's authorial agenda, one that, we would argue, should not be merely to translate *Beowulf* into an "authentic" version of itself.

Indeed, the detail in Barnhouse's *The Coming of the Dragon* that most sus-pended our disbelief necessary to enjoy this engaging YA adventure concerns neither an historical detail nor a distortion of *Beowulf* as source text, but a picayune matter: the description of the dragon's hoard includes a "glittery tapestry hanging from a wall," but how on earth could a dragon hang a tapes-try?[34] Then again, who are we to say that dragons cannot hang tapestries? Indeed, *Beowulf* mentions this somewhat silly detail—"Swylce he sioman geseah segn eallgylden/heah ofer horde, hondwundra mæst" ("There he also saw a golden standard/hanging over the hoard, intricate weaving/of wondrous skill"),[35] and so, according to the logic of fidelity to one's sources, Barnhouse should be credited for her inclusion of this detail; nonetheless, no matter how this tapestry found its way into a dragon's lair, dangling above the rest of the treasures, it strains the reader's credulity to see it there. But to fixate on this tapestry in *Beowulf* and *The Coming of the Dragon* is both to find miniscule faults with a masterpiece and its retelling and to nitpick a small detail while overlooking the larger one staring readers in the face: dragons do not exist. All fictions necessitate that readers suspend their disbelief, and in large measure, the success of a work of fiction depends on readers' willingness to do so in spite of lapses in historical reality, credible motivation, or any other part of the fantasy that constitutes all fiction, whether for children or adults.

Running through much analysis of "medieval" children's literature is the assumption that it should, even as fantasy, teach about the real Middle Ages, but not all children's literature is didactic in purpose, and many stories revel in the creation of a carnivalesque realm in which the rules of ordinary life are turned upside-down. As Alison Lurie emphasizes: "[children's] books are, in the deepest sense, subversive. ... [T]hey make fun of adults and expose adult pretensions and failings; they suggest, subtly or otherwise, that children are braver, smarter, and more interesting than grown-ups, and that grown-up rules are made to be broken."[36] Cressida Cowell's *How to Train Your Dragon* refreshingly illustrates this carnivalesque perspective: on the novel's copyright page, well before the story begins, the text's declared author Hiccup Horrendous Haddock III has scrawled in an ungainly penmanship, "Please note: Any relationship to any historical fact whatsoever is entirely coincidental."[37] Cowell's novel plays with the rules of authorship, claiming for herself merely the role of Hiccup's translator of his Old Norse original text, and her dismissal of history allows her text to revel in the pleasures of a fantasy Middle Ages. In the eponymous how-to manual "How to Train Your Dragon" that is included in her novel of Hiccup's misadventures, a child has scribbled in the margins, "Beowulf is a softy," a notation that highlights Cowell's pleasure in the play of the past rather than her shackled subservience to it.[38]

Within the realms of "medieval" children's literature, the Middle Ages is often a place of fantasy, but so too was the very construction of the Middle Ages as other to the Renaissance: medieval people could never realize their "medievalness," not knowing that subsequent generations would label them as such. In this regard, Fradenburg avows, "the notion that the Middle Ages was fully present to itself is as problematic as is the notion that we need to reconstruct such fullness of self-understanding, or the notion—for that matter—that the 'past' is indeed over, that 'past' and 'present' can be distinguished with absolute certainty."[39] Children's and YA literature with medieval settings recognizes this indistinguishability, accepting both the alterity of the Middle Ages and its multivalent use as a time and place that embraces change and multiple points of view. Instead of assuming a clean distinction between past and present, these narratives seem to understand that various points of contact with the Middle Ages generate the truth of their fiction, if they also trip over some historical facts along the way. Accepting the "radical discontinuity" of the details of the past, while simultaneously asserting certain aspects of shared humanity between them, is finally a somewhat medieval, or, at least, a medieval narrative, view, along the lines of Chaucer's engagement with Troy and Athens.

In the end, these liminal fantasies do not provide young readers with an authentic view into an historical past, unmediated by contemporary sensibilities, but a medievalized mode of reading, in which the space between past and present collapses and the two are bound together. Following medieval examples, the past becomes a place to explore the concerns of the present: Pagan's Jerusalem and France are simultaneously then and now, just as Chaucer's Troy in *Troilus and Criseyde* is both the classical past and the fourteenth-century present. In describing her experience of reading Augustine's *Confessions* at the Newbury Library, Catherine Brown notes that "there came a moment in which 'I' and 'other,' 'subject' and 'object' simply ceased to be adequate categories through which to think about the relations between reader and read, present and past." She adds that this was a "moment when two historical live wires crossed—and changed both me and what I was reading ... in a very real sense, no medieval text will ever be the same again." If young readers are not exactly interacting with truly medieval works, they are still "coincident in space and time," or as Brown coins it, "*coeval*" with these fictions that help them to make sense of themselves in the alien world of the present, through a fantasy vision of the past.[40] For neither today's children nor yesteryear's history are intrinsically innocent to the extent that the past can pollute the present; on the contrary, the past allows children to consider their present lives, not through the perversity of an eternal innocence, but in the quest for knowledge—of the self and of the other—that constitutes one of reading's greatest pleasures, alongside the equally pleasurable pitfalls of ahistoricism and anachronism that cannot help to be constructed into current fantasies of the past.

Notes

1 It is beyond the scope of this chapter to precisely distinguish children's literature from its YA counterparts, except for the presumed difference that children's literature is written for a slightly younger, and YA literature for a slightly older, audience of children and adolescents. The fact that many adults enjoy children's and YA literature blurs these ostensibly distinct genres further. For overviews of children's literature as contrasted to YA literature, see Michael Cart, *Young Adult Literature: From Romance to Realism* (Chicago: American Library Association, 2010); and Charles Frey and Lucy Rollin, ed., *Classics of Young Adult Literature* (Upper Saddle River, NJ: Pearson, 2004), 1–13.

2 In this chapter we refer to "medieval" children's literature to register its post-medieval creation and to distinguish it from children's literature written during the Middle Ages. For studies of medieval children's literature, see Seth Lerer, *Children's Literature: A Reader's History, from Aesop to Harry Potter* (Chicago: University of Chicago Press, 2008), esp. 57–80; and Nicholas Orme, "Children and Literature in Medieval England," *Medium Aevum* 68.2 (1999): 218–46.

3 John Ganim, *Medievalism and Orientalism: Three Essays on Literature, Architecture, and Cultural Identity* (New York: Palgrave Macmillan, 2005), 4.

4 Jacqueline Rose, *The Case of Peter Pan, or the Impossibility of Children's Fiction* (1984; Philadelphia: University of Pennsylvania Press, 1992), 10.

5 Lady Charlotte Guest, qtd. in Erica Obey, *The Wunderkammer of Lady Charlotte Guest* (Bethlehem: Lehigh University Press, 2007), 105.

6 Erica Obey, *The Wunderkammer of Lady Charlotte Guest*, 105.

7 Judith Hillman, *Discovering Children's Literature*, 2nd ed. (Upper Saddle River, NJ: Merrill, 1999), 24.

8 Sidney Lanier, "Introduction to *The Boy's King Arthur*," *The Centennial Edition of the Works of Sidney Lanier*, ed. Clarence Gohdes and Kemp Malone, 10 vols. (Baltimore: Johns Hopkins University Press, 1945), 4.355–69, at 369.

9 Madalen Edgar, *The Boy's Froissart: Selected from Lord Berners' Translation of the Chronicles* (London: Harrap, 1912), 9. Edgar's *Boy's Froissart* is a separate edition of Froissart's *Chronicles* than Lanier's, yet the two editors agree on the moral value of chivalry for the children of their present day.

10 Sidney Lanier, "Introduction to *The Boy's Froissart*," *The Centennial Edition of the Works of Sidney Lanier*, 4.346–54, at 346.

11 Thomas Nelson Page, *Two Little Confederates* (1888; New York: Grosset & Dunlap, 1916), 20.

12 Thomas Nelson Page, *Two Little Confederates*, 101.

13 Thomas Nelson Page, *Two Little Confederates*, 85.

14 Kim Moreland, *The Medievalist Impulse in American Literature: Twain, Adams, Fitzgerald, and Hemingway* (Charlottesville: University Press of Virginia, 1996), 7.

15 Catherine Brown, "In the Middle," *Journal of Medieval and Early Modern Studies* 30.3 (2000): 547–74, at 547.

16 Catherine Brown, "In the Middle," 548.

17 Rebecca Barnhouse, *Recasting the Past: The Middle Ages in Young Adult Literature* (Portsmouth, NH: Boynton/Cook, 2000), x. Barnhouse's book is the most extended study of the Middle Ages in literature for young adults, and it therefore asserts an authority on the subject that limits more than it uncovers. While many scholarly studies address "medieval" children's and YA literature, they tend to focus on individual authors and novels rather than exploring the genre as a whole.

18 Rebecca Barnhouse, "Of Trenchers and Trestle Tables: Recent Young Adult Novels Set in the Middle Ages," *Medieval Academy News* (September 2009), 8.

19 James Kritzeck, *Peter the Venerable and Islam* (Princeton: Princeton University Press, 1964), 164–65.

20 Headnote to "All the World Shall Come to Serve Thee," ("V'yehehtayo Kol L'avdechah"), *Machzor: High Holiday Prayer Book*, ed. Rabbi Morris Silverman (Hartford, CT: Prayer Book, 1951), 363.

21 Rebecca Barnhouse, *Recasting the Past*, 13 and 10.

22 Louise Fradenburg, "Voice Memorial: Loss and Reparation in Chaucer's Poetry," *Exemplaria* 2.1 (1990): 169–202, at 172–73.

23 In Stephanie Spinner's *Damosel* (New York: Knopf, 2008), Damosel and her cousin Nimue are both bound by a series of *Rules Governing the Ladies of the Lake*, capable of various sorts of magic, yet involved in authentic crafts such as jewelry and sword making.

24 Catherine Brown, "In the Middle," 547.

25 For series that provide a more magical perspective, see, for instance, T. A. Barron, *The Great Tree of Avalon* series, *The Lost Years of Merlin*, or *Merlin's Dragon*. More classic examples include Lloyd Alexander's *Chronicles of Prydain* and Susan Cooper's *The Dark Is Rising* series. These novels operate in a liminal space more enchanted than anything seen in medieval romance, yet they too draw from the spirit of medieval romance, observing conventions of the quest narrative, the Arthurian story, and the magic seen in medieval texts.

26 Catherine Jinks, *Pagan's Crusade* (Cambridge, MA: Candlewick, 1992), 2–3.

27 Catherine Jinks, *Pagan's Crusade*, 6.

28 Michael Spradlin, *Orphan of Destiny: The Youngest Templar, Book 3* (New York: Putnam, 2010), 240.

29 Catherine Jinks, *Pagan's Crusade*, 242.

30 Catherine Jinks, *Pagan in Exile* (Cambridge, MA: Candlewick, 1994), 320.

31 Catherine Jinks, *Pagan's Vows* (Cambridge, MA: Candlewick, 1995), 327.

32 Rebecca Barnhouse, *The Coming of the Dragon* (New York: Random House, 2010), 306.

33 Rebecca Barnhouse, *The Coming of the Dragon*, 290.

34 Rebecca Barnhouse, *The Coming of the Dragon*, 210.

35 *Beowulf*, ed. Franz Klaeber (Lexington, MA: Heath, 1950), lines 2767–69. The translation is by Howell Chickering, ed. and trans., *Beowulf: A Dual-Language Edition* (New York: Doubleday, 1977), lines 2767–69.

36 Alison Lurie, *Boys and Girls Forever: Children's Classics from Cinderella to Harry Potter* (New York: Penguin, 2003), xi.

37 Cressida Cowell, *How to Train Your Dragon* (New York: Little Brown, 2004).

38 Cressida Cowell, *How to Train Your Dragon*, 54.

39 Louise Fradenburg, "Voice Memorial," 192.

40 Catherine Brown, "In the Middle," 553.

5 King Arthur's and Robin Hood's Adventures in Medievalism

Mythic Masculinities (and Magical Femininities)

One is a king, the other an outlaw, but both men illustrate the allure of mythical versions of medieval masculinity. King Arthur rules over a Golden Age Britain, one in which disparate factions have united to protect the land, whereas Robin Hood resists the tyrannical authority of an unjust and corrupt monarchy, creating a pastoral fellowship fighting on behalf of oppressed commoners. As the leaders of their respective companies of knights and foresters, King Arthur and Robin Hood stand as the preeminent figures in the legends celebrating their valiant achievements, yet their contrasting, and at times overlapping, brands of heroism testify to the looseness of the medieval heroic tradition and its modern incarnations. While culturally celebrated as paragons of mythic heroism, Arthur and Robin Hood also ironically embody the inherent instabilities of lionized masculinities, thereby exposing the lurking solecism implicit in viewing medieval masculinities as transhistorically triumphant. As Holly Crocker forcefully demonstrates, masculinity has historically been shielded as a topic of critical inquiry due to its culturally invisible status: "Masculinity's presumption of universality is [a] myth," she argues, as she proceeds to unpick the ways in which "medieval categories of sex, gender, race, and sexuality were culturally constructed."[1] King Arthur and Robin Hood function within this framework of invisibility, in that their masculinities are so naturalized and lionized as to appear to be eternal truths of male honor, morality, and virtue; their heroic genders, both in their medieval and post-medieval incarnations, nonetheless demand exploration for the contradictions at their core.

In many instances, medieval heroes are modern creations: knights, kings, and other medieval heroes of modern popular culture attest to the continued appeal of the Middle Ages, yet, as Martha Driver and Sid Ray note, the gap between heroes of medieval literature and their modern avatars is striking. "The hero as conceived in postmodern America usually bears little resemblance to a medieval knight with his storied *nobilitas*, *genealogie*, or *gentilesse*,"[2] they declare, and medieval heroes such as King Arthur and Robin Hood, through a continual process of accretion and renewal, frequently mirror the exemplary values of the periods of their rewriting more than of their original creation. Today's versions of King Arthur and Robin Hood often resemble action heroes of Hollywood cinema rather than a knight of medieval romance or an outlaw from medieval ballads. Jill Mann outlines the characteristics of romance heroes, which differ markedly from those of protagonists of action-adventure films: "The romance hero does not seek to execute a consciously developed plan; rather, he seeks 'adventures' in general, and allows chance … to dictate the shape they will take. His role is to respond rather than to initiate, to suffer rather than to struggle."[3] Also, despite their superiority in arms and strength over their foes, romance heroes do not display the bloody aggression of their modern-day descendants: for instance, mercy stands as a key virtue of medieval knights, yet heroes of Hollywood blockbusters frequently slaughter without hesitation all opponents impeding their paths. From a medieval perspective, Robin Hood is not a romance hero but a figure from folk and ballad culture, yet he is frequently treated as a romance hero in retellings of his legend, thus blurring the parameters of medieval heroism further both in its historical roots and in its modern retellings.

Part of the mythical allure of King Arthur and Robin Hood lies in the possibility—slight though it may be—that they were real men, and this possibility humanizes their mythic masculinities: if they once lived in the past, their achievements can be realized again in the present, inspiring many aficionados of their legends with visions of morally triumphant masculinity. If an historical Arthur existed, he likely lived sometime near or during the fifth century C.E., and his heroic status perhaps arose from defending the native Britons against invading Saxon warriors when the land was left vulnerable to attack following the Romans' retreat from the British Isles in 410. Gildas's *On the Downfall and Conquest of Britain* (*De excidio et conquestu Britannaie*, c. 540) describes such a conflict between Britons and Saxons, and the Venerable Bede also mentions this conflict in his *Ecclesiastical History of the English People* (*Historia ecclesiastica gentis Anglorum*, 731). Somewhat problematic to the historical reconstruction of King Arthur's biography is that these histories refer to this hero as Ambrosius Aurelianus. Nennius's *History of the Britons* (*Historia Brittonum*, c. 800) is the first Latin chronicle to cite Arthur by name, and even in this early account of his reign, his outsized masculinity defines his heroic accomplishments. The *History of the Britons* details a long struggle between the native Britons and the invading Saxons, in which Arthur triumphs due to an amazing display of heroic prowess during their twelfth battle: "Duodecimum fuit bellum in monte Badonis, in quo corruerunt in uno die nongenti sexaginta viri de uno impetu Arthur; et nemo prostravit eos nisi ipse solus, et in omnibus bellis victor extitit" ("The twelfth was the battle of Mount Badon, in which nine hundred and sixty men fell from a single attack of Arthur, and nobody put them down except him alone, and in every one of the battles he emerged as victor"). Nennius also testifies to Arthur's Christianity, affirming that "Arthur portavit imaginem sanctae Mariae perpetuae virginis super humeros suos, et pagani versi sunt in fugam in illo die, et caedes magna fuit super illos per virtutem Domini nostri Jesu Christi et per virtutem sanctae Mariae virginis genitricis ejus" ("Arthur carried an image of St. Mary, the Perpetual Virgin on his shoulders, and the pagans were put to flight on that day, and there was a great massacre of them through the power of Our Lord Jesus Christ and his mother Mary").[4] Notwithstanding the implausibility of Arthur's superhuman martial abilities and his unlikely adoption of Christianity for his religion (well prior to Augustine of Canterbury's late sixth-century mission to convert the people of England to Christianity), Nennius's account of the king's victory creates a unvanquishable Christian as the hero of this legend, proving the righteousness of his faith in a land of conflicting religious beliefs. For Nennius, Arthur's masculinity and military prowess are inextricably linked to his spiritual leadership, with martial and religious values uniting throughout the land due to his leadership. From these relatively scant beginnings, the Arthurian legends grew, and in his *History of the Kings of Britain* (*Historia regum Britanniae*, c. 1138–47), Geoffrey of Monmouth compiles key components of Arthur's heroic legend, including the mysterious circumstances of his birth, his decapitation of the giant of Mont St. Michel, and his calamitous battle with his son Mordred. Geoffrey claims a "Britannici sermonis librum uetustissimum" ("certain very ancient book written in the British language") as the source for his history, yet his contemporaries and modern scholars agree that this source is likely a fabrication.[5] In his detailed account of Arthur's assumption of the throne and his ensuing exploits, Geoffrey transformed a quasi-historical warrior of little more than a name into the preeminent hero of his age (and of subsequent ages as well).

As with the quasi-historical accounts of Gildas, Bede, Nennius, and Geoffrey of Monmouth in regard to King Arthur, Robin Hood's legend is elliptically recorded in medieval chronicles, providing the possibility of a factual foundation for the many legends surrounding his career. These chroniclers debate the heroic status of the outlaw, staking out opposing positions in regard to his criminality, with some excoriating and others lionizing him. Andrew Wyntoun praises Robin in his *Oryginale Chronicle* (c. 1420)—"Litil Iohun and Robert Hude/Waythmen [hunters] war commendit gud/In Ingilwode and Bernnysdaile"[6]—but Walter Bower's *Continuation* of John of Fordun's *Scotichronicon* (c. 1440) condemns Robin and his men as criminals: "Then arose the famous murderer, Robert Hood, as well as Little John, together with their accomplices from among the disinherited, whom the foolish populace are so inordinately fond of celebrating both in tragedies and comedies, and about whom they are delighted to hear the jesters and minstrels sing above all other ballads."[7] By locating Robin's devotees among the "foolish populace" and placing his legend in the ballad tradition, Bower denigrates the hero as one who appeals to low-culture tastes. In his *History of Greater Britain* (*Historia Majoris Britanniae*, 1521), John Major censures Robin's crimes while praising his motivations: "About this time it was, as I conceive, that there flourished those most famous robbers Robert Hood, an Englishman, and Little John, who lay in wait in the woods but spoiled of their goods those only that were wealthy. ... The robberies of this man I condemn, but of all robbers he was the humanest and the chief."[8] In these documents, Robin Hood emerges as a larger-than-life figure, one who simultaneously attracts contempt and praise due to the morally ambiguous nature of his enterprise.

From their ephemeral foundations in history, the stories of King Arthur and his glorious knights and of Robin Hood and his devoted huntsmen multiplied. For King Arthur this metamorphosis entailed transcending his pseudo-historical roots and flourishing in the genre of medieval romance. The twelfth-century French poet Chrétien de Troyes elevated Arthurian narratives into literary art in the romances *Erec and Enide*, *Cligés*, *Lancelot*, *Yvain*, and *Perceval*, yet Arthur is a curiously peripheral character in Chrétien's narratives, one who, for the most part, resides comfortably in his castle as the eponymous questing knights set forth on their adventures. The French Vulgate Cycle (c. 1215–35), comprising *The History of the Holy Grail* (*Estoire del Saint Graal*), *The Story of Merlin* (*Estoire de Merlin*), *Lancelot*, *The Quest for the Holy Grail* (*Queste del Saint Graal*), and *The Death of Arthur* (*Mort Artu*), proved profoundly influential in setting the basic parameters of the characters, personalities, and quests of Arthurian narratives, and throughout these adventures, King Arthur is famous not merely for his own exploits, but also for those of the many knights associated with him. Such figures as Lancelot, Perceval, Galahad, Bors, and Tristan, among others, are celebrated in their own legendary stories and accomplishments that redound to the benefit of Arthur's reputation. Indeed, King Arthur is such a peripheral character in many Arthurian legends that his name is merely mentioned as a touchstone figure of exemplary kingship, as in several of the *Tristan* romances and in Heldris of Cornwall's thirteenth-century romance *Silence*. In establishing the excellence of King Evan's rule in *Silence*, the narrator need only compare him favorably to Arthur: "Si maintint bien en pais la terre/Fors solement le roi Artu/N'i ot ainc rien de sa vertu" "([King Evan] maintained peace in his land;/with the sole exception of King Arthur,/there never was his equal)."[9]

Despite these strong roots in French literary traditions, King Arthur's legend has inspired numerous English authors as well. The single finest Arthurian romance of the English Middle Ages, the anonymously penned *Sir Gawain and the Green Knight*, recounts Gawain's quest to preserve his honor after failing to vanquish his monstrously verdant adversary at Camelot. Arthur's role in this fourteenth-century legend is mostly decorative, as he presides over his court in the manner of an impetuous child: "[Arthur] watz so joly of his joyfnes, and sumquat childered" ("[Arthur] was so jolly in his youthfulness—and just a bit juvenile)."[10] Hardly a model of masculine authority, Arthur's impetuous youth in this romance implicitly questions his fitness for the spiritual duties of kingship. Sir Thomas Malory's *Morte D'Arthur*, printed in 1485 by William Caxton, relies heavily on the Vulgate Cycle as its source. In Malory's encyclopedic work, Arthur's role is most prominent in its beginning and end, as these sections respectively detail his rise to the throne and then the final fall of Camelot. In Malory's telling of the legend, the defining irony of Arthur's status as masculine ideal is stressed: despite the greatness of his reign, he is cuckolded by Guinevere and Lancelot. Moreover, upon discovering their infidelity, Arthur regrets the loss of his men rather than of his lady, as he laments: "And much more I am soryar for my good knyghtes losse than for the losse of my fayre queen; for quenys I myght have inow [enough], but such a felyship of good knyghtes shall never be togydirs in no company."[11] Arthur more esteems the service offered by his devoted knights than Guinevere's fidelity or affection; as Arthurian romances emphasize gendered dynamics in which a knight abases himself to prove his devotion to his lady, Arthur's nonchalant reaction to losing Guinevere places him outside this courtly tradition.

In 1684 John Dryden, the leading literary figure of his day and author of such works as *All for Love*, "Absalom and Achitophel," and *Fables, Ancient and Modern*, wrote a dramatic opera entitled *King Arthur, or the British Worthy*, with Henry Purcell composing the music. Dryden praises King Charles II in the play's dedication, comparing the king with his legendary forebear to their mutual advantage (although, as Dryden declares, the king "liv'd not to see the Performance of it, on the Stage)."[12] For Dryden, the Arthurian legends bespeak an ideal figure of masculine kingship, as evident in this description of the title character:

> ... In battle brave;
> But still Serene in all the Stormy War,
> Like Heaven above the Clouds; after Fight,
> As Merciful and Kind, to vanquisht Foes,
> As a Forgiving God.[13]

Dryden's portrait of King Arthur in this passage focuses on his quasi-divine qualities, and by linking Charles II to Arthur, the poet skillfully deploys the legendary aura of Arthur to curry favor with the successors of the recently deceased king. With most of the traditional story expunged, such as the Lancelot and Guinevere plotline, Dryden proves the utility of Arthur's legendary masculinity in establishing bonds among men, as one man's complimentary assessment of another's manliness builds relationships of mutual support.

Arthur's reputation as England's legendary king could not forever ensure him praise from all quarters, and in the early nineteenth century, Samuel Taylor Coleridge tartly pondered of English literature, "An Epic poem must either be National or Mundane. As to Arthur, you could not by any means make a poem national to Englishmen. What have *We* to do with him?"[14] As the Industrial Revolution effected tremendous shifts and innovations throughout England, Arthur appeared a relic to some, an archaic reminder of yesteryear's failures. In contrast, other poets turned to the legendary king as the ideal representative of England's lost Golden Age. Alfred, Lord Tennyson's *Idylls of the King* revitalized interest in England's mythic sovereign, as this masterwork ascribes to Arthur the highest ideals of chivalry, loyalty, and honor. Similar to Dryden in praising Charles II, Tennyson begins his idylls with a dedication to Queen Victoria's husband Prince Albert, extolling this ruler's virtues by comparing him to Arthur's chivalrous men: "And indeed He seems to me/Scarce other than my king's ideal knight."[15] For Tennyson, Arthur represents the epitome of knightly virtue due to his innate ability to ennoble all mankind, as the opening of his poem emphasizes: "But man was less and less, till Arthur came," the narrator proclaims. He then describes Arthur's reign as a Golden Age because he succeeded in uniting England's warring factions, in contrast to the failures of his predecessors Aurelius and Uther in this regard:

> And after these King Arthur for a space,
> And thro' the puissance of his Table Round,
> Drew all their petty princedoms under him,
> Their king and head, and made a realm, and reign'd.[16]

Tennyson includes among his idylls numerous narratives without Arthur as their focus, including the stories of Gareth and Lynette, Geraint and Enid, Balin and Balan, Merlin and Vivien, Pelleas and Ettare, and Lancelot and Elaine. The vision of Arthur as a triumphant and just ruler provides a thematic touchstone to gauge the honor of Tennyson's other male characters, as the court faces internal dissolution due to sexual duplicity. In this regard Ettare's emasculation of Pelleas, who hisses in spite, "I have no sword," after she betrays him with Gawain, presages the tragic consequences of Lancelot and Guinevere's cuckolding of Arthur.

For the Pre-Raphaelite Brotherhood, a group of British painters and poets of the late nineteenth century including Dante Gabriel Rossetti, William Holman Hunt, and John Everett Millais, the Middle Ages represented an ideal period characterized by humanity's immediate access to nature, when people lived happily tied to the rhythms of the natural world. Their nostalgia for the past was particularly attuned to Arthurian chivalry and the quest motif. Rossetti was a poet as well as a painter, and he proclaimed, undoubtedly with exaggeration, that Malory's Arthurian legends were his sole source of reading: "I never read any [books] at all, except King Arthur and the Knights of the Round Table, which I find overwhelmingly stunning."[17] Rossetti planned (but did not complete) a poem entitled "God's Graal," which he described in a letter to Algernon Charles Swinburne as detailing "Lancelot losing the Sancgrail ... wherein God and Guinevere will be weighed against each other by another table of weights and measures."[18] William Morris, a poet and artist associated with the Pre-Raphaelites due to his friendship with Rossetti, and whose Kelmscott Press issued lavishly illustrated editions of many medieval and medieval-inspired works, wrote a number of Arthurian poems in 1858, including "The Defence of Guenevere," "King Arthur's Tomb," "Sir Galahad: A Christmas Mystery," and "The Chapel in Lyoness." In "The Defence of Guenevere," the queen rebuts Gawain's accusations of adultery, and she obliquely undercuts Arthur's image when referring to her betrothal as "the time ere I was bought/By Arthur's great name and his little love."[19] Despite this "little love," Guinevere discloses her frustrated affection for Arthur in Morris's "King Arthur's Tomb," in which Lancelot and Guinevere reunite at the titular location and Guinevere wonders, "Launcelot, Launcelot, why did he take your hand,/When he had kissed me in his kingly way?"[20] Morris's revisioning of the Arthurian legend casts Arthur as an ambivalent figure, one whose reputation merits respect despite his inability to quell the erotic tensions in his household. Morris implicitly criticizes Arthur for concentrating on his role as monarch rather than as husband, thus anticipating the need for twentieth-century feminist retellings of the archetypal gender roles on display in much Arthurian legend.

Within the American literary tradition, numerous poets, including Ralph Waldo Emerson, Sara Teasdale, Edna St. Vincent Millay, Dorothy Parker, Sinclair Lewis, and Edgar Lee Masters, have written verses with Arthurian themes, despite the incongruity between the values of a legendary English monarchy and American democratic individualism. Keenly aware of this cultural divide between England and America, Mark Twain pillories the Arthurian legend in *A Connecticut Yankee in King Arthur's Court* (1889), casting Arthur as tainted by his aristocratic privilege. The titular Yankee, Hank Morgan, assesses how the tyranny of monarchy corrupts Arthur when he (Arthur) advocates returning escaped peasants to their cruel lord: "There it was, again. He could see only one side of it. He was born so, educated so, his veins were full of ancestral blood that was rotten with this sort of unconscious brutality, brought down by inheritance from a long procession of hearts that had each done its share toward poisoning the stream."[21] Reviling the anti-democratic nature of monarchy, Twain casts Arthur as more an ignorant man than a tyrant, but his lack of empathy for his suffering subjects earns him the opprobrium of the novel's protagonist. Twain's condemnation of Arthur contrasts sharply with the more adulatory tone with which his legend is generally treated, and despite the anti-monarchical sentiments of many Americans, other writers concentrate on the inspiring potential of this legendary material. Almost one hundred years after Twain's *Connecticut Yankee*, John Steinbeck, author of *East of Eden* and *The Grapes of Wrath*, translated and revised Malory's *Morte D'Arthur* in his *Acts of King Arthur*. This work was published posthumously in 1976, and it captures his belief in the inherent nobility of the Arthurian legend. In the Prologue to this work, Steinbeck explains his desire to bring Malory's text to a modern audience—"For a long time I have wanted to bring to present-day usage the stories of King Arthur and the Knights of the Round Table. These stories are alive even in those of us who have not read them"[22]—and he also declares his belief in the moral value of the *Morte D'Arthur*: "I don't know any book save only the Bible and perhaps Shakespeare which has had more effect on our morals, our ethics, and our mores than this same Malory."[23] For Steinbeck, Arthur and his questing knights bespeak a desire for earthly perfection, and although this dream is preordained to fail, it is nonetheless an inspirational experience for those undertaking it, as well as for those reading of it. Arthur serves as a masculine avatar of all virtues for Steinbeck, illuminating for his readers moral lessons necessary to live righteous lives.

In contrast to these literary treatments of King Arthur, many of which are regarded as canonical achievements in the history of English and American letters, Robin Hood's legend remains more firmly in the realm of popular culture. Also, Robin's masculinity borders on the illicit due to his criminality, and thus contrasts with Arthur's regal authority, a factor that contributes further to his status as an outsider. The medieval ballads in which his legend grew, an artistic tradition attuned to folk (rather than literary) culture, paint Robin Hood as a (mostly) selfless hero fighting against a corrupt nobility, and he is often portrayed as an ethical scamp due to his propensity for outwitting his foes. Sometimes strongly imbued in medieval popular religion, Robin Hood can comfortably and sincerely thank the Virgin Mary for putting people to rob in his path. In "Robin Hood and Guy of Gisborne," he kills his enemy Guy and then impersonates him, claiming in this disguise that he has killed himself so that he can rescue Little John:

> "But [since] now I have slaine the master," he sayd,
> "Let me goe strike the knave;
> This is all the reward I aske,
> Nor noe other will I have."[24]

With this ploy, Robin Hood deceives the Sheriff of Nottingham into believing he will dispatch Little John, but frees him instead. Little John then succeeds in killing his captor: "But Little John, with an arrow broade,/Did cleave [the Sheriff's] heart in twinn [in two]."[25] Through a combination of deceit and martial skill, Robin Hood and Little John defeat their enemies, many of whom are seeking to bring these outlaws to justice. Certainly, Robin Hood is also known for his strength in battle, as in "Robin Hood and the Monk," when he kills twelve men in a day.[26]

Beyond his characterization as a trickster and huntsman, Robin Hood is a desirable lover, further contributing to his idealized masculinity. In "Robin Hood and the Potter," his courtesy to ladies—"All wemen werschepyd he"—models the chivalric treatment of women expected from knights of the medieval romance tradition.[27] At the same time, Robin is often paired romantically with strong female characters, which testifies to the suppleness of gender roles even in the early texts of this legendary material. Maid Marian, Robin Hood's traditional love interest, is known for her beauty, but she is often depicted as Robin's equal as a warrior. In the ballad "Robin Hood and Maid Marian," they fight while both are wearing disguises and thus remain unknown to each other:

> They drew out their swords, and to cutting they went,
> At least an hour or more,
> That the blood ran apace from bold Robins face,
> And Marian was wounded sore.[28]

Proving her ability to match Robin blow for blow, here Marian rejects the damsel-in-distress role that she fulfills in other versions of this legendary material. Likewise, in the ballad "Robin Hood's Birth, Breeding, Valour, and Marriage," Robin Hood's romantic interest is another strong woman. Clorinda, "queen of the shepherds," kills the fattest buck of the herd, to Robin Hood's amazement: "'By the faith of my body,' said bold Robin Hood/'I never saw woman like thee.'"[29] He soon decides, "[H]ow sweet it would be,/If Clorinda would be my bride!"[30] Unlike the knights of the romance tradition, who abase themselves for their ladies by obeying their every whim, Robin enjoys egalitarian relationships with women, as both Maid Marian and Clorinda are characterized as powerful women able to defend themselves from their enemies without the assistance of their suitor.

Although the renegade Robin Hood superficially bears little resemblance to the regal King Arthur, shared tropes in the depictions of these men point to the likelihood of crossings between ballads, with their roots in folk culture, and romances, with their roots in literary culture. For example, in such romances as *Sir Gawain and the Green Knight*, King Arthur refuses to eat his dinner unless he hears a tale or witnesses a marvel—"he wolde neuer ete/Vpon such a dere day er hym deuised were/Of sum auenturus thing an vncouthe tale" ("For he had established the noble custom that he never would sup/On a high and holy day until he had first heard/An unusual account of some adventuresome affair")[31]—and Robin Hood likewise eschews food in preference of adventure in "A Gest of Robyn Hode": "To dyne have I noo lust,/Till that I have som bolde baron,/Or som unkouth gest."[32] Furthermore, if Robin Hood is established as a countercultural hero in various ballads, he nonetheless bears himself royally and wins deference from his followers. King Edward marvels at the dedication of Robin's men:

> "Here is a wonder seemly syght;
> Me thynketh, by Goddes pyne [pain],
> His men are more at his byddynge
> Then my men be at myn."[33]

More respected than the king himself, Robin Hood embodies the oxymoron of a royal outcast: he leads his men as the prince of thieves, as he is sometimes dubbed, who rules more justly than the corrupt authorities with whom he battles, thereby proving the allure of masculinity predicated on a man's moral actions rather than on his royal lineage (and potential perversion of the social contract).

The many ballads of Robin Hood testify to his popularity in folk-culture traditions, yet they also underscore his relative absence from the literary realm. As Stephen Knight summarizes, "The Robin Hood tradition has always been popular in the sense of being highly successful with audiences, but it is also popular in a more searching sense, apparently resisting elevation to the high literary canon. Major writers have either refused to enter the greenwood of the Robin Hood tradition or have done so without much commitment or success."[34] Knight mentions several examples of canonical authors who address the Robin Hood legend in their literature, including Ben Jonson, John Keats, Sir Walter Scott, Thomas Love Peacock, and Alfred, Lord Tennyson, but, as he suggests, none of these efforts are as sustained or artistically accomplished as, for instance, *Sir Gawain and the Green Knight* or Tennyson's *Idylls of the King*. These literary treatments of the Robin Hood legend nonetheless illustrate key aspects of the hero's allure and his enduring appeal, as well as the ways in which his masculinity is predicated upon resistance to external corruption.

In Keats's short poem "Robin Hood: To a Friend" (1818), the narrator laments the loss of the greenwood heroes and expresses his nostalgic longing for the camaraderie of this legendary past:

> But you never may behold
> Little John, or Robin bold;
> Never one, of all the clan,
> Thrumming on an empty can
> Some old hunting ditty.[35]

The simplicity of the image—Robin Hood and his men enjoying a ballad, perhaps one recounting their own triumphs—evokes a sense of regret for the lost hero and the times he represents. Tennyson's passion for medieval legends is best attested by his rewriting of Arthurian legends in *Idylls of the King*, but toward the end of his life, he wrote *The Foresters* (1892), a play based on Robin Hood. R. B. Dobson and J. Taylor declare the play to be "well below the level of Tennyson's best work,"[36] yet it nonetheless evinces a jauntiness appropriate to the plucky adventurer. Friar Tuck encourages Robin to retire to the woods, where his men will follow him—"Be thou their leader and they will all of them/Swarm to thy voice like bees to the brass pan"—to which Robin breathlessly replies:

> "—By St. Nicholas
> I have a sudden passion for the wild wood—
> We should be free as air in the wild wood—
> What say you? shall we go? Your hands, your hands!"[37]

Such unrestrained eagerness for a life in nature marks the Robin Hood legend as unequivocally pastoral in its imagination: escaping the corruption of city life by relocating to the wild woods, Robin Hood is acutely attuned to the natural world and models a unity with nature appealing to many alienated by urban tensions.

The fact that Robin Hood has mostly avoided the realm of high culture does not imply that he has remained static; on the contrary, the various popular-culture treatments of his adventures testify to the protean adaptability of this outlaw legend. As John Marshall notes: "Robin [has shifted] in shape over the years from the sometimes violent, anti-authoritarian yeoman of the late medieval ballads and games through the genteel, dispossessed nobleman of Renaissance plays and Victorian novels to the Green Lord of the Wildwood, the incarnation of spring, of new age literature"; throughout these transformations, "he and his adventures have epitomized the Middle Ages."[38] So too for King Arthur: his legends, despite their differing treatments in the literary canon, converge in modern popular culture as defining exemplars of medieval heroism and masculinity. The countless (and often seemingly random) examples of King Arthur and Robin Hood in popular culture testify to the enduring legacy of these heroes: numerous videogames and comic books retell their legends, but they are also encoded in tourism (e.g., the Excalibur Hotel and Casino in Las Vegas) and even housing tracts (e.g., suburban subdivisions named Sherwood Forest in Detroit, Michigan; Memphis, Tennessee; Baton Rouge, Louisiana; and Charlotte, North Carolina).

Within the realm of popular culture, the continued appeal of King Arthur and Robin Hood is most apparent in Hollywood cinema, as both heroes are the subject of numerous films recording and expanding on their legends. The many Arthurs and Robin Hoods of cinematic history vary remarkably in their characterizations, proving once again the malleability of the medieval hero tradition. Notable entries in the Arthurian cinematic corpus include *A Connecticut Yankee in King Arthur's Court*, starring Bing Crosby and Rhonda Fleming (dir. Tay Garnett, 1949); *Camelot*, starring Richard Harris and Vanessa Redgrave (dir. Joshua Logan, 1967); *Excalibur*, starring Nigel Terry, Nicholas Clay, and Helen Mirren (dir. John Boorman, 1981); *First Knight*, starring Sean Connery and Richard Gere (dir. Jerry Zucker, 1995); and *King Arthur*, starring Clive Owen and Keira Knightley (dir. Antoine Fuqua, 2004). The most acclaimed entries in the Robin Hood cinematic canon include *Robin Hood*, starring Douglas Fairbanks and Wallace Beery (dir. Allan Dwan, 1922); *Adventures of Robin Hood*, starring Errol Flynn, Basil Rathbone, and Olivia de Havilland (dir. Michael Curtiz, 1938); *Robin and Marian*, starring Sean Connery and Audrey Hepburn (dir. Richard Lester, 1976); *Robin Hood: Prince of Thieves*, starring Kevin Costner and Morgan Freeman (dir. Kevin Reynolds, 1991); and *Robin Hood*, starring Russell Crowe and Cate Blanchett (dir. Ridley Scott, 2010).[39]

The heroism on display in these films shifts from one retelling of the legend to another, as is evident in the various incarnations of masculinity performed by the stars playing the lead role. In *A Connecticut Yankee in King Arthur's Court*, Bing Crosby plays the cool Yankee in contrast to Cedric Harwicke's ineffective Arthur, whereas Richard Harris's introspective musings on justice and fidelity imbue *Camelot* with a melancholic air. *Excalibur* features Nigel Terry as a young Arthur seeking to revive his land through a grail quest, whereas Sean Connery's Arthur in *First Knight* is a warrior past his prime, one distraught by Guinevere and Lancelot's infidelity yet steadfastly true to his people. *King Arthur* queries the ethics of serving an unjust Roman regime, with Clive Owen taciturnly performing the role of a stalwart Arthur faced with the ethical ramifications of his violent actions. The numerous cinematic Robin Hoods likewise depict varying and even contradictory paradigms of masculinity, ranging from Douglas Fairbanks's silent swashbuckling and Errol Flynn's plucky adventuring to later revisions of such jaunty heroism, including Sean

Connery's impotent salvos of an aging man past his warrior prime in *Robin and Marian*; Kevin Costner's laconic introspection in a politically correct medieval world in *Robin Hood: Prince of Thieves*; and Russell Crowe's moody archer called to impersonate nobility in *Robin Hood*.

As King Arthur and Robin Hood inspire allegiance from their knights and foresters, as well as from their modern-day fans, they likewise inspire feminist revisions of their legends, as various authors rewrite the cultural meanings of femininity, and of masculinity as well, in these narratives. Female writers, including Marion Zimmer Bradley, Sharan Newman, Persia Woolley, and Rosalind Miles, have challenged the overarching masculine ethos of Arthurian legend by depicting in greater psychological depth the challenges facing the tradition's women. Their stories recast the gendered politics of Arthurian romances by exploring the knightly world of chivalry through the perspectives of such characters as Guinevere, Morgan le Fay (Arthur's sister and frequent antagonist), and Igraine (his mother). For example, in Bradley's *The Mists of Avalon* (1982), Morgaine retells the Arthurian legend from her perspective, implicitly (and at times explicitly) absolving herself of her characterization in much Arthurian literature as a villain:

> *In my time I have been called many things: sister, lover, princess, wise-woman, queen. Now in truth I have come to be wise-woman, and a time may come when these things may need to be known. But in sober truth, I think it is the Christians who will tell the last tale. For ever the world of Fairy drifts further from the world in which the Christ holds sway.*[40]

No longer a character of pure (and often irrational) malevolence, Morgaine speaks her truths throughout Bradley's novel, rewriting literary and religious traditions that, from her viewpoint, have stifled women's roles in the western world. Although Bradley's *The Mists of Avalon* is the most influential of feminist retellings of the Arthurian legend, other such novels in this tradition similarly explore the desires of Arthurian women hidden from view in a literature that has historically been written more by men than by women.

Counterbalancing the mythic masculinities of Arthurian knights, these feminist visions of Arthurian women celebrate a magical and mystical view of femininity, in which female characters are graced with deep insights and keen spiritual awareness about the challenges, both sacred and secular, of their world. If these novels follow *The Mists of Avalon* in their ambitions to revise the reputations and motivations of the story's female characters, Guinevere is a particularly popular figure for resurrection, and she seems to lend herself to a tripartite structure, appearing in trilogies by Sharan Newman (*Guinevere* [1981], *The Chessboard Queen* [1983], *Guinevere Evermore* [1985]); Persia Woolley (*Child of the Northern Spring* [1987], *Queen of the Summer Stars* [1990], *Guinevere: The Legend in Autumn* [1991]); Nancy McKenzie (*Queen of Camelot* [2002], *Guinevere's Gift* [2008], *Guinevere's Gamble* [2009]); and Rosalind Miles (*Guenevere: Queen of the Summer Country* [1998], *Knight of the Sacred Lake* [2000], *Child of the Holy Grail* [2001]). Although the shadow of the adulterous affair with Lancelot that brings down the Arthurian kingdom inflects many of these narratives with a melancholy air, Guinevere takes on a different role and personality (and sometimes spelling) for each author. For Miles, Guinevere stands at the mercy of narrative forces she cannot control, but she shows herself far stronger, more resolute, and more determined than Arthur, who is easily swayed by the magical machinations of Morgan and Morgause. She is also at the center of a battle between the Christianity and the "old religion," centered on the isle of Avalon, for which she serves as protector and representative, the true owner of the Round Table, and, ultimately, the only person able to salvage the values of Arthur's court. Indeed, she proves resistant to the court's demise in several versions: at the end of Sharan Newman's *Guinevere Evermore*, she finds a place for herself in the new world of Saxon-controlled Britain, gamely trying to speak Old English to a group of terrified orphans, assuring them that there are no ghosts (or, we might imagine, only literary ones) in Camelot, which has become something of an orphanage for wayward children under her care. Looking back after a visit from Lancelot, she ruminates: "Being with him again had shown her the gap between her old half-Roman world and this vibrant one of eager newcomers. She had accomplished what she wanted. Arthur would not be forgotten, nor, she believed, his dream. Her home was safe. It had even become a refuge."[41] Her death is coupled with a promise to return to the land of magic, where people have pet unicorns and she can be united with Lancelot forever.

Such a "new age" Guinevere occupies a different position in goddess religion than she does in *The Mists of Avalon*, in which Morgan is charged with the preservation of Avalon, yet the connection of women with magic and pre-Christian religious traditions runs rife in many of these Arthurian novels by, or from the point of view of, women. In her novels *The Dragon Queen* (2001) and *Raven Warrior* (2003), Alice Borchardt envisions a Guinevere closely allied (somewhat mysteriously) with Norse themes and (again) pagan religion: Lancelot is a shape-shifting Raven, and Guinevere is a warrior princess who must protect her land and whose love affairs are primarily alliances to strengthen her forces against the powers of evil. In complementary fashion to her Guinevere trilogy, Miles's trilogy loosely based on the Arthurian version of Tristan and Isolde—*Isolde: Queen of the Western Isle* (2002), *The Maid of the White Hands* (2003), and *Lady of the Sea* (2004)—explores similar themes: Isolde is a "Princess of Erin," one of the last upholders of the old religion in Ireland.

In these reformulations of the gendered dynamics of medieval romance, the Arthurian legends are reclaimed from their masculine ethos, as these authors shift the focus to a powerful femininity that is tied to magic, spirituality, and often pacifism. Arthurian women, bound to a dying religious system that values them and that is embattled by the rise of Christianity, become protectors, warriors, queens, princesses, and healers, warding off a masculine force that can only be held off briefly against an inevitable demise. Ironically, this pattern is similar to the way Arthur emerges, if in reverse: in the chronicles, Arthur's masculinity and martial prowess are inevitably tied to his Christian leadership, joining military and spiritual forces together in the service of political unity, but in these feminist retellings, the characters' femininity is embodied in the intersection of their military (or strategic) and spiritual leadership, although this authority ultimately is what destroys, rather than unites, their worlds, if not the larger Arthurian world in which they function. Feminine potentiality is played out against masculine forces of narrative, and the characters in these novels seem as confined and threatened by the narratives that have been and will continue to be told about them as they are likewise constrained by the forces of patriarchal, monotheistic religion.

If less engaged with preserving and claiming the feminine forces of paganism and pre-Christian religious traditions, retellings of the Robin Hood story from Maid Marian's point of view are equally engaged in reclamation (usually from the intermediary, rather than the actual medieval versions of the stories), depicting Marian as a lively, witty, intelligent, and sincere woman, one who is as important a member of Robin Hood's band as any of the Merry Men. In Robin McKinley's *Outlaws of Sherwood* (1988), Marian is as accomplished an archer as Robin and his male compatriots, and as loyal and powerful a friend, although to enact several of her talents, she must dress as a boy. In doing so she poses various challenges to the legend's masculinity, positing by her actions that the ideal man is really a woman. Marian's disguise blurs gender boundaries, as it also allows her to explore the novel's possibilities for social justice constructed from outlawry. As a female hero (albeit a quiet one; most of the novel is told through Robin's voice), she becomes a much more essential actor in the story, one who embodies all its values, while simultaneously introducing romance values of love. Kathryn Lasky's *Hawksmaid* (2010) and Esther Friesner's *The Sherwood Game* (1995), which sets its story in the world of computer games, construct Marian in similar ways, making her, and her heroics, essential to the story and to Robin's success. Cate Blanchett's performance in Ridley Scott's film *Robin Hood* clearly draws on these same impulses: she is not only essentially the lord of the manor in place of her father, who is too infirm to uphold his duties, but she also serves as the source of the film's romance values (and, in the final battle scene, proves a ferocious and skilled fighter as well).

Feminist retellings of the legends of King Arthur and Robin Hood redress some of the legendary materials' cultural biases, and caricatures and parodies of these corpora likewise reassess their standard plotlines and characters, albeit in a comic mode, to question the desirability of medieval mores. Arthur's and Robin's heroic masculinities cast them as all but invincible warriors—although they die in many versions of their legends—but these seamless performances of triumphant strength invite reimaginings of their legends and their masculinities for the purposes of humor and satire. The classic parody *Monty Python and the Holy Grail* envisions an Arthur (as played by Graham Chapman) who proudly proclaims, "I am Arthur, King of the Britons," only to be met by sneering French soldiers throwing excrement, and revolutionary peasants rolling in muck.[42] At the conclusion of his Grail Quest, Arthur is arrested by the British police for the murder of an historian, and this ending ironically comments on the relationship between the past and those who attempt to interpret it. Mel Brooks's *Robin Hood: Men in Tights* begins with the clichéd sequence of a village under attack, prompting a townsman to complain, in a postmodern and metacinematic interruption of the film's narrative: "Every time they make a Robin Hood movie, they burn our village down." Robin, as played by Cary Elwes, affirms his heroism by itemizing his martial objectives in a list that quickly degrades into ridiculousness: "And tell them also that I vow to put an end to the injustice, right the wrongs, end the tyranny, restore the throne, protect the forest, introduce folk dancing, demand a four-day work week, and affordable health care for Saxons and Normans." The boy he has saved from attack merely agrees, "Yes, yes, good, good," indicating his growing impatience with the hero's inflated ego.[43] *Robin Hood: Men in Tights* follows the standard trajectory of many Robin Hood films, in which Robin battles the Sheriff of "Rottingham" and the usurping Prince John, but his primary adversary in this comic retelling of the legend appears to be the chastity belt circling Maid Marian's waist.

Such comic perspectives on the legends of Arthur and Robin Hood ironically prove the enduring legacy of their heroism: they would not stand as targets of parody if they did not so clearly communicate cultural values still esteemed so many years after the Middle Ages. Within contemporary culture, both King Arthur and Robin Hood appear unlikely to lose their prized positions in the popular imaginary, as their stories are continually resurrected and rewritten for new audiences. As with these new narratives, so too with both heroes, who transcend their deaths and promise their eventual return, as recorded in the foundational texts of their narratives. Certainly, their death scenes depict their loss as devastating to their communities. In *Idylls of the King*, Tennyson envisions Arthur's demise with a sense of heart-wrenching loss, as Bedivere laments his lord's passing:

> "For now I see the true old times are dead,
> When every morning brought a noble chance,
> And every chance brought out a noble knight.
> Such times have been not since the light that led
> The holy Elders with the gift of myrrh."[44]

In these lines Arthur represents an exemplary kingship analogous to Jesus's authority in Christianity: as the preeminent ruler of a lost age of chivalry, his passing signals the changing times, in which all men's heroism consequently dims. The lines also encode a potential anachronism: should Bedivere refer to the recent history of Arthur's reign as "the true old times"? This solecism suggests the ones truly suffering Arthur's loss are all those who have come after his glorious reign, including, not merely the characters of the story, but those reading Tennyson's poetry. Several ballads of Robin Hood likewise end with the hero's death, such as in "The Death of Robin Hood," in which a prioress bleeds Robin Hood, ostensibly to cure him, but in fact conspires with his enemy Red Roger to kill him. In his final moments, he shoots an arrow to mark the location of his grave—"And where this arrow is taken up,/There shall my grave digged be"[45]—and this final act establishes a mystical bond between the man and archery that transcends his death. "Robyn and Gandelyn" begins and ends with the refrain, "Robynn lyth in grene wode bowndyn [bound in his funeral shroud],"[46] and these lines establish a mournful tone for this ballad detailing Robin's death at the hands of Wrennok of Donne, and Gandelyn's avenging of this treachery.

Key to the enduring legacy of King Arthur and Robin Hood is the promise that, despite their deaths, they continue to protect England and her citizenry: Arthur is the *rex quondam rexque futurus*, the once and future king, as proclaimed in numerous legends (and in the title of T. H. White's modern masterpiece of the Arthurian legend).[47] Geoffrey of Monmouth avers, "Sed et inclitus ille rex arturus letaliter volneratus est qui illuc ad sananda uulnera sua in insulam avallonis euectus" ("Arthur himself, our renowned king, was mortally wounded and was carried off to the isle of Avalon, so that his wounds might be attended to").[48] This hint that Arthur survived the conflict with Mordred became a defining feature of his legend, and Wace states more explicitly in his twelfth-century *Roman de Brut*:

> Arthur, si la geste ne ment,
> Fud el cors nafrez mortelment;
> En Avalon se fist porter
> Pur ses plaies mediciner.
> Encore i est, Bretun l'atendent,
> Si cum il dient e entendent;
> De la vendra, encor puet vivre.

> Arthur, if the chronicle is true, received a mortal wound to his body. He had himself carried to Avalon, for the treatment of his wounds. He is still there, awaited by the Britons, as they say and believe, and will return and may live again.[49]

Indeed, the promise of Arthur's return inspires new additions to the corpus of his kingship, such as in Mike Barr and Brian Bolland's *Camelot 3000*, a space-age science-fiction and superhero graphic novel that takes its inspiration from the prophecy of Arthur's return at Britain's moment of greatest need: "How *long*—how many nights has slept Arthur Pendragon, King of Britain, Lord of the Roman Empire?", Arthur asks as he wakes from his centuries of slumber and then quickly prepares to defeat an incoming army of aliens and his old nemeses, Morgan le Fay and Mordred.[50] Likewise, Robin Hood is seen as an almost saintly figure in death, as Richard Grafton details in his *Chronicle at Large* (1569), in which the popular acclamation accorded to the hero ascribes to

him the preternatural ability to give hope and comfort to travelers on dangerous roads: "And the cause why she buried him there was for that the common
passengers and travailers knowyng and seeyng him there buryed, might more
safely and without feare take their jorneys that way, which they durst not do in
the life of the sayd outlawes."[51] Eternally inspiring the commoners long after
his death, Robin Hood's legend provides hope to those seeking succor while
traveling England's dangerous roads.

A king and an outlaw, yet their paths converge in the creation of mythical
paradigms of medieval manhood. Respectively representing the monarchy and
resistance against the tyranny of the monarchy, they conflict in their social
positions yet unite in modeling virtues of bravery, loyalty, honor, chivalry, and
fellowship. Perhaps their differences are best symbolized by their respective
weapons: for Arthur, the glorious Excalibur, a sword befitting a king and an
emblem of courtly knighthood; for Robin Hood, a simple bow and arrow, an
instrument of the hunt and a requisite for life in the forest. No matter the many
times that their stories are rewritten and their values re-signified for new audiences, the images of King Arthur's and Robin Hood's masculine strength and
honor persist, coloring their legends with the heady allure of an inviolate masculinity, no matter the contradictions and paradoxes in their stories' presentation of such heroism. As enduring models of medievalisms' investment in
gender and masculinity, Arthur and Robin Hood prove the longstanding allure
of men valiantly fighting for justice and honor, as they also attest to the malleability of gender roles in the many retellings of their tales, for these heroes, no
matter the consistencies and variations among their legends, can always be
re-envisioned to incarnate distinct and unique versions of masculinity reflective
of modern desires.

Notes

1 Holly Crocker, *Chaucer's Visions of Manhood* (New York: Palgrave Macmillan, 2007), 3.
2 Martha Driver and Sid Ray, "Preface: Hollywood Knights," *The Medieval Hero on Screen*, ed. Martha Driver and Sid Ray (Jefferson, NC: McFarland, 2004), 5–17, at 5.
3 Jill Mann, "Sir Gawain and the Romance Hero," *Heroes and Heroines in Medieval English Literature*, ed. Leo Carruthers (Cambridge: D. S. Brewer, 1994), 105–17, at 107.
4 Nennius, *British History and the Welsh Annals*, ed. John Morris (London: Phillimore, 1980), 76. The translation is from James J. Wilhelm, "Arthur in the Latin Chronicles," *The Romance of Arthur: An Anthology of Medieval Texts in Translation*, ed. James J. Wilhelm (New York: Garland, 1994), 3–9, at 5.
5 Geoffrey of Monmouth, *The History of the Kings of Britain*, ed. Michael Reeve (Cambridge: Brewer, 2007), at 2.9–10. A particularly fine translation of Geoffrey of Monmouth is available in *The History of the Kings of Britain*, ed. and trans. Lewis Thorpe (London: Penguin, 1966), 52.
6 Stephen Knight and Thomas Ohlgren, ed., *Robin Hood and Other Outlaw Tales* (Kalamazoo: Medieval Institute Publications, 2000), 24.
7 Stephen Knight and Thomas Ohlgren, *Robin Hood and Other Outlaw Tales*, 26.
8 Stephen Knight and Thomas Ohlgren, *Robin Hood and Other Outlaw Tales*, 27.

9 Heldris of Cornwall, *Silence*, ed. and trans. Sarah Roche-Mahdi (East Lansing: Colleagues, 1992), 7, lines 108–10. The text and translation are both Roche-Mahdi's.

10 J. R. R. Tolkien and E. V. Gordon, ed., *Sir Gawain and the Green Knight*, 2nd ed., ed. Norman Davis (Oxford: Clarendon, 1967), 3, line 86; the translation is James J. Wilhelm, *Sir Gawain and the Green Knight*, *The Romance of Arthur*, 403, line 86.

11 Thomas Malory, *Works*, ed. Eugène Vinaver, 2nd ed. (London: Oxford University Press, 1971), 685.

12 John Dryden, *King Arthur, or The British Worthy: A Dramatick Opera*, in *Dryden: The Dramatic Works*, ed. Montague Summers (New York: Gordian, 1968), 6.231–89, at 239.

13 John Dryden, *King Arthur*, 248.

14 Samuel Taylor Coleridge, *Table Talk*, *The Collected Works of Samuel Taylor Coleridge*, ed. Carl Woodring (Princeton: Princeton University Press, 1990), 14.441, for the discussion dated 2 September 1833.

15 Alfred, Lord Tennyson, *Idylls of the King*, ed. J. M. Gray (London: Penguin, 1983), 19, lines 6–7.

16 Alfred, Lord Tennyson, *Idylls of the King*, 21, lines 12, 16–19.

17 William Fredeman, ed., *The Correspondence of Dante Gabriel Rossetti: The Formative Years, 1835–1862: Volume I, 1835–1854* (Cambridge: D. S. Brewer, 2002), 300, for the letter of 19 December 1853, to William Bell Scott.

18 Oswald Doughty and John Robert Wahl, ed., *Letters of Dante Gabriel Rossetti* (Oxford: Clarendon, 1965–67), 2.779; qtd. in David Staines, *Tennyson's Camelot: The Idylls of the King and Its Medieval Sources* (Ontario: Wilfred Laurier University Press, 1982), 157.

19 William Morris, "The Defence of Guenevere," *Arthur, the Greatest King: An Anthology of Modern Arthurian Poems*, ed. Alan Lupack (New York: Garland, 1988), 56–65, at 58.

20 William Morris, "King Arthur's Tomb," *Arthur, the Greatest King*, 67–79, at 74.

21 Mark Twain, *A Connecticut Yankee in King Arthur's Court* (1889; London: Penguin, 1986), 272.

22 John Steinbeck, *The Acts of King Arthur and His Noble Knights: From the Winchester Manuscripts of Thomas Malory and Other Sources*, ed. Chase Horton (New York; Farrar, Straus, & Giroux, 1976), xiii.

23 Elaine Steinbeck and Robert Wallsten, ed., *Steinbeck: A Life in Letters* (New York: Viking, 1975), 540.

24 Stephen Knight and Thomas Ohlgren, *Robin Hood and Other Outlaw Tales*, 179, lines 199–202.

25 Stephen Knight and Thomas Ohlgren, *Robin Hood and Other Outlaw Tales*, 180, lines 233–34.

26 Stephen Knight and Thomas Ohlgren, *Robin Hood and Other Outlaw Tales*, 40, line 110.

27 Stephen Knight and Thomas Ohlgren, *Robin Hood and Other Outlaw Tales*, 62, line 12.

28 Stephen Knight and Thomas Ohlgren, *Robin Hood and Other Outlaw Tales*, 495, lines 42–45.

29 Stephen Knight and Thomas Ohlgren, *Robin Hood and Other Outlaw Tales*, 532–33, lines 106, 129–30.

30 Stephen Knight and Thomas Ohlgren, *Robin Hood and Other Outlaw Tales*, 533, lines 147–48.

31 J. R. R. Tolkien and E. V. Gordon, ed., *Sir Gawain and the Green Knight*, 3, lines 91–93; the translation is from James J. Wilhelm, *Sir Gawain and the Green Knight*, 404, lines 91–93.

32 Stephen Knight and Thomas Ohlgren, *Robin Hood and Other Outlaw Tales*, 90, lines 22–24.

33 Stephen Knight and Thomas Ohlgren, *Robin Hood and Other Outlaw Tales*, 139, lines 1561–64.

34 Stephen Knight, "'Meere English flocks': Ben Jonson's *The Sad Shepherd* and the Robin Hood Tradition," *Robin Hood: Medieval and Post-Medieval*, ed. Helen Phillips (Dublin: Four Courts, 2005), 129–44, at 129.

35 John Keats, "Robin Hood: To a Friend," *John Keats*, ed. Elizabeth Cook (Oxford: Oxford University Press, 1994), 82–84, at lines 23–27.

36 R. B. Dobson and J. Taylor, ed., *Rymes of Robin Hood: An Introduction to the English Outlaw* (Pittsburgh: University of Pittsburgh Press, 1976), 25.

37 Alfred, Lord Tennyson, "Extracts from *The Foresters*," R. B. Dobson and J. Taylor, *Rymes of Robin Hood*, 243–49, at 249.

38 John Marshall, "Riding with Robin Hood: English Pageantry and the Making of a Legend," *The Making of the Middle Ages: Liverpool Essays*, ed. Marios Costambys, Andrew Hamer, and Martin Heale (Liverpool: Liverpool University Press, 2007), 93–117, at 93.

39 For more extensive filmographies of King Arthur and Robin Hood, see Kevin Harty, "Cinema Arthuriana: A Comprehensive Filmography and Bibliography," *Cinema Arthuriana: Twenty Essays*, ed. Kevin Harty, rev. ed. (Jefferson, NC: McFarland, 2002), 252–301; and Mike Dixon Kennedy, *The Robin Hood Handbook: The Outlaw in History, Myth, and Legend* (Phoenix Mill: Sutton, 2006), 429–32.

40 Marion Zimmer Bradley, *The Mists of Avalon* (New York: Del Rey, 1982), ix; italics in original.

41 Sharan Newman, *Guinevere Evermore* (New York: St. Martin's, 1985), 373.

42 *Monty Python and the Holy Grail*, dir. Terry Jones and Terry Gilliam, perf. Graham Chapman, John Cleese, and Eric Idle (Python [Monty] Pictures, 1974).

43 *Robin Hood: Men in Tights*, dir. Mel Brooks, perf. Cary Elwes, Richard Lewis, and Amy Yasbeck (Twentieth-Century Fox, 1993).

44 Alfred, Lord Tennyson, *Idylls of the King*, 298–99, lines 397–401.

45 Stephen Knight and Thomas Ohlgren, *Robin Hood and Other Outlaw Tales*, 598, lines 131–32.

46 Stephen Knight and Thomas Ohlgren, *Robin Hood and Other Outlaw Tales*, 230–32, lines 1 and 76.

47 Thomas Malory, *Works*, 717. See also T. H. White, *The Once and Future King* (New York: Putnam, 1958).

48 Geoffrey of Monmouth, *Historis Regum Britanniae of Geoffrey of Monmouth*, ed. Acton Criscom, trans. Robert Ellis Jones (Geneva: Slatkine, 1977), 501. The translation is Geoffrey of Monmouth, *The History of the Kings of Britain*, ed. and trans. Lewis Thorpe, 261.

49 Wace, *Wace's Roman de Brut: A History of the British*, ed. and trans. Judith Weiss (Exeter: Exeter University Press, 1999), 332–34, lines 13, 275–81.

50 Mike Barr and Brian Bolland, *Camelot 3000: The Deluxe Edition* (New York: DC Comics, 2008), 9.

51 Stephen Knight and Thomas Ohlgren, *Robin Hood and Other Outlaw Tales*, 29.

6 Movie Medievalisms

Five (or Six) Ways of Looking at an Anachronism

Proprieties of place, and especially of time, are the bugbears which terrify
mankind from the contemplation of the magnificent.

—Edgar Allan Poe[1]

When a clock chimes in *Julius Caesar*, the mighty Shakespeare's fallibility
comes to the fore: his tragedy concerns events transpiring in the first century B.C.E.,
yet chiming clocks were not invented until the Middle Ages, and, according to
anti-anachronistic logic, such mistakes detract from the authenticity necessary
to create a sufficiently credible setting for a literary masterpiece.[2] As Hans
Magnus Enzensberger tartly observes, "The temptation to judge anachronism
on moral grounds is difficult to resist," for an anachronism of this sort is
undoubtedly an error—one easily correctible if the author conscientiously
undertakes the research necessary to write historical fiction—and errors should,
we are taught in school and life, be corrected. "But perhaps [anachronism's]
actual scandalousness lies precisely in its indifference to such judgments,"[3]
Enzensberger posits, and, truly, the critical reputation of *Julius Caesar* has not
unduly suffered from a chiming clock: Mark Antony's soaring rhetoric alone
trumps this small error of historical fact.

It is a simple enough matter to brush aside the anachronisms of such great
writers as Shakespeare and Chaucer, whose genius is universally acclaimed
despite anachronisms small (e.g., Shakespeare's chiming clock) or large (e.g.,
Chaucer's rewriting of medieval knighthood into classical legend, as in his
Knight's Tale and *Troilus and Criseyde*). Other artists, including those who
create "medieval" films, transgress more broadly in their historical errors, and
frequently their works are judged harshly as a result.[4] Anachronisms appear
throughout many "medieval" films in terms of the costumes, settings, and props
that are intended to convey historical authenticity yet fail to denote the factual
contours of medieval life. Indeed, one need look no further than the actors'
mouths to discover anachronisms in "medieval" films: only rarely is the dialogue written in Latin or the early precursors of modern languages, and even
when the actors smile, aesthetic anachronisms shine across the screen in their
perfectly straight teeth gleaming with the striking whiteness typical of Hollywood
stars but mostly alien to the pre-orthodontic milieus of earlier centuries. As

these brief examples of tongues and teeth demonstrate, however, anachronism need not detract from the narrative artistry of "medieval" films, for some anachronisms, such as modern languages instead of archaic ones, are essential for reaching contemporary audiences. Also, would a "medieval" film achieve a greater aesthetic pitch if its characters suffered from bleeding gums and discolored teeth? Draconian realism is not always pleasant to view.

Cinematic anachronisms need not be seen merely as careless flaws distracting from historical verisimilitude, for anachronisms achieve striking aesthetic, narrative, and pleasurable effects. As Joseph Luzzi suggests, anachronisms bear a diachronic purpose in their "capacity … to collapse the boundaries between a literary work's internal means of reference and its external referential compass"; in Luzzi's view, the intertemporal insights available from anachronism outweigh concerns over historical solecisms.[5] Because anachronisms range widely in their aesthetic and narrative effects, it is necessary to assess them according to their unique deployments in individual films rather than summarily dismissing them as evidence of a filmmaker's ignorance. Thomas Greene proposes five types of anachronism, each of which is apparent in various "medieval" films: *naïve anachronisms*, which put forth no pretense of historical authenticity; *abusive anachronisms*, which adapt history "crudely, tactlessly, without attention to context"; *serendipitous anachronisms*, which create beneficial readings of the past despite their historical errors; *creative anachronisms*, which employ the past to comment on and interpret the contemporary historical moment of the artwork at hand; and *tragic anachronisms*, which engage with the decline of the present moment in relationship to the past.[6] It should be noted as well that anachronisms involve not only the intrusion of artifacts from the present into the past but the reemergence of otherwise antiquated entities from the past to the present, a dynamic that, by definition, must be enacted in every film depicting the Middle Ages.

Gauging the effects of anachronism on "medieval" cinema becomes more challenging in light of the vast array of films within this genre, as it is constituted of numerous complementary subfields. Many "medieval" films depict the exploits of legendary figures such as King Arthur or Robin Hood, and a related subgenre is comprised of biographical films of historical figures, such as Sergei Eisenstein's *Alexander Nevsky* (1938), Peter Glenville's *Beckett* (1964), and Anthony Harvey's *The Lion in Winter* (1968). Films in this vein often strive for historical accuracy while simultaneously enhancing the dramatic appeal of their protagonists' lives, and the melding of medieval settings with storylines updated to address modern concerns often obscures the historical portraits of their protagonists. Within the field of medieval biopics, films featuring Joan of Arc, including George Méliès's *Joan of Arc* (1899), Victor Fleming's *Joan of Arc* (1948), and Luc Besson's *The Messenger* (1999), establish her as a preeminent figure in cinematic re-creations of the past. Many "medieval" films are based on the acclaimed literature and legends of iconic authors, including Pier Paolo Pasolini's *Decameron* (1971) and *Canterbury Tales* (1972), Hans-Jürgen Syberberg's *Parsifal* (1982), and Kevin Reynolds's *Tristan + Isolde* (2006); these films, and others of their ilk, rewrite the literature of such authors as Giovanni Boccaccio, Geoffrey Chaucer, Wolfram von Eschenbach, and Gottfried von Strassburg, among others, often adapting their storylines to comment on contemporary social issues. Action-adventure films with medieval themes frequently address the exploits of Vikings (such as Richard Fleischer's *The Vikings* [1958], Clive Donner's *Alfred the Great* [1969], and Terry Jones's *Erik the Viking* [1989]) or the Crusades (such as Cecil B. DeMille's *The Crusades* [1935], Youssef Chahine's *Saladin* [1963], and Ridley Scott's *Kingdom of Heaven* [2005]), often thematically commenting on the historical ramifications of clashes between cultures. Still others attempt to address a sort of "serious" Middle Ages, or at least what they perceive as the period's serious issues, such as Lesley Megahey's *The Advocate* (1993), which engages medieval law and animal trials; Chris Newby's *Anchoress* (1993), concerned with women's religious enclosure and witchcraft; and Vincent Ward's *The Navigator* (1988), whose subjects encompass the black death and affective piety, along with time-travel. How effective these films are at being serious, or truly expressing an authentic Middle Ages, especially when they include time-travel to contemporary Australia, is debatable, but their visions of the medieval period differ significantly from the more standard versions found in films drawn from subjects with a more idealized medieval history.

Lighter subgenres of "medieval" films include fantasy (such as Matthew Robbins's *Dragonslayer* [1981], Richard Donner's *Ladyhawke* [1985], and Rob Cohen's *Dragonheart* [1996]) and comedy (such as Melvin Frank and Norman Panama's *The Court Jester* [1956], Ray Austin's *The Zany Adventures of Robin Hood* [1984], and David Green's *Your Highness* [2011]). The Middle Ages provides a preferred setting for children's cinema, as evident in such animated films as Frederick Du Chau's *Quest for Camelot* (1998) and Disney's *Sword in the Stone* (1963), *Robin Hood* (1973), and *The Hunchback of Notre Dame* (1996). Mark Twain's *A Connecticut Yankee in King Arthur's Court* has been filmed several times, most notably the 1949 version directed by Tay Garnett and starring Bing Crosby, and its plotline serves as a template for numerous adventures in which modern-day protagonists time-travel to the medieval past, including Russ Mayberry's *Unidentified Flying Oddball* (1979), Michael Gottlieb's *A Kid in King Arthur's Court* (1995), Jean-Marie Poiré's *Les Visiteurs* (1993) remade in English as *Just Visiting* (2001), and Richard Donner's *Timeline* (2003). Popular cinematic genres primarily set in the present but that can nonetheless be transposed to medieval settings include horror (Sam Raimi's *Army of Darkness* [1992]), mystery (Jean-Jacques Annaud's *The Name of the Rose* [1986]), and, despite the implausibility of merging the past and the future, science fiction (Graham Baker's *Beowulf* [1999] or Howard McCain's *Outlander* [2008]). Kevin Harty documents a subgenre of medieval erotica, films "that flirt with soft-core pornography" including Richard Kanter and Erwin Dietrich's *The Ribald Tales of Robin Hood* (1969) and Adrian Hoven and David Friedman's *The Erotic Adventures of Siegfried* (1971).[7] Even films set beyond the temporal boundaries of the Middle Ages can be productively viewed as "medieval" when they engage with medieval themes, often by lamenting the loss of a mythical past, including Michael Powell and Emeric Pressburger's *A Canterbury Tale* (1944) and Terry Gilliam's *The Fisher King* (1991).

As the preceding paragraphs tacitly indicate, it is beyond the scope of this chapter to attempt a history of "medieval" cinema; nevertheless, Greene's rubric of anachronisms as naïve, abusive, serendipitous, creative, and tragic illuminates the shifting relevance of the past to the present in these films and the necessity to assess anachronisms for the varying narrative objectives that they achieve. As John Aberth remarks, filmmakers alter history, not merely by failing to adhere to its factual contours, but, purposefully, so as to create a film in line with their artistic vision: "In nearly every case, filmmakers have altered history in order to make their movies, or so they believe, more meaningful and appealing to their audience. Therefore, even though the history may be wrong, the way it is presented in the film reflects ... the ways in which modern audiences ... wish to remember their past."[8] As historiographers have long observed, history is written not simply to record the past but to create a narrative of the past for consumption in the present, and the same is true with "medieval" films and their frequent use of anachronisms to impart messages about the past through the present. The ensuing analysis of five Arthurian films accentuates the oscillating resonance of Greene's rubric of anachronisms and their interpretive potential for "medieval" cinema, showcasing in each instance the ways in which anachronisms are central to the director's deployment of the Arthurian legend to engage with the present moment of the film's creation. By concentrating the ensuing analysis on five Arthurian films—*Black Knight* (2001), *King Arthur* (2004), *Monty Python and the Holy Grail* (1975), *King Arthur Was a Gentleman* (1942), and *Knightriders* (1981)—we also aim to explore the utility of anachronism to the Arthurian legend in films of varying genres and sensibilities, despite their shared, if at times peripheral, attention to King Arthur. For even when directors of "medieval" films proclaim their desire for realism, they practice—they cannot help but practice—anachronism in the creation of new narratives that are dependent upon modern technologies and inescapable from modern perspectives, despite any roots, deep or shallow, in the medieval past.

Naïve anachronisms, those which evince little interest in historical veracity and play with the past for the sheer pleasure of reimagining it, percolate throughout Gil Junger's *Black Knight*, a film whose Arthurian roots are shallow yet nonetheless evident as an urban homage to Mark Twain's *A Connecticut Yankee in King Arthur's Court*.[9] The protagonist Jamal Walker (Martin Lawrence) travels through time to the year 1328 to achieve the knightly masculinity as yet unavailable to him in the narrative present. Despite the fact that this film is based on the fantasy of time-travel, Junger declares that he sought authenticity in many aspects of its medieval setting, implicitly denying allegations of anachronism. In describing the costuming, he states, "We ... wanted everything to be very realistic," and in regard to the props, he affirms that his property master undertook "a tremendous amount of research and just did a phenomenal job. Every single sword was historically accurate, and the weight and the size and—he just did a wonderful job." He likewise applauds his casting agents for locating actors and extras who appear especially "medieval": "they look believable; they don't look like contemporary American faces." He also states, "Again, if you look at all these people, they look very realistic." Although one might wonder which facial physiognomies are particularly suggestive of the Middle Ages in Junger's view, as well as how these actors' faces signify this past, his words express a determination to eschew anachronism and thereby to create a realistic setting for an unabashedly unrealistic film featuring time-travel, implausible battle scenes, and a hackneyed plot.

Junger's affirmations of *Black Knight*'s historical authenticity notwithstanding, his film, as part of the *Connecticut Yankee* tradition, must engage with anachronism, for anachronism lies at the heart of its storyline. The humor of the *Connecticut Yankee* narrative and its descendants arises in large part from the comic disjunctions of transposing elements from the present to the medieval past, and *Black Knight* revels in such naïve anachronisms for the sheer pleasure of disrupting linear temporality. The film's soundtrack relies heavily on 1960s and 1970s soul and funk standards, including the diegetic use of Sly and the Family Stone's "Dance to the Music" for its riotous dance sequence and the nondiegetic use of James Brown's "Get Up Offa That Thing" for a training montage. Junger mentions that the dance sequence pays homage to the famed dance show *Soul Train*—"I wanted to duplicate the shots from *Soul Train*," he declares—with little regard for the inherent contrast between historically accurate props and wildly anachronistic music and choreography. His decision to film an anachronistic dance results in a lively and humorous scene, one with enthusiastic energy and an electric pulse, but no such comparable emotional or aesthetic achievement is attained by the film's swords, which Junger pronounces to be historically accurate but which bear little effect on the film's humor or fantasy.

Black Knight does not suffer from its naïve anachronisms; on the contrary, it flourishes with them, as the film tackles the inherent instability of the present due to simulacra of the past and thereby achieves a thematic depth surprising in light of its adolescent humor. As Laurie Finke and Martin Shichtman observe, "*Black Knight* spoofs the cultural industries that turn everything they touch into a reproduction of reality; at the same time, though, it participates in that very enterprise."[10] The true focus of the film, and its deeper humor, arises not in historical veracity but in naïve anachronisms that illuminate its treatment of reproduction as a theme. When Jamal arrives in the medieval past, he mistakes King Leo's castle (which represents reality within the film's medieval past) for Castle World (which represents a theme-park simulation of reality within the film's narrative present). Astounded by the competition that his employer Ms. Bostick, the proprietor of the theme park Medieval World, will soon face, Jamal praises Castle World, which he believes to be a pop-culture anachronism in his modern world, for its successful deployment of the necessary semiotics to convey an "authentic" Middle Ages: "Castle World's got it going on—horses, costumes, smells," he muses. For Jamal, this perceived simulation of the past becomes immersed in unpleasant reality when he visits the castle's indoor privy and is disgusted by its stench and when, at the execution of a rebel, he declares, "Sorry, I didn't mean to interrupt your rehearsal," as he then realizes in shock that this simulation is, in fact, authentic. When the rebel's head rolls to his feet, he wonders, "How do they make it look so real?", only then to discover the horror of a severed human head and the dire threat within this reality that he believed to be a simulacrum. The virtual Middle Ages of the film's present teaches Jamal that his reality is merely an illusion, while the reality of his adventures in the medieval past allow him to attain a heroic identity unavailable to him through mere simulacra.

The humor and play of *Black Knight*'s naïve anachronisms thus pave the way for Jamal's assumption of a more honorable masculinity at the film's close: to achieve manhood, he must embody the anachronism of knightly chivalry in a modern world where it is long lost (as evidenced by his own boorish behavior in the film's opening scenes). After triumphing as the eponymous Black Knight over the usurping King Leo and his evil henchman Percival, the newly reinstated Queen knights him: "In acknowledgment for your service to the Crown, I dub thee Sir Sky Walker, the Black Knight," and the film quickly returns to its narrative present with its hero enacting his renewed sense of chivalry. When a co-worker urges him to sue Ms. Bostick for his fall into the moat, he tersely replies, "There ain't no honor in that, man," and he explains to her his rediscovered dedication to her commercial endeavors: "I know things can get a little scary, but courage isn't the absence of fear. It is the presence of fear, yet the will to go on." In her refurbished theme park and its freshly scrubbed simulation of the past, where she now rules as a queen seated on her throne, Ms. Bostick compliments him, "I always knew you had it in you, Jamal." After his adventure in the "reality" of the past, which is suffused with the incongruity of the modern in the medieval, Jamal is no longer an empty simulacrum of a man, the film posits, but a man made real through the heady and disruptive force of anachronistic adventure. These anachronisms may be naïve, but they are nonetheless effective in the cultural work that they perform in rehabilitating Jamal.

Abusive anachronisms, those which pay little attention to history or its contexts, and often claim "truth" for wildly speculative and inaccurate representations, are evident throughout Antoine Fuqua's *King Arthur*, a cinematographically lush film that seeks to restore Arthur to his rightful place in history.[11] With little sense of irony, the film's opening screen declares the truthfulness of the ensuing narrative: "Historians agree that the classical fifteenth century tale of King Arthur and his Knights rose from a real hero who lived a thousand years earlier in a period often called the Dark Ages. Recently discovered archeological evidence sheds light on his true identity." The film thus begins with a truth claim without verifiable truth, and this stated concern for historical veracity merges with Fuqua's desire to create an Arthurian legend based on realism rather than fantasy, as the director declares: "I figured, if you're going to make a film about King Arthur, why not try to find some sort of reality to it?" The paradox of building a realist film from chimerical history, one only fleetingly recorded in historical documents, subverts its foundations, as Fuqua holds his work to historical standards only to be undone by the emptiness of its anachronistic play. The film begins in 452 C.E. yet depicts Arthur as a contemporary of Pelagius (354–c. 430), and is ostensibly set during the twilight years of Rome's occupation of Britain, although Rome's Emperor Honorius ordered British cities to provide for their own defenses in his rescript of 410 C.E.[12] Furthermore, Fuqua and screenwriter David Franzoni adapt the so-called Sarmatian hypothesis—which identifies Arthur's knights as Sarmatian soldiers conscripted into service of Rome—into their plotline, although this thesis is completely unproven.[13]

The anachronistic and historical mishmash in *King Arthur* aspires to allegorical depth, and traces of creative anachronisms, those that use the past to consider the present, are apparent in these efforts. Fuqua sketches the parallels between his Sarmatian knights fighting Saxon invaders and American soldiers in Vietnam: "We discussed Vietnam quite a bit, because when I read the script I thought this was more like a Vietnam situation, in the knights being the American soldiers, or even the French, and the British, the Picts, would be the V.C. ... The Woads were guerilla fighters, just like the V.C." Franzoni also sees American history in the film: "After that it became for me the American GI experience—strangers in a strange land, killing to stay alive and hating doing it"; he also states that he used "Ho Chi Minh as a model for Merlin."[14] History is conscripted in service of a message intended to resonate with the film's modern audience, yet the allegory is not as much fundamental to *King Arthur* as it is incidental, with Arthur representing neither the king of legend nor of history but an anachronistic American soldier tacitly questioning the ethical authority of his leaders and the morality of the Vietnam War.

If the film fails in the impossible task of rescuing the historical King Arthur from his ahistorical treatment in other films, its attempted dismissal of the legend's origins in romance correspondingly fails to banish this material from the film. Indeed, fiction proves inescapable, as Fuqua finds himself justifying the essential elements of the Arthur story that never appear in the so-called historical materials (the chronicles of Gildas and Nennius, or the Celtic triads). The love triangle of Arthur, Lancelot, and Guinevere imbues Arthurian legend with latent tragedy, but Fuqua emphatically rejects these roots in romance, despite their centrality to the narrative's overarching themes:

> The triangle with Arthur, Guinevere, and Lancelot in traditional stories always ended in this betrayal ... I've always had a difficult time with that part of the Arthur story, especially when you do research about people who lived this way [when] loyalty and friendship and honor meant something ... And I didn't want to see Lancelot sleep with her ... I needed for them *not* to do that because where I grew up you wouldn't do that. ... That's kind of a sick romance.

Fuqua's sense of personal ethics as derived from his childhood lessons derails his retelling of the Arthurian legend, imbuing the narrative with an anachronistic reticence—one of his own design—to tell the story as it is recounted in numerous medieval sources. Moreover, despite Fuqua's desire to expunge sexual betrayal from the film, Lancelot and Guinevere express their mutual attraction in several scenes. They never consummate their affections, but their flirtatious banter marks their romantic interest in each other, with Lancelot proclaiming to her, "If you represent what heaven is, then take me there," and she recognizing her affinity with him: "So you see, Lancelot, we are much alike, you and I." Their interactions sparkle with ironic and humorous flirtations, such as in the suspenseful battle with the Saxons on the frozen lake (which is modeled on the famed ice battle of *Alexander Nevsky*), when Lancelot warns Guinevere, "There's a large number of lonely men out there," to which she coolly replies, "Don't worry. I won't let them rape you." In a film mostly devoid of humor, Guinevere's words inject a hint of levity that also establishes the mutuality of the pair. Fuqua's solution to this developing sexual tension is simply to kill Lancelot in the climactic battle with the Saxons, thus rendering infidelity impossible and tempering the Arthurian legend's investment in the complex intersections of courtly love, adultery, and masculine fidelity to one's martial leader (those essential themes of medieval romance). Likewise, the challenge of atoning spiritually for one's sexual transgressions, as Guinevere and Lancelot seek in the conclusion of Malory's *Morte D'Arthur*, is absent from the film.

In spurning the narrative's roots in romance and thereby bolstering its foundations in pseudo-history, Fuqua depicts Guinevere as a warrior woman rather than as a princess, and she rejects fairy-tale romance when speaking with Arthur: "My father told me great tales of you. ... Fairy tales. The kind you hear about people so brave, so selfless, that they can't be real." With these words she implies that fairy-tale romances are untrue and that Arthur's literary image fails to correspond with the reality of the man before her, but romance nonetheless seeps into the film and further subverts its claims to history. Fuqua declares that his Guinevere would never wear a flowered dress because she is a warrior, but when she marries Arthur, her wedding dress is indeed embroidered with a floral pattern. According to his assessment of his film, Fuqua prefers historical realism over romance, yet the power of romance is stronger than history in *King Arthur*, with the marriage plot subsuming the knights' military victory into a communal celebration of proto-American freedom from tyranny. The anachronistic foundations of the film—its blending of Woads (which, historically, is a name of a particular sort of war paint, not a tribe) with the V.C., its recasting of Arthur as a disciple of Pelagius, its application of the filmmaker's personal ethos to Lancelot and Guinevere's adultery—fail to achieve any unified purpose: these abusive anachronisms cannot unite into any organic theme and thus pull the narrative into too many disjointed strands to cohere, as a "happily ever after" ending of marriage trumps the film's investment in an ultimately spurious history, thus insistently, if unintentionally, reminding audiences of its inherent fictionality.

Serendipitous anachronisms illuminate important truths of the past despite their historical errors, and this dynamic percolates humorously throughout Terry Jones and Terry Gilliam's *Monty Python and the Holy Grail*.[15] With knights prancing about without horses, with coconuts clapped together providing sound effects, and with policemen swooping in to arrest King Arthur at the film's conclusion, it is blatantly apparent that the Pythons were unconcerned about historical solecisms disrupting their play with the past, despite their greater claims to knowledge of that past than many other Arthurian filmmakers.[16] The film is set in 932 C.E., and this declaration of a definitive temporal setting for the film makes a mockery of history, as its various depictions of the medieval past are too ridiculous and free-floating to be given any ballast by the pronouncement of a specific year circumscribing the narrative's events. For instance, the date 932 C.E. renders the appearance of French soldiers in various castles incongruous since they predate William the Conqueror's 1066 invasion. To correct this anachronism, the Pythons might simply have changed the temporal setting to a date after 1066, but doing so would express a respect for historical accuracy gleefully lacking throughout the film.

For all of its lampooning of the Middle Ages, *Monty Python and the Holy Grail* provides striking insights into the Arthurian legend and its literature, for even trivial scenes resonate with obscure Arthurian allusions. Arthur's discussion with a castle guard concerning the flight velocities of coconut-laden European and African swallows is a comic masterpiece of misdirected dialogue, yet it echoes the musings of the narrator in Gottfried von Strassburg's *Tristan* over a nesting swallow:

> Si lesent an Tristande,
> daz ein swalwe ze Îrlande
> von Kurnewâle kæme,
> ein frouwen hâr dâ naeme
> ze ir bûwe und zir geniste,
> (ine weiz, wâ sîz dâ wiste)
> und fuorte daz wider über sê.
> geniste ie kein swalwe mê
> mit solhem ungemache,
> sô vil sô sî bûsache
> bî ir in dem lande vant,
> daz si über mer in fremediu lant
> nâch ir bûgeræte streich?

One reads in the old Tale of Tristan that a swallow flew from Cornwall to Ireland and there took a lady's hair with which to build its nest—I have no idea how the bird knew that the hair was there—and brought it back over the sea. Did ever a swallow nest at such inconvenience that, despite the abundance in its own country, it went ranging overseas into strange lands in search of nesting materials?[17]

Because they set their film in 932 C.E., the Pythons render such witty allusions to Arthurian literature into anachronisms, since Gottfried's tale dates to the early thirteenth century. Numerous other scenes mirror moments from an Arthurian tradition that are anachronistic within the film's fictions, yet these serendipitous anachronisms nonetheless encourage deep insights into Arthurian literature. The Pythons' depiction of Sir Galahad's sexual misadventures in the Castle Anthrax recall Gawain's temptations in the fourteenth-century romance *Sir Gawain and the Green Knight*. When Galahad attempts to escape the seductress Zoot, she reminds him of his duties as an Arthurian knight: "Sir Galahad! You would not be so ungallant as to refuse our hospitality." Trapped by her words, Galahad simply stammers, "Well, I—I, uh" and proceeds further into temptation. Zoot's rhetorical ploy directly echoes that of Bertilak's lady in *Sir Gawain and the Green Knight* when she attempts to win a kiss from Gawain by denying that he is the man before her. "Bot that ye be Gawan, hit gotz in mynde" ("Yet to think that you're the brilliant Gawain boggles my mind!") she proclaims, to which Gawain replies confusedly: "'Querfore?' quoth the freke, and freschly he askez,/ Ferde lest he hade fayled in fourme of his castes" ("'But why?' asked the bed-dweller, blurting it out/And fearing he had failed in his flawless behavior").[18] For all of the sexual farce of the pure knight Galahad warding off the advances of a bevy of nubile maidens in *Monty Python and the Holy Grail*, the scene captures a key aspect of the gender dynamics of medieval romance in which women demand action from knights simply by reminding them of their chivalric code.

Monty Python and the Holy Grail also humorously highlights the exaggerated masculinity expected of medieval knights, as evident in Arthur's dismembering of the Black Knight, who refuses to concede defeat and, as an armless and legless stump, still demands combat when Arthur departs. The scene greatly exaggerates the military masculinity of some Arthurian villains, yet it also recalls Lancelot's dispatching of Meleagant when this villain refuses to yield despite losing his arm in Chrétien de Troyes's *Lancelot*:

> Mes Lanceloz le haste fort,
> si li done un grant cop et fort
> devant l'escu a descovert
> el braz destre de fer covert;
> si a li colpé et tranchié.
> Et quant il se sant domagié
> de sa destre qu'il a perdue,
> dist que chier li sera vandue.
> ...
> ...
> ...
> Vers lui cort, que prendre le cuide.

But Lancelot presses his opponent close and gives him a great hard blow past his shield directly onto his mail-clad right arm, severing it at a stroke. Feeling the loss of his right arm, he declared that Lancelot would pay dearly for it ... [Meleagant] runs towards him, trying to grapple with him.[19]

How does a knight grapple an opponent—a warrior armed both corporeally and with weaponry—after losing an arm? Likewise, Lancelot's slaughter of a wedding party while rescuing the imprisoned "maiden" Herbert in *Monty Python and the Holy Grail* is reminiscent of the knight's indiscriminate slaughter of Guinevere's prosecutors in Malory's *Morte D'Arthur*, most notably his allies Gareth and Gaheris:

> And so in thys russhynge and hurlynge, as sir Launcelot thrange here and there, hit mysfortuned hym to sle sir Gaherys and sir Gareth, the noble knyghts, for they were unarmed and unwares. As the Freynshe booke sayth, sir Launcelot smote sir Gaherys and sir Gareth upon the brayne-pannes, wherethorow that they were slayne in the felde. Howbeit in very trouth, sir Launcelot saw them [nat].[20]

Numerous other serendipitously anachronistic pairings of post-932 C.E. medieval literature and history with the Pythons' modern parody structure the film: Dennis the revolutionary peasant anachronistically foreshadows the Peasants' Revolt of 1381; the Pythons' tale of the cowardly Sir Robin makes manifest the parodies of medieval romance evident in the Middle Ages, such as in Chaucer's "Tale of Sir Thopas"; and Arthur and his knights' confrontation with a deadly bunny, in which they ultimately triumph by detonating their holy hand grenade, mirrors the legend of Arthur and the Devil Cat from the *Prose Merlin*.[21] Through these anachronistic allusions and their serendipitous illumination of the tropes of medieval romance, the Pythons play with the themes and motifs of their source texts, all the while enlightening their meaning through their parody's insistent puncturing of pretense. With the humorous pleasure of anachronism uniting with the filmmakers' deep knowledge of medieval literature and history, the term *anachronism*, in this instance, almost becomes an oxymoron, for these tropes, in their play as purposeful mistakes, enlighten the film's very knowledgeable humor; in all its anachronism, *Monty Python and the Holy Grail* may be the most accurately medieval movie ever made.[22]

Filmmakers employ creative anachronisms to reflect on the present moment through the past, and this tendency is strikingly apparent in Marcel Varnel's *King Arthur Was a Gentleman*, a British film of the "why we fight" tradition.[23] This genre of cinematic propaganda bolstered morale for the ongoing military efforts during the trying times of World War II, when British citizens were asked to sacrifice in defense of their homeland. As Anthony Aldgate and Jeffrey Richards document, the nation's film industry mobilized in patriotic accordance to the precepts of Lord Macmillan, the first wartime Minister of Information, who "issued a memorandum in 1940 suggesting three themes for propagandist feature films: what Britain was fighting for, how Britain was fighting, and the need for sacrifice."[24] In *King Arthur Was a Gentleman*, a charming musical comedy telling the story of a milquetoast transforming into military manhood to proudly defend his nation, the medieval past anachronistically illuminates the nation's ambition to defeat Nazi Germany, inspiring men, women, and children to fight heroically for their homeland through the glorified image of King Arthur.

The film's title proclaims that *King Arthur Was a Gentleman*, but here too is a potential anachronism, for Arthur, in his literary roots, is a king, and in this role he adheres to the precepts of gentility as etymologically encoded in *gentleman*. The word *gentleman*, however, also denotes a modern-day democratic ideal in which any man, no matter his lineage, may achieve this lofty designation. David Castronovo observes the liminality of the English gentleman, inherent in this figure's ability "to poise himself between the world of privilege and the world of democracy. His peculiar resiliency as a model for English society was the direct result of his ability to open and close his ranks according to no fixed principle."[25] The medieval image of Arthur as king, and thus as the apex of the aristocracy, seamlessly unites with this new image of Arthur as gentleman, a category without rank in modern times and achievable by all men who respond to the necessity of war by fighting for their homeland. Within the film's fictions, the actor Arthur Askey, representative of a mild-mannered Everyman, portrays Arthur King, a man eager to serve his nation despite his puny stature. Jane Stokes describes Askey's typical cinematic persona as a satirist of social pretension and authority: "Always critical of arbitrary authority, the 'Little Man,' as Askey was known, used the tools of his trade—satire and silliness—to lambaste autocratic prigs. ... [He] reserved special opprobrium for the BBC mandarins who seemed to dictate public taste."[26] In this film, however, in line with its "why we fight" ethos, Askey's Arthur King stands solidly in support of the prevailing social order and idolizes King Arthur as its sterling representative.

Proving the transtemporal and anachronistic allure of Arthurian romance, Askey's Arthur King childishly re-enacts the legendary king's valiant deeds. In the sequence in which he is introduced, Arthur King is little more than a child as he plays with maps and toys to re-create King Arthur's Saxon campaigns dated to 493 C.E.: "And that's how they squashed the invasion," he explains to a young girl who works with him as a volunteer in the civil service. She responds skeptically, "What? With one knight on horseback?", but Arthur King replies: "One knight? He wasn't a knight. He was King Arthur! He had the strength and courage of fifty knights." He continues his ode to Arthur with a stirring account of the monarch's heroism: "Ah, but King Arthur was a gentleman. Do you know, at the first sign of danger, he'd put on his armor, he'd grab his sword Excalibur, leap onto his horse, and face the enemy without fear or reproach!" In contrast to his namesake's accoutrements, Arthur King's armor is a wastepaper basket, his sword merely a blackboard pointer, and a stepladder serves as his mount; more importantly, no enemy—that is, no Nazi—is present for him to attack. Rather, the young girl to whom he speaks reminds him that he would be an ineffective avatar of Arthurian masculinity: "No one expects you to fight. You're a reserve!" Similar depictions of Arthur King throughout the film accentuate his failed masculinity: effeminizing scenes show him knitting socks and dressing in drag to sneak into the women's barracks, and several characters disparage him as a "twerp." His girlfriend Susan (Evelyn Dall) defends him, "He's not helpless; he's just a little too romantic for everyday life," but she later exasperatedly asks him, "Arthur King, are you a man or aren't you?" As the film's touchstone creative anachronism, King Arthur stands as a transhistorical ideal of masculinity, inspiring Arthur King to join an active brigade and access the latent manhood within him. He requests Colonel Duncannon to deactivate him from the civil service and enroll him in the fusiliers: "Well, let me tell you, there's a lot of us nothingses. And if someone would only put us all together, we'd amount to a very big something." He also proclaims to Susan, "I'm going to be the biggest little man in the British Army." With the image of King Arthur guiding him, Arthur King succeeds in defeating Nazis and rescuing British soldiers, proving his manhood to all who doubted him.

In merging the "why we fight" tradition with Arthurian legend, *King Arthur Was a Gentleman* provocatively, if humorously, argues for an anachronistic vision of England as its defining identity amid the horrors of a modern war. The girl with whom Arthur King volunteers in the civil service derides his fantasy—"Of course, this King Arthur stuff is only a fairy story, isn't it?"—but Arthur King's response proves the enduring appeal of the legendary in the present: "Certainly not. King Arthur was the greatest man who ever lived. If he were alive today, he'd make history." The film views history as temporally elastic and thus eternally available and inspirational to all British citizens. As Susan affirms of her suitor, "Lots of little people are like that. They hitch their wagon to a star—something to look up to, that's all. Arthur's picked history." History, in Susan's perspective, potentially elevates all Britain's milquetoasts into military masculinity, but her words suture over the distinction between the nation's factual history and its literary foundations in medieval romance. In many of his earliest romance incarnations, King Arthur is always already a glorious anachronism, a transtemporal icon of Britain's lost Golden Age. *King Arthur Was a Gentleman* posits the possibility of King Arthur as the nation's eternal creative anachronism, ever available and always inspiring during moments of present crisis. During his military training, Arthur locates his battalion in the vale of Avalon—"This is the actual spot where Arthur had his Round Table"—creating a truth claim as implausible as those of Fuqua's *King Arthur* but one in which the truth is the spirit of Arthurian romance rather than of empty history. Arthur King's subsequent adventures with Excalibur—which is proven an authentic relic of the Arthurian era when he tosses it in a lake at the film's conclusion and a hand miraculously reaches forth, catches, and brandishes it—assert the eternal truth of the British legendary. *King Arthur Was a Gentleman* posits that anachronistic visions from the past are truths worth dying for in the present, and that as long as Arthurian history lives in the land, Britain will take up arms in its defense. Arthur again proves himself the once and future king.

Tragic anachronisms highlight the failures of the present in light of the glories of the past, and this elegiac theme imbues George Romero's *Knightriders* with much of its haunting power.[27] Best known for his horror films, Romero ventures into modern-day Arthuriana with this cinematic critique of American consumer society, much as he satirized mindless consumerism in his zombie romp *Dawn of the Dead* (1978), in which the undead attempt to feed on the living in a shopping mall. *Knightriders* tells the story of King Billy (Ed Harris) and his traveling medieval fair, in which its eponymous knights joust on motorbikes and enjoy a countercultural oasis from prevailing social mores. Pippin, the announcer at the games, avows the troupe's affinity for its Arthurian forebears: "Welcome to the games of the court of Sir William the King. When T. H. White wrote down the magical tale of Arthur and the Round Table, he called him the Once and Future King. Once honor and nobility ruled; in the future may they also reign." Pippin's words imply that honor and nobility are lacking in the present day: these virtues guided knights of the past and may return in the future, but in an American cultural wasteland where dollars trump honor, King Billy's court acts as an antidote to this sterility.

In lionizing purportedly anachronistic values of honor and chivalry, King Billy foregrounds his ethos of personal honor, and this sense of integrity is masterfully realized in Ed Harris's searing portrayal. When a young boy asks for Billy's autograph for his *Cycle Riders* fan magazine, the king refuses: "I'm sorry. I don't like this kind of stuff. … I can't … This is like Evel Knievel or something like that. It's got nothing to do with what we're doing." As the epitome of 1970s motorbike dare-devilism and self-promotion, Evel Knievel represents the gaudy inverse of Billy's asceticism, and Billy rejects the child's adulation as inherently complicit in degrading his personal integrity. In contrast, Billy's rival Morgan signs the magazine for the child, revealing his shallow understanding of his king's code, but the code nonetheless stands as the film's predominant value. When Steve, the troupe's lawyer, attempts to lure Billy into commercialism, the king refuses: "We're not an act," he declares, but Steve replies, "It's money, Billy. It's all to do with money. Money makes the world go round. Even your world." In response, Billy pronounces the enduring challenge of his code: "It's tough to live by the code. I mean, it's real hard to live for something you believe in." He then rejects financial motivations altogether: "You can keep the money you make off this sick world, lawyer. I don't want any part of it." As Susan Aronstein observes, "Billy is right not to accept economic compromise, even in the service of 'survival' … ; however, as a king, he has the obligation to provide for his people, if not economically then spiritually. But 'the truth' he offers instead of money is never—beyond its chivalric trappings, roots in violence, and vague ideas of self-sacrifice and community— clearly articulated."[28] The film implies that even an undefined and anachronistic code is superior to prevailing American mores, as Billy's kingship and moral example allow others to be true to themselves.

Within this dissipated vision of an America undone by consumerism, manhood suffers, and Arthurian virtue thus provides an anachronistic template against which to measure modern masculinity. Novelist Stephen King, with whom Romero collaborated on his 1982 feature *Creepshow*, plays an extra in a crowd scene who confesses his failed masculinity to his wife: "You know, I don't have the balls to wear anything like that," he states as the camera cuts to a crotch shot of a well-endowed juggler in tights, proving visually the masculinity of the medieval troupe. Morgan, the ostensible antagonist of the film who hopes to depose King Billy and reign in his stead, derides the Arthurian tradition that should inspire him: "I wasn't into this King Arthur crap anyways. I was into the bikes, man, the bikes." As Pippin reports, Morgan's assumption of the name of Arthurian villainess Morgan le Fay reveals his ignorance: "He just recently found out Morgan le Fay was a woman." Due to the allure of crass commercialism, Morgan leaves the troupe, falling under the seductive sway of the publicists and promoters Bontempi and Sheila, but his departure is short-lived. He quickly realizes that, in contrast to the masculine puissance available to modern-day knights who practice Billy's code, consumerism emasculates him: he learns that Sheila's financial dependence on another man entails that she will sleep with him but will never commit herself to him, and he subjects himself to a humiliating photo shoot during which the photographer wheedles his models with the plea, "Now, everyone, think medieval sex." Finally, after witnessing a hotel-room brawl fought by hooligans without honor, Morgan returns to Billy's troupe and wins his lord's crown honorably.

In this manner, Billy's exemplary lifestyle of truth and honor saves his followers from degrading themselves, and the film's Christological thematics come to the fore. Morgan tells his girlfriend Angie that Billy's crown is a crown of thorns, and a guitar player, one of the motley members of Billy's troupe, thanks Billy for rescuing them from the meaninglessness surrounding them: "You give us everything, man. You've given us a chance." Morgan's redemption is evident when he rejects Bontempi and the allure of commercialism—"You know those contracts? Burn 'em, baby"—and the fair's randy Friar Tuck, who engaged in lascivious carnality while eating pizza with a female photographer hoping to sell her shots of the knightriders, now counsels her against profiting from her work: "Hey, hey, baby, let's just keep it in the family." Billy avenges himself against the corrupt policeman who harassed his troupe earlier in the film, throwing the cop's gun into the deep fryer at a restaurant and then dispensing soft-serve ice-cream on his head to the applause of the restaurant's patrons in a sequence that, in Tony Williams's words, "seems a self-conscious ironic deed from a director who has commented elsewhere on the 'McDonaldization of America.'"[29] In a final act of atonement, Billy gives his sword to the boy who asked for his autograph and then dies tragically in a head-on collision with a truck. Billy's earlier words forcefully resonate: "You've got to fight for your ideals, and if you die, your ideals don't die. The code that we're living by is the truth. The truth is our code." The name of Billy's troupe, "Fight or Yield," concisely captures the challenge of living in a post-medieval world, where Billy's anachronistic lifestyle inspires those around him to surpass the ordinary and achieve the extraordinary feat of adhering to antiquated values. Fittingly for a film suffused with tragic anachronisms, Billy's death elicits a mournful and melancholic regret for the lost Middle Ages, yet because the Middle Ages never dies but is continually reborn in film and other media, so too does hope pierce through the sadness.

Films of the Middle Ages without anachronisms are impossibilities, but as Greene's rubric illuminates, anachronisms function in a range of complementary and distinct ways to build thematic depth within a given artistic work. Directors may at times proclaim their abhorrence for anachronism, but they should instead affirm the essential nature of anachronism in "medieval" movie-making, since their films do this, despite their intentions. As this overview of naïve, abusive, serendipitous, creative, and tragic anachronisms and their meanings in various Arthurian films illustrates, it is not the presence of anachronisms in a film that merits analysis and investigation as much as their function, and so we would be well advised to add a sixth category of anachronism to Greene's rubric of five: the essential anachronisms, the ones without which a "medieval" film would degenerate into meaninglessness, or, perhaps worse, tediousness. Anachronisms perform important cultural work, bridging yesterday and today (and often tomorrow as well), and in so doing, whether naïvely, abusively, serendipitously, creatively, or tragically, they clarify the continued appeal of the Middle Ages to contemporary society in the movies that turn to the past for insights into the present.

Notes

1 Edgar Allan Poe, "The Assignation," *The Collected Tales and Poems of Edgar Allan Poe* (New York: Modern Library, 1992), 293–302, at 301.

2 For the clock in question, see William Shakespeare, *The Tragedy of Julius Caesar*, *The Riverside Shakespeare*, ed. Blakemore Evans, et al., 2nd ed. (Boston: Houghton Mifflin, 1997), 2.1.191; for a history of clocks, see Gerhard Dohrn-van Rossum, *History of the Hour*, trans. Thomas Dunlap (Chicago: University of Chicago Press, 1996), esp. 45–123.

3 Hans Magnus Enzensberger, *Zig Zag: The Politics of Culture and Vice Versa* (New York: New Press, 1997), 48.

4 Tison Pugh and Lynn Ramey address the inherent anachronism and paradox of the term "medieval" cinema, noting the "patently obvious technological impossibility" of such a conflation yet suggesting the need "to confront that incongruity, acknowledging that even when it is granted that medieval cinema refers to modern films depicting the Middle Ages, the possibility of paradox inheres" ("Introduction: Filming the 'Other' Middle Ages," *Race, Class, and Gender in "Medieval" Cinema*, ed. Lynn Ramey and Tison Pugh [New York: Palgrave Macmillan, 2007], 1–12, at 1).

5 Joseph Luzzi, "The Rhetoric of Anachronism," *Comparative Literature* 61.1 (2009): 69–84, at 70.

6 Thomas Greene, *The Vulnerable Text* (New York: Columbia University Press, 1986), 220–22. Greene employs his rubric of anachronism to consider the relationships between Renaissance writers and their classical forebears, yet its utility extends to other artists and their refashionings of the past.

7 Kevin Harty, *The Reel Middle Ages* (Jefferson, NC: McFarland, 1999), 6.

8 John Aberth, *A Knight at the Movies: Medieval History on Film* (New York: Routledge, 2003), xi.

9 *Black Knight*, dir Gil Junger, perf. Martin Lawrence, Tom Wilkinson, and Marsha Thomason (Fox, 2001). All quotations of Junger are taken from his commentary track accompanying the DVD release of the film.

10 Laurie Finke and Martin Shichtman, *Cinematic Illuminations: The Middle Ages on Film* (Baltimore: Johns Hopkins University Press, 2010), 357.

11 *King Arthur*, dir. Antoine Fuqua, perf. Clive Owen, Keira Knightley, and Ioan Gruffudd (Touchstone, 2004). All quotations of Fuqua are taken from his commentary track accompanying the DVD release of the film.

12 The precise meaning of Honorius's rescript is subject to debate; see Peter Salway, *Roman Britain* (Oxford: Clarendon, 1981), 442–45. Despite the ambiguity of this document, it is clear that the Romans were withdrawing from the British Isles in the early fifth century.

13 For the Sarmatian hypothesis, see Scott Littleton and Linda Malcor's *From Scythia to Camelot* (New York: Garland, 1994). For a study of truth claims in Arthurian films, see Roberta Davidson, "The Reel Arthur: Politics and Truth Claims in *Camelot*, *Excalibur*, and *King Arthur*," *Arthuriana* 17.2 (2007): 62–84.

14 John Matthews, "The Round Table: The 2004 Movie *King Arthur*," *Arthuriana* 14.3 (2004): 112–25, at 116–17.

15 *Monty Python and the Holy Grail*, dir. Terry Jones and Terry Gilliam, perf. Graham Chapman, John Cleese, and Eric Idle (Python [Monty] Pictures, 1975).

16 The Monty Python crew is highly educated, with all but Terry Gilliam having attended either Cambridge or Oxford, and some having specifically medieval credentials as well; John Cleese at one time taught Latin, History, and Literature; Terry Jones has, since the film, written several books with medieval themes, including two books on Chaucer, *Chaucer's Knight: The Portrait of a Medieval Mercenary* (Baton Rouge: Louisiana State University Press, 1980) and *Who Murdered Chaucer? A Medieval Mystery*, co-written with Terry Dolan, Juliette Dor, Alan Fletcher, and Robert Yeager (New York: St. Martin's, 2004).

17 Gottfried von Strassburg, *Tristan*, ed. Karl Marold (Leipzig, 1906), 123, lines 8605–17. Translation from Gottfried von Strassburg, *Tristan*, ed. A. T. Hatto (London: Penguin, 1967), 154. Thanks to Robert Squillace for assistance with the Middle High German.

18 *Sir Gawain and the Green Knight*, ed. J. R. R. Tolkien and E. V. Gordon, 2nd ed., ed. Norman Davis (Oxford: Clarendon, 1967), 36, lines 1293–95; the translation is James J. Wilhelm, *Sir Gawain and the Green Knight*, *The Romance of Arthur: An Anthology of Medieval Texts in Translation* (New York: Garland, 1994), 434, lines 1293–95.

19 Chrétien de Troyes, *Lancelot, of the Knight of the Cart*, ed. and trans. William W. Kibler (New York: Garland, 1984), lines 7059–66; 7073; the translation is from Chrétien de Troyes, *Arthurian Romances*, ed. D. D. R. Owen (London: Everyman, 1993), 280.

20 Thomas Malory, *Works*, ed. Eugène Vinaver, 2nd ed. (London: Oxford University Press, 1971), 684.

21 For Arthur's battle with a devilish cat, see John Conlee, ed., *Prose Merlin* (Kalamazoo: Medieval Institute Publications, 1998), 312–17.

22 The accuracy of *Monty Python and the Holy Grail*'s medieval details, and therefore its feeling, was often observed by Joan M. Ferrante, to whom we are grateful for this insight.

23 *King Arthur Was a Gentleman*, dir. Marcel Varnel, perf. Arthur Askey and Evelyn Dall (Gainsborough Pictures, 1942).

24 Anthony Aldgate and Jeffrey Richards, "Why We Fight," *Best of British: Cinema and Society from 1930 to the Present* (London: Tauris, 1999), 57–78, at 57.

25 David Castronovo, *The English Gentleman: Images and Ideals in Literature and Society* (New York: Ungar, 1987), 17.

26 Jane Stokes, "Arthur Askey and the Construction of Popular Entertainment," *British Cinema: Past and Present*, ed. Justine Ashby and Andrew Higson (London: Routledge, 2000), 124–36, at 124.

27 *Knightriders*, dir. George Romero, perf. Ed Harris and Tom Savini (Laurel, 1981).

28 Susan Aronstein, *Hollywood Knights: Arthurian Cinema and the Politics of Nostalgia* (New York: Palgrave Macmillan, 2005), 138–39.

29 Tony Williams, *The Cinema of George A. Romero: Knight of the Living Dead* (London: Wallflower, 2003), 112.

7 Medievalisms in Music and the Arts
Longing for Transcendence

Longing, as Susan Stewart posits, is always implicated within temporalities of desire; as she explains, "the direction of force in the desiring narrative is always a future-past, a deferment of experience in the direction of origin and thus eschaton, the point where narrative begins/ends, both engendering and transcending the relation between materiality and meaning. Yet the particular content of this desire is subject to historical formation."[1] Such a conception of longing is particularly relevant for examining medievalism in music and the arts. The goal of displaying an object of medieval art is often to create a future and transcendent past, a potential Middle Ages whose "real" meaning is deferred in exchange for a moment of mystical origin that simultaneously projects a potential future. Between the music or the art and its meaning lies the medieval, an historical formation that is both made of and outside of actual history. It is a Middle Ages that negotiates between the post-industrial awareness of difference between "book as object and book as idea," in Stewart's particular formulation, and the pre-modern relationship of object to transcendent meaning or purpose. In the attempt to make (or remake) the medieval for the modern world, musicians, artists, and curators take authentic objects of the past and ask them to live in the present in a way that speaks both within and across time. Musicians who perform medieval music for modern audiences or borrow medieval forms and subjects for contemporary genres, artists who paint medieval themes, and museums that display medieval art are all faced with the same process of "engendering and transcending" this relationship, of seeking to "'realize' a certain formulation of the world."[2] In music and the arts, the "medieval" is not a neutral signifier, a simple reference to an historical time and space, unless one views those terms as Geoffrey Chaucer does in the General Prologue to the *Canterbury Tales*, as an invitation to suspend the boundaries of the real and enter into the fiction.[3] And while the fictional Middle Ages can play many roles, what is found in music and the fine arts is an attempt at transcendence, an attempt to create an experience in which art regains a kind of ritual and spiritual function that separates it from works arising in (and influenced by) both earlier and later periods.

The rich heritage of medieval music, literature, and history has proved a fertile ground for musicians. In performance, form, and subject matter, music composed during the Middle Ages, as well as contemporary music that draws its influences from medieval music or medieval subject matter, constructs "medieval" as a category, rather than reflecting an historically accurate vision of the medieval period and its musical forms. Indeed, performance, form, and subject matter offer categories for exploring the function of medieval music in the post-medieval world: medieval music continues to be performed and studied in the contemporary world; medieval musical forms influence contemporary composers; and medieval subject matter informs music that draws little structurally from the period.

Medieval music continues to draw audiences, and while its relationship to the classical repertoire is complex, it is common to see early music offerings in concert series, and the number of groups performing medieval music continues to flourish, from the most established, such as Anonymous 4, Sequentia, and the Tallis Scholars, to more recent entries such as Trio Mediæval and AOI: Brooklyn's Finest Medieval Band.[4] An example of a twentieth-century composer heavily influenced by medieval forms is Arvo Pärt, whose tintinnabuli style, Leopold Brauneiss suggests, shows a "lack of egotism, a leaning toward anonymity, a tendency to withdraw the subject of the composer."[5] Brauneiss views these traits as essentially medieval; he notes that Pärt's harmonies are "a function of the relationships between the voices and not vice versa," and sees him drawing performance ideology, methodology, and form from his medieval antecedents. In a sense, Pärt can be said to have taken "the modes of medieval polyphony and translated them into his own system of rules; this is why his music sounds old and new at the same time."[6] More common, however, is the use of medieval subjects. Although one may immediately think of Wagner's *Ring Cycle*, *Lohengrin*, and *Tristan und Isolde* as the primary examples, this operatic medievalism begins much earlier, in operas such as John Dryden and Henry Purcell's 1691 *King Arthur* (which draws more from the versions of the Arthurian legend found in works like the *Alliterative Mort Arthure* rather than Thomas Malory), and continues into the present. Examples such as Harrison Birtwhistle and David Harsent's *Gawain* (1991) and J. D. McClatchy, Elliot Goldenthal, and Julie Taymor's *Grendel* (2006) suggest the broad appeal of the genre in high culture.

Popular music is equally filled with medieval themes, such as when, in the 1960s and 1970s in western rock and folk music, folk musicians drew parallels between themselves and the medieval lyric tradition, imagining themselves as "troubadours" offering secular music to the people. Arthurian themes in particular became popular as "Camelot … became the hallmark of a new form of Western escapism,"[7] offering images of "the world as it might have been" as well as a fantasy of what it might yet come to be.[8] Examples include Crosby, Stills, & Nash's "Guinevere," in 1969, Uriah Heep's "Merlin" on *Heroes and Visions* in 1972, and Rick Wakeman's *The Myths and Legends of King Arthur* (in 1975), an album comprised entirely of Arthurian-themed songs, although these examples only scratch the surface of the genre. Arthurian and other medieval themes and forms—Michael Rewa points out, for instance, that Neil Young's

1970 album *After the Gold-Rush* is essentially a dream vision[9]—express both a nostalgic longing for a lost bucolic past as well as aspirations for a vague but peaceable, idyllic future.

This popular musical engagement with medieval themes and forms continues into the present. For instance, Philadelphia's MewithoutYou's second album *Catch for Us the Foxes* (2004) vocalizes an Augustinian struggle against illicit desires, proclaiming: "When I looked down, like if to pray,/Well, I was looking down her dress./Good God, please! Catch for us the foxes in the vineyard."[10] The speaker also realizes, "When I satisfied each need invented by my eye/It was nothing like I'd imagined," and includes a longing for salvation: "If there was no way into God/I would never have laid in this grave of a body for so long."[11] The band's *It's All Crazy! It's All False! It's All a Dream! It's Alright* (2009) can be heard as a response to the *Canterbury Tales*, as it draws from Chaucer's rich and varied storytelling, religious themes, metafictional issues, and narrative structures. Titles like "The Fox, the Crow, and the Cookie" sound echoes of Chaucer's *Nun's Priest's Tale*, and this song similarly uses a beast fable to tell a moral story; moreover, the album engages in an exploration of Chaucer's concerns about "sentence and solaas," resulting in thematic concerns both distinct from and appropriate for the Middle Ages.[12]

The "medieval" roots of such popular-culture traditions cannot be pinned down to the Middle Ages, however, for their more immediate sources may well be found in T. H. White's *The Once and Future King* rather than in Malory's *Morte D'Arthur*. Indeed, the ideologies and views of the Middle Ages often stem more from Victorian medievalism than from the Middle Ages, appropriating a vision of the medieval period similar to that of the Pre-Raphaelite Brotherhood's, in which the Middle Ages is celebrated as a time of gloriously resplendent beauty and simplicity. A Middle Ages is created tied only to its fictions rather than to its realities; there is nothing in this music to suggest any sense of the difficulty, danger, or abjection of medieval life, although to be fair, the medieval secular musical tradition does not concentrate on these elements of medieval life either.

This fantasy of medievalism operates across musical genres, including those of popular and high cultures, and certain examples might be seen as looking back to the past and then coming to stand for that same past itself. A striking such example is Carl Orff's *Carmina Burana*, which draws from medieval sources by setting a series of medieval Latin poems to music. Although there is nothing stylistically medieval about the piece, it becomes a "medieval" touchstone, standing in for "real" medieval music. The simple melodies of the original *Carmina Burana*, many of which can be sung to the simple rhythm and tune of the Christmas carol "Good King Wenceslas," are transformed into high-culture orchestral works. The medieval *Carmina Burana* has been recorded several times, but has never achieved the same popularity as Orff's adaptation, which appears in many medieval movies, such as John Boorman's *Excalibur* (1981), and thus demonstrates the deeper medievalness of the adaptation than the original.

Against these contemporary examples, real medieval music continues to be performed, often paired with a medievalized pageantry designed to evoke a ritualized past that parallels elements of the music itself. The popularity of these concerts, particularly around Christmastime, is a potent example of the way the Middle Ages is constructed as a simpler, more ritualized, and homogeneous past while overlooking the fact that Christmas, as it is currently celebrated, is a Victorian, not a medieval phenomenon. This combination of the two eras arises from the Victorian fascination with and ultimate reconstruction of the medieval period. The projection backward collapses time and turns it all into an undifferentiated fantasy. "Medieval" performances require a particular kind of access for the modern listener, one suggesting a distance from the material different from that of later classical music performance while nonetheless appropriate for enabling the experience of religious transcendence.

Contemporary performances of medieval music are rife with a set of anxieties not experienced by musicians performing compositions from the Baroque or other later periods. While groups that perform Baroque music often characterize their repertoire as "Early Music" and concern themselves with the authenticity of their performances, such adaptations typically entail using original instruments and different tunings, rather than creating an experience for the audience that is as much theater as concert. Ross Duffin's collection *A Performer's Guide to Medieval Music* makes clear that medieval music is considered differently, and therefore performed differently, than its later counterparts. Musicians must seek a balance between historical background and conjecture due to the lack of information about the specifics of medieval performance. In describing the parameters of his volume, Duffin notes:

> this book is rather more laden with historical background than most "how to" manuals, and rather more sprinkled with conjecture and "best guesses" than is typical for scholarly publications. Although definitive answers to many pertinent performance questions are frequently unavailable, our silence on such issues would almost certainly mean fewer performances and a perpetuation of the very situation we are trying to remedy. It would also mean the eventual loss of the beautiful and effective performance approaches evolved by many of these authors over a period of decades, a loss that in a small way, perhaps, would mirror the loss of the original performance traditions. Future generations may well choose to perform medieval music differently from the ways described or recommended in these pages, but at least they will not be totally ignorant of the thought that informs some of today's best performances.[13]

He notes of performers of medieval music: "No one wants to be criticized for being 'inauthentic' or worse yet, 'musically immoral.' But we are all, in a way, 'troubadours,' seeking after beautiful, meaningful performances of this music, and we will not experience them if we are hesitant about performing."[14] It seems that the less that is known about how medieval music was performed and experienced, the greater the anxiety about the authenticity of contemporary performance. What it would mean to be "musically immoral" in regard to the performance of medieval music for a contemporary audience then becomes the key question. Because so little is known about what medieval music performance looked or sounded like, contemporary performers are consigned to construct a musical Middle Ages built out of a combination of research, conjecture, and invention.

That this invention can be used for multiple purposes divorced from the music's content can be seen in the recent fascination with Hildegard of Bingen, whose status as a woman author, healer, preacher, mystic, and musician has made her ripe for reclamation in medieval studies and equally appealing to a variety of popular projects. Jennifer Bain notes that Hildegard becomes famous for creating a unique form of "ecstatic" chant, defined by musical leaps and relationships that are actually more conventional than recent studies acknowledge.[15] Bain shows Hildegard's musical similarity, at least in her use of soaring jumps, to many of her contemporaries; not only does Hildegard include fewer of these defining phrases than she is given credit for, but many of her contemporaries employ the same stylistic features. Hildegard's interest, then, arises from a desire to construct her difference rather than from an actual difference in the music itself. An example of this conventional assumption is put forward on the Hildegard of Bingen Music Page:

> In contrast to the narrow scope of most chants in her day, Hildegard's music has a very wide range. She uses extremes of register as if to bring heaven and earth together. According to Pfau, by adding and omitting pitches and pitch groups in repetitions of melodic phrases, Hildegard stretches and contracts melodic phrases to create the "soaring arches" that we are familiar with in her music.[16]

In contrast, Bain views Hildegard's identity as constructed not from material but from performance; she notes that "despite Hildegard's clear historical significance, rather than Hildegard herself it is Gothic Voices and Sequentia who have created her 'ecstatic' chants. Many performers and scholars since have used the notion of ecstasy as a 'hook' to promote her music."[17] Thus the nature of Hildegard's medievalness is another invention, a creation of both author and material as a New Age mystic designed to connect contemporary audiences to a notion of an experiential past that replicates current interest in felt spirituality rather than any liturgical commonplaces of medieval religious life. Although Bain demonstrates convincingly the ways in which Hildegard is typical of her own musical period, this contemporary construction of her as different (as "ecstatic") makes her a medieval icon. Instead of being "medieval" because of her consistency with all things medieval, Hildegard becomes "medieval" because of the Middle Ages constructed around her, which make her simultaneously of her time and completely exceptional and anomalous.[18]

Bain notes that Gothic Voices "adopts a rapid tempo and rhythmically animated performance style," a style of chant performance that she calls "remarkably original" although the style originates in 1982 rather than 1182.[19] Given these comments, and her note that it is "important ... that we at least attempt to produce early performance styles," Bain points to a key difficulty in performing medieval music: the tension between a desire for authenticity and an inability to offer more than conjectures about medieval performance style, which leads to a medieval-ish construction that stands in the place of the real. Bain declares:

> The impact of virtuosic recordings of Hildegard's music on our perception of her as a composer cannot be overstated. Without the recordings would everyone—church choirs, university chorales, early music ensembles—put Hildegard on their programmes? Without recordings would the New Age recording industry have appropriated Hildegard so enthusiastically? ... Probably not. ... Hildegard's status as an ecstatic is the "hook" that has been used to promote her music, but often it has obscured the music's historical context.[20]

Thus Bain reveals how medievalism supplants the medieval, how invented medieval music transcends its real identity. As aficionados of Hildegard's music seek transcendence in the experience of listening to her works, the medieval qualities of this music must be re-signified into an expression of ecstasy situated in but not of its very past.

Even a casual fan of medieval music will note that its performance is fundamentally different than that of other musical periods, even other periods, such as Baroque music, that fall under the umbrella of "Early Music." In short, more medieval music is performed in costume, as drama (liturgical and secular), and "on location" in churches or museums than its later counterparts, which are generally heard in concert halls and performed in conventional dress. The Metropolitan Museum's *Concerts and Lectures 2011–2012 Season* lists several holiday events, which are "presented in front of the Museum's Christmas Tree and Neapolitan Baroque Crèche in the Medieval Sculpture Hall." The Metropolitan Museum's famous tree, with its eighteenth-century crèche and angels decorations, is annually displayed in front of the Choir Screen from the Cathedral of Valladolid, attributed to Rafael Amezúa of Ellorio and completed c. 1763, which is the centerpiece of the museum's Medieval Hall. The fact that neither work is actually medieval seems to be beside the point; the atmosphere created supersedes any drive toward art-historical correctness. In this fascinating pastiche, multiple pasts, real and invented, collide. In regard to the various concerts, the medieval ones—A Chanticleer Christmas (which quickly sells out three performances), Anonymous 4, and Voices of Ascension—are held in this location, whereas Judy Collins and the Ebony Ecumenical Ensemble perform in the auditorium. The fervor for a medieval experience at Christmas is echoed in the annual sold-out Christmas concerts by the Waverly Consort at the Cloisters, which are described on the group's website:

> Many have come in a yearly pilgrimage to hear this beautiful seasonal music from the great cathedrals of Europe in an original setting. In addition to the performances at The Cloisters, The Christmas Story travels each year to communities throughout North America.
>
> In the spirit and pageantry of the medieval church dramas and mystery plays, eight singers and five instrumentalists playing reproductions of medieval instruments recount the events of Christmas—the message of the archangel Gabriel to the shepherds, the journey of the Magi to the manger at Bethlehem, the intrigue of Herod and his court, the flight into Egypt—in an uplifting and moving celebration of ritual drama and song.[21]

The language of pilgrimage and performance attempts to replicate a medieval experience as much as medieval music itself does. Annette Kreutziger-Herr describes a 1995 concert by the Hillary Ensemble in the Main Church of St. Michael's in Hamburg in which the performers moved throughout the church, "their heads bent like monks who were absorbed in some secret vision."[22] As an experience, she suggests, it was "somewhere between the secular and the sacred. It was a kind of religious experience, but one that permitted either participation or uninvolved observation."[23] The pleasures of such performances are obvious, and the sense of necessity that this affords to medieval music is striking; Kreutziger-Herr notes that "most people today do not realize that the classical music they admire and love was composed for specific contexts (church, court, salon) and conceptualized in circumstances totally different from ours today," but performers of medieval music instead stress the need to reconstruct (or, perhaps better, reinvent) those contexts for their modern audience.[24] Reconstruction and performance of medieval music, Kreutziger-Herr adds, "is something between creative, reproductive and scientific medievalism, and the mix of those three approaches is guided by imagination: medieval music is an especially convincing dream of the Middle Ages."[25]

Katherine Bergeron, in response to a similar concert, suggests that it "strained the limits of 'authenticity' at the same time that it opened a new arena on which the 'authentic' might be reimagined: the virtual space of neither/nor."[26] Fueled by nostalgic desires for meaning and purpose, emotion and feeling, and mystical wisdom that humans lost with the humanism of the Renaissance, contemporary medieval music performance, despite its attempts to reconstruct an authentic style and method, is consigned to produce only a medieval fantasy. In its reconstructions of the past, performed in quasi-medieval clothing (such as the trousers and blouses of the Waverly Consort, or gowns of Trio Mediæval and Anonymous 4, and Sequentia's Benjamin Bagby's unique ensembles) and often in quasi-medieval settings, it serves to create an invented "stable" Middle Ages, as much a product of the Gothic Revival as of the real past. Kreutziger-Herr notes that, "around 1800 the Middle Ages blossom out into an object of longing," and the music was envisioned as "the embodiment of the natural, the innocent, and the divine." This ultimately came to represent "harmony" in political, aesthetic, and musical contexts,[27] so that clear harmonies called forth a harmony of humans and the universe. Performing medieval music, then, can transcendently connect listeners to a "time without time, an era in which the narration of its own historicity ... was stopped," a "gain of time, of timeless possibilities, an encounter with 'timelessness,' an exploration of 'eternity,'" as Kreutziger-Herr describes it.[28]

At the same time that medievalism drives the performance of medieval music, aligning an imaginary Middle Ages with a desire for methodologically accurate musical styles, medievalism also drives reimaginings in contemporary music with a more secular focus. Elizabeth Aubrey, in her introduction to performing non-liturgical monophony, comments that "vernacular monophony is perhaps more difficult than other medieval music to communicate effectively to a modern audience."[29] This is an interesting, and perhaps counterintuitive, observation due to the secular character of most contemporary medievalism. In many of its cultural moments, "medieval" and its descendant medievalisms seem divorced from the religious assumptions that led Will and Ariel Durant to call the medieval volume of their eleven-volume *The Story of Civilization* "The Age of Faith."[30] Whereas for many performers of medieval music, the liturgical repertory is where modern audiences can find the most to connect to, for contemporary musicians looking to the Middle Ages for inspiration, it is elements of the secular world, and often the vestiges of pagan religions, that inform their canon.

While not exactly "non-liturgical monophony," although perhaps non-liturgical cacophony, medievalism, particularly Scandinavian medievalism, becomes a reference point for the subgenre of heavy metal music often called "Viking Metal," with parallel engagement with the past happening in Folk and Pagan Metal, which similarly draw on shared themes and ideas about the past beyond Viking Metal's specific focus on Norse mythology.[31] "Viking Metal," Gregg Moffitt declares in *Decibel* magazine's recent feature on the band Amon Amarth, "the words conjure a certain ring to them. Like iron striking steel or hammer on anvil amid the mist of sand, they render vivid images with which to conjure. Musically, too, it appears a perfectly balanced equation—a marriage of might and majesty, a quickening of the pulse and a stirring of the blood."[32] In terms of its overarching qualities, Viking Metal features lyrics inspired by Norse mythology, a somewhat frenetic tempo, and the acoustic trappings of heavy metal. The origin of Viking Metal is often attributed to the band Bathory, whose album *Blood, Fire, Death* (1988) featured the title song and "A Good Day to Die," which are laced with Viking themes, and it was followed in 1990 by *Hammerheart*. Described as having "lengthy epics, ostentatious arrangements, chorused vocals, and ambient keyboards,"[33] *Hammerheart* became the originary work of Viking Metal, trading Satanic themes for Norse mythology. Bathory was soon joined by other groups such as Amon Amarth and Enisferum, each offering its unique perspective on a musical genre and mythological world that came to embody an anti-establishment (particularly religious establishment), violent, creative philosophy that draws its inspiration from both the medieval "past" of the Norse *Eddas* and the nineteenth-century Viking revival.[34]

Bathory's *Blood, Fire, Death* depicts *The Wild Hunt of Odin* on its cover, a painting by the nineteenth-century Norwegian artist Peter Nicolai Arbo, rather than an image from the illuminated medieval manuscripts in the Arni Magnusson Institute collection in Reykjavik. Although elements of the genre seem quite silly—bands generally perform in Viking costumes, for instance—their connection to the past is not simply frivolous. While "they're certainly not averse to a swill or two of mead," for most of these bands, Viking Metal implies a philosophy of life.[35] Johan Hegg, Amon Amarth's frontman, comments that "the Vikings viewed man as a being with all his faults, but also with all the fantastic things man can accomplish. That's inspired me to review my own life at certain points."[36] Beyond this realization, the philosophy of Viking Metal is strongly pagan and anti-Christian, demonstrating resentment for the Christianization of northern Europe along with a powerful attachment to beliefs in individual freedom; such ideas find their parallels in Norse literature, such as in *Egil's Saga*, in which the main character repeatedly struggles against what might be called the "westernization" of Norway under King Harald Fine-Hair and ultimately moves to Iceland to escape these pressures. One element of this philosophy dear to Hegg is the idea that "even though you had different classes of people—leaders, warriors, farmers—people took care of each other … the leaders didn't take everything from them, the taxes were moderate. But as soon as Christianity came in, they assumed divine right!"[37] This is certainly interesting in Scandinavia, whose countries are often considered the last vestiges of the true welfare state, offering a connection between an originary ideology (real or imagined) and contemporary political systems (not unlike what readers find in the British nineteenth-century attempts to tie their political system to the Magna Carta by building Big Ben and the Houses of Parliament in the style of Westminster Abbey rather than in the popular neoclassical architecture often seen in civic buildings).[38]

Most Viking Metal groups seek to reclaim the images of the Vikings, calling them "very open-minded to different cultures and even beliefs," and adding that "they were smart, courageous people. Way before anyone else could sail over open seas, they had compasses" and "a vast knowledge of astronomy." The groups also profess that their Viking forebears "had art, culture, an economic system, and were probably the first people in Europe to have civil laws and a judicial system."[39] These systems of order remain more ideology than structure for the Viking Metal performers, with Moffitt noting that "the greatest impact they have is through the brute force of their music," an observation that draws on the Vikings' reputation as warriors looting, pillaging, and wreaking havoc.[40] Yet, in a larger sense, this genre presents a worldview in which "the ancestral culture of the north is at the heart of the band's imagination, whether expressed through Viking material culture, landscapes, or creative vignettes drawn from

Scandinavian mythology and culture." This is not just the musical subject, however; "the recurring metaphor of life as a battle, as a struggle" is the allegorical purpose behind the somewhat "animalistic and barbaric" and, of course, violent imagery that the practitioners of Viking Metal produce.[41] Simon Trafford and Aleks Pluskowski suggest that this ideology may be a response to contemporary (particularly contemporary Scandinavian) society: "escape into a stirring past, like rock 'n' roll decadence, may be an understandably attractive alternative to the horrors of respectable middle-class life in an affluent, enlightened, European democracy."[42] Such a response itself represents an example of Viking medievalism, in that the Norse Sagas are replete with heroes seeking to escape from the changes taking place in mainland Scandinavia as a result, often, of Christianization, which leads them to Iceland, a land that stands for rugged individualism, collective government, and anti-monarchical sentiment. If the anti-Christian response is less overt in the Sagas, Christianity does not govern or play much role in the lives of the Saga figures, whose destinies are often tied to mystical forces of both Norse mythology and a larger, encompassing sense of fate.

Authenticity is hardly the point, however; as Trafford and Pluskowski point out, "historical representation or context is not really an aim: what matters is what they (Vikings) stand for in popular cultural terms, as that has been communicated by books and films, and as it is understood by performers and audience." The qualities these authors see in the appropriation of Vikings for music purposes are "freedom, masculinity, adventure, and chaos."[43] While these qualities are appealing to the bands who find their medievalism in the Vikings, their initial point may well be taken for all musical responses to the Middle Ages. In contemporary performance of authentically medieval music, in folk songs on Arthurian subjects by the 1960s and 1970s troubadours, in the construction of Hildegard of Bingen as a medieval feminist composer for a modern spiritual age, and in the invention of the Viking world for heavy metal audiences, the Middle Ages is not so much what is found in the dusty documents of the past, but what successive periods have chosen to make of this period in pursuit of transcendence. And if these admittedly divergent examples offer a variety of auditory fantasies, what they share is that sense of fantasy. Ironically, it is a fantasy created to produce an authentic experience, a listening engagement that is as emotional as it is intellectual. In an interview with Lawrence Rosenwald, Barbara Thornton, described as "one of the most eminent medieval voices of our time" in Klaus Neumann's obituary in *Early Music*,[44] describes the troubadour as working "out in the open imagination and chart[ing] with each song a new and infallible system, a heuristic system, intended to stimulate the inner and outer senses into an actual experience of word and tone."[45] Her sense of the performer's responsibility is significant, as she affirms that as "the creator shows the way into the piece, the living interpreter must make the journey."[46] She views this process as "intended to stimulate the imagination," which she believes is the essence of communication, adding that "imagination is *the* medium for knowledge. The process of turning knowledge into wisdom is tradition, *ruminatio*, practice (a medieval attitude, of course). It is generally acknowledged that this is a very mysterious process and needs a lot of time."[47] She adds:

> the mesh created between text and music in the medieval world is so fine that it needs to be kept alive with active imagining at all times. That is what we mean when we say the singer is not only re-constructing the piece, but re-composing it as he goes along. He is so active in this process that his own poetic soul moves the performance, his poetic core has met the poetic core of the work.[48]

Difficulties in performing or connecting to the music, she suggests, are finally resolved when one's "innate medievalism ... rises up from within one to save the day."[49]

If performers of medieval music are reconstructing and recomposing, it is hardly a stretch to think of them reconstructing this "innate medievalism" as well. What is important about the medievalism present in music—as performance, form, or subject matter—is a fantasy of authenticity, of the blending of the contemporary poetic soul with the (imagined) poetic soul of the past. In discussing the issue of authenticity and counterfeits, Mary McAleer Balkun notes, "the ostensibly real thing may not be 'authentic' and the fake may have an authenticity of its own; ... what appears genuine on the surface may be a careful construction; and finally what appears to be performance or obfuscation may in fact reveal something genuine."[50] This layered examination explains the ways music engages the medieval: performances of medieval music may be a construction, while the invented medieval worlds of Viking Metal may offer an authentic method of exploring real anxieties about contemporary life, and both can ultimately reveal something profound and real, even if the "real" is not an historically accurate Middle Ages. Whether the fantasy is an authentic performance of medieval music, an authentic folkloric history that links past and present, or an authentic image of Vikings and Viking philosophy, it essentially functions in the same way—a longing for a kind of direct experience, of an emotional journey, that like the ideas about Hildegard's music, can produce an ecstasy that uses this auditory (and visual) form to take listeners out of the contemporary world, into both a nostalgic past and an imagined harmonious future.

Similar quests for transcendence accompany the display of medieval art, and the Antioch Chalice (see Figure 7.1), currently held at the Cloisters, provides a representative anecdote for understanding medievalism in the fine arts. Made in the first half of the sixth century in Antioch or Kaper Koraon, the chalice contains an internal silver cup encased in a silver-gilt footed shell. The shell's rinceau pattern of a grapevine, inhabited by birds and animals, curls over twelve seated figures holding scrolls, and while the identities of some figures are uncertain, two of them represent Christ, while the others have been variously considered to be apostles or classical philosophers. When the chalice was

Figure 7.1 The Antioch Chalice. The Cloisters, Metropolitan Museum of Art, New York.

discovered in the early twentieth century, the interior cup was identified as the Holy Grail. As the museum website affirms:

> The identification of the "Antioch Chalice" as the Holy Grail has not been sustained, and even its authenticity has at times been challenged. The work has usually been considered a sixth-century chalice for the Eucharist. Most recently, however, its shape has been recognized as more closely resembling

sixth-century standing lamps, its decoration possibly in recognition of Christ's words "I am the light of the world. (John 8.12)"[51]

The object, itself a composite, incarnates the layering of history and fiction inherent in medievalism; the chalice may come from a particular time and place, but its meaning and value were found for those who believed it to be the Holy Grail in its embodiment of a medieval legend. The story it actually tells becomes supplanted by a fantasy, an imposed narrative that understands the Middle Ages as mysterious and transcendent, yet that transcendence is not the "real" transcendence of the chalice's possible participation in the Eucharist, but in a mythographic transcendence of the Holy Grail story, whose potency comes both from its religious significance and its narrative importance in the King Arthur legends.

Miriam Murphy, in a review of Gustavus Eisen's two-volume work on the chalice, *The Great Chalice of Antioch on Which are Depicted in Sculpture the Earliest Known Portraits of Christ, Apostles, and Evangelists*, comments that because the outer shell was considered a reliquary, that "transition is easy from this thought to the suggestion that here may be indeed the Holy Grail, Christ's own Chalice at the Last Supper," but adds that "the fame of the Chalice does not, however, need to depend upon its identity with the Holy Grail. Its finding is exceedingly important on artistic and historical bases, for it proves positively, the truth of the documents which maintain that the Church founded by Christ and His apostles is identical with the Church presided over by Peter's successor, the bishop of Rome."[52] In either case, the Chalice is used to authenticate a story, to produce a meaning about the Middle Ages outside itself. Read either as the Holy Grail or as eyewitness portraits of the apostles, the object is asked to perform more than its aesthetic or ritual function. And yet, the chalice itself invites the same kind of reading, for it is an object both functional and symbolic, even if its symbolism merely connects classical philosophers to the Christian tradition. Whatever its actual use, chalice or lamp, the Antioch Chalice produces its own symbolic narrative through the patterned rinceau of the outer cup, a story that is as multiply interpretive as the contemporary meaning assigned to it. Therefore, as an artifact, both then and now, it serves to join past and present, history and fiction.[53]

Medievalism in art can be evaluated through the same converging historical tensions that influence medieval music: post-medieval works are mediated through medieval forms, imagery, and subjects, and the presentation of historically medieval art is mediated for modern audiences. In defining medievalism, Michael Alexander notes that it is the "offspring of two impulses: the recovery by antiquarians and historians of materials for the study of the Middle Ages; and the imaginative adoption of medieval ideals and forms."[54] This formulation is particularly useful for thinking about art, as it acknowledges the primary division one may see, yet that division may ultimately be insufficient, since the analysis and display of the "materials" are often engaged in the same "imaginative adoption" of ideals and forms. The Pre-Raphaelite Brotherhood is often credited with the creation of medievalism, and while it is readily apparent that various medievalisms predate those of the Victorian era, such a longing for a fictional past, created by a confluence of artistic and narrative forms and a drive toward confraternity, characterizes some of the first conscious theories of medievalism. If earlier medievalism was essentially an attempt to revise medieval subjects for modern times, the Pre-Raphaelites spoke to a different nostalgia for the past: instead of bringing the Middle Ages to the present, they sought a return to a "Middle Ages" that stood for all that was antithetical to contemporary Victorian life. In doing so, they created a visual Middle Ages, an image of the past that combined certain simplicity of form with a focused detail, a movement away from realism that did not, however, move toward abstraction. This nostalgic visualization implicitly governs contemporary displays of medieval art, which more than later works, are treated as if they stand on the border between art and anthropology. England's finest medieval collections are housed in the British Museum and the Victoria and Albert Museum, the latter known primarily for decorative arts, rather than in the National Gallery, which houses the country's most esteemed paintings (including only one medieval example, the Wilton Diptych). At the Metropolitan Museum in New York, the bulk of its medieval collection is housed at the Cloisters, a museum that attempts to create a medieval "experience" in its removed location from the hustle and bustle of downtown Manhattan and in its architecture as well as its collection.

In "The Work of Art in the Age of Mechanical Reproduction," Walter Benjamin comments that:

> even the most perfect reproduction of a work of art is lacking in one element: its presence in time and space, its unique existence at the place where it happens to be. This unique existence of the work of art determined the history to which it was subject throughout the time of its existence. This includes the changes which it may have suffered in physical condition over the years as well as the various changes in ownership.[55]

Benjamin's point is evident in contemporary images of the starkness of classical temples and medieval cathedrals. Because the polychrome has for the most part worn away, our understanding of this art is inherently created by the ravages of time, rather than the experience of the material that its original audience would have enjoyed. Medieval art, and particularly architecture, therefore is imagined as bare stone rather than as a riot of painted colors, making the experience of buildings where the full color remains, such as the Cathedral in Siena, seem particularly anomalous instead of authentic. Even if, as Benjamin theorizes, "[t]he presence of the original is the prerequisite to the concept of authenticity,"[56] contemporary audiences' notions of what constitutes that authenticity may themselves be inventions created by a combination of modern concerns and the ravages of time. Benjamin suggests that "the authenticity of a thing is the essence of all that is transmissible from its beginning ranging from its substantive duration to its testimony to the history which it has experienced,"[57] a definition that encompasses both contemporary interpretations and the functions of history. The loss of that history shows that "what is really jeopardized when the historical testimony is affected is the authority of the object."[58]

For context—cultural, geographical, temporal—affects any interpretation or transcendent enjoyment of art. As Benjamin adds, "The uniqueness of a work of art is inseparable from its being imbedded in the fabric of tradition. This tradition itself is thoroughly alive and extremely changeable."[59] Here Benjamin looks at the example of Venus, who for the Greeks was an object of veneration, but for medieval clerics, he claims, was "an ominous idol."[60] He locates the "unique value of the 'authentic' work" in its "basis in ritual, the location of its original use value."[61] This ritual sense of art, which "is still recognizable as secularized ritual even in the most profane forms of the cult of beauty," operates in opposition to "the doctrine of *l'art pour l'art*," which, he feels, gives rise to a "negative theology in the form of the idea of 'pure art,' which not only denied any social function of art but also any categorizing by subject matter."[62] The Antioch Chalice is a case in point, as its various imagined values are inherently representational and symbolic, not physical or even particularly visual. The shift he identifies, then, is the movement from art with a ritualistic function and useful purpose to art whose emphasis lies primarily in its exhibition value.[63]

Medieval art might be said to occupy the space between these distinctions in the contemporary museum world. Sites such as the Metropolitan Museum of Art's Cloisters, the medieval annex that displays art in partially original buildings on top of a bluff in New York City's Fort Tryon Park, offers both authentic objects and what Helen Evans, Curator of Medieval Art at the Metropolitan and the Cloisters, calls "the purity of the romantic period," an evocation of what the Middle Ages should be as much as what it was.[64] The museum attempts to connect place and time, and with its nearly unchanging collection, it replicates the fantasy of the Middle Ages as a time of unity, stability, and stasis. Anything that is added, Associate Curator Melanie Holcomb notes, needs to look like it was always there, which creates its own kind of pressure on the museum: what is medieval becomes stuck in the ideal of a common civic experience.[65]

As with the contemporary performance of medieval music, the display of medieval art in a modern museum attempts to evoke an authentic experience that owes its vision of the Middle Ages to similar impulses of Victorian medievalism that influenced the Pre-Raphaelites. Nineteenth-century medievalist impulses can be seen in the Metropolitan Museum of Art in New York, where the side stairways on either side of the Medieval Hall preserve the original building's 1874 gothic design; when they were renovated in 1995, the stairwells were repainted to suggest an original polychrome, and the marble floor was re-created in the image of the original. The Medieval Hall that these surround is designed to evoke the Middle Ages (and the Victorian Middle Ages) in its design and presentation of its art. The Metropolitan Museum is not alone in these attempts at evocative re-creation. The Toledo Museum, for instance, dims the lights in its cloister to make it feel more authentically "medieval," almost making literal the idea of the Dark Ages.[66]

Medieval art was originally collected as Decorative, rather than Fine Arts,[67] and its emphasis on functional objects—chalices, pyxes, choir stalls, and reliquaries, and even the more massive tombs and baptismal fonts—creates an image of the artifacts *in situ*, interesting as much for what they do as what they look like. Of course this is a false dichotomy; it does not replicate the way people experienced art, at least until the development of the museum. Art, even paintings, are most authentically experienced along with the decorative arts that surround them. Still, one sees that the methods of display found in many medieval galleries contrast strongly to even the temporally close Old Master Paintings, which are generally grouped by time and country (even city) of origin. So whereas a medieval exhibit might include both a Spanish religious sculpture and a late-medieval French tapestry, the painting galleries will distinguish twelfth-century Siennese works from thirteenth-century Florentine ones.[68] Perhaps this is because, as Benjamin points out, "Painting simply is in no position to present an object for simultaneous collective experience, as it was possible for architecture at all times, for the epic poem in the past, and for the movie today."[69] However, this seems to be more than a distinction of form; the Cloisters, for example, displays the Annunciation Triptych (see Figure 7.2) in a room that looks nearly exactly like the one depicted in the painting, with many of the same objects in their places and similar furniture along the walls.[70]

The anachronism of the painting (found in much medieval art), in which a biblical subject is set in the artist's own time, is a similar anachronism found in the displays of medieval art that also disregard the categories of time and space in their presentations. And yet, to take the point further about the false distinction between decorative and fine arts, medieval art might thus be said to be more authentic in its presentation, since it more clearly replicates the experience of art-in-life, both of its own time and of our own time. So, while it is easy to suggest that "medieval" in the world of art becomes a kind of exotic, foreign land that requires a different kind of interaction than later, and even earlier, art, medievalism in the visual arts, just as in music, treads the fine line between the authentic and the imaginary. While the Middle Ages it offers is more fantasy than history in its methods of transmission, it finds itself in a surprisingly medieval, and therefore authentic, place. Although the Antioch Chalice is not the Holy Grail, it continues to perform symbolic work, bringing the present and past together in an attempt to transcend the boundaries of both. For as transcendence defines for many patrons of music and the fine arts the ultimate pleasures of these pastimes, such transcendence is achieved by transcending, or ignoring, or reinventing, the contours of the Middle Ages in favor of a fantasy, but no less real, Middle Ages that speaks to a present, if not eternal, quest for artistic experiences that liberate ourselves from our very selves.

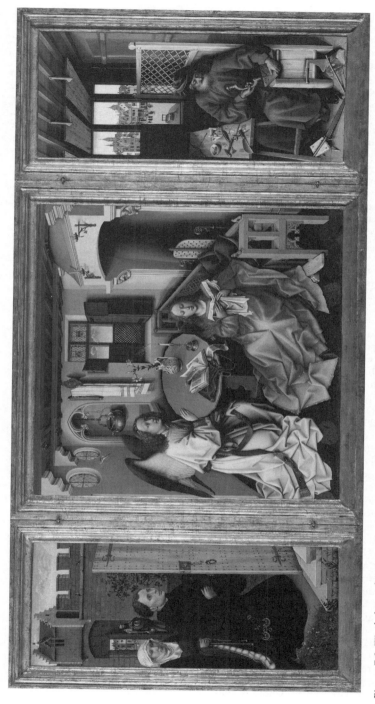

Figure 7.2 Workshop of Robert Campin. The Annunciation Triptych. The Cloisters. Metropolitan Museum of Art, New York.

Notes

1 Susan Stewart, *On Longing: Narratives of the Miniature, the Gigantic, the Souvenir, the Collection* (Durham: Duke University Press, 1993), x.

2 Susan Stewart, *On Longing*, xi.

3 See, for instance, the opening of the General Prologue to the *Canterbury Tales*. When Chaucer declares, "But nathelees, whil I have tyme and space" (1.35), he invites the reader into a world of fiction, where a narrator can speak to twenty-nine people in an evening and know their most intimate secrets: time is time suspended, and space, of course, is the space of the page. Together, for Chaucer, these two terms signify the movement from reality into fiction, as well as his particular consciousness of doing so (Geoffrey Chaucer, "The General Prologue," *The Riverside Chaucer*, ed. Larry Benson [Boston: Houghton Mifflin, 1987], 23–36, at line 35).

4 Information, history, and discography for these performers can be found at the following websites (all accessed 24 January 2012): Anonymous 4 at anonymous4.com; Sequentia at sequentia.org; Tallis Scholars at thetallisscholars.co.uk; Trio Mediæval at triomediaeval.no, and AOI: Brooklyn's Finest Medieval Band at singaoi.com.

5 Leopold Brauneiss, "Arvo Pärt's Tintinnabuli Style: Contemporary Music toward a New Middle Ages?" *Studies in Medievalism XIII: Postmodern Medievalisms*, ed. Richard Utz and Jessie Swan (Cambridge: D. S. Brewer, 2005), 27–34, at 29.

6 Leopold Brauneiss, "Arvo Pärt's Tintinnabuli Style," 33.

7 Florin Curta, "Pavel Chinezul, Netru Vodă, and 'Imagined Communities': Medievalism in Romanian Rock Music," *Studies in Medievalism XIII*, 3–16, at 3. Curta's article, while beyond the scope of this chapter, focuses on a particular use of medievalism in Romanian folk music under Ceausescu as a way of creating a national identity and community. In doing so, Curta also notes the ways medieval influences appear in popular music (primarily rock and folk) in other Eastern-Bloc countries.

8 Michael Rewa, "The Matter of Britain in British and American Popular Music (1966–1990)," *Popular Arthurian Traditions*, ed. Sally Slocum (Bowling Green, OH: Bowling Green State University Press, 1992), 104–10, at 105.

9 Michael Rewa, "The Matter of Britain," 105.

10 MewithoutYou, "The Soviet," *Catch for Us the Foxes* (Tooth and Nail Records), 2004.

11 MewithoutYou, "Carousels," *Catch for Us the Foxes* (Tooth and Nail Records), 2004.

12 The material on MewithoutYou was investigated and compiled by Kevin Stevens, to whom we express thanks for his insights into their use of medieval themes in popular music.

13 Ross Duffin, "Preface," *A Performer's Guide to Medieval Music*, ed. Ross Duffin (Bloomington: Indiana University Press, 2000), ix–xi, at ix.

14 Ross Duffin, "Preface," x.

15 Jennifer Bain, "Hooked on Ecstasy: Performance 'Practice' and the Reception of the Music of Hildegard of Bingen," *The Sounds and Sights of Performance in Early Music*, ed. Maureen Epp and Brian Power (Farnham, Surrey: Ashgate, 2009), 253–73.

16 hildegard.org/music/music.html, accessed 22 June 2011.

17 Jennifer Bain, "Hooked on Ecstasy," 271.

18 Thanks to Karen Gevirtz for her help in working out this formulation.

19 Jennifer Bain, "Hooked on Ecstasy," 271.

20 Jennifer Bain, "Hooked on Ecstasy," 272–73.

21 "The Christmas Story," The Waverly Consort, waverlyconsort.org/concerts.php, accessed 11 June 2011.

22 Annette Kreutziger-Herr, "Imagining Medieval Music: A Short History," *Studies in Medievalism XIV: Correspondences: Medievalism in Scholarship and the Arts*, ed. Tom Shippey with Martin Arnold (Cambridge: D. S. Brewer, 2005), 81–109, at 101.

23 Annette Kreutziger-Herr, "Imagining Medieval Music," 101.

24 Annette Kreutziger-Herr, "Imagining Medieval Music," 83.

25 Annette Kreutziger-Herr, "Imagining Medieval Music," 85. Kreutziger-Herr helpfully points to four kinds of medievalism: creative (old works forming new ones); reproductive (the reconstruction of old works to seem authentic); scientific (the study of medieval authors, works, or events in order to explain them in their context); and political or ideological (the exploitation of medieval themes or works for political reasons and used to legitimate actions) ("Imagining Medieval Music," 84).

26 Katherine Bergeron, "Finding God at Tower Records: The Virtual Sacred," *The New Republic* (27 February 1995); qtd. in Kreutziger-Herr, 101.

27 Annette Kreutziger-Herr, "Imagining Medieval Music," 85, 87, 88.

28 Annette Kreutziger-Herr, "Imagining Medieval Music," 102.

29 Elizabeth Aubrey, "Non-Liturgical Monophony," *A Performer's Guide to Medieval Music*, ed. Ross Duffin, 105–14, at 112.

30 Will and Ariel Durant, *The Story of Civilization, Vol. 4: The Age of Faith* (New York: Simon & Schuster, 1950). This is not to claim that the Durants have any particular authority in defining historical periods, but to show that one of the most popular histories of the twentieth century, which contributed to many people's perspectives, viewed the Middle Ages as an essentially religious period, distinct from those that came before and after.

31 Many thanks to Gesina Phillips, DJ and Promotions Director, and Michcella Tiscornia, DJ and Technical Operations Director, of WSOU Radio, South Orange, New Jersey, for their helpful walk-through of Viking Metal, its history, and its characteristics. Bands like the Russian group Arkona, for instance, draw on national pagan mythologies that are not specifically Viking, but share a great deal with the philosophies of Viking Metal. The Napalm Records video for Arkona's best-known song, "Goi, Rode, Goi," ("Hail, Rod, Hail," a reference to the Slavic equivalent of Thor), shows a Viking longboat sailing in a storm while Masha, "Scream," their lead vocalist, alternates between a stage performance and singing standing on an isolated North Sea island. In both scenes, she is dressed in medieval clothing, with an emphasis on furs, and in the concert sections, a horned helmet. At the end of the video, the longboat is wrecked on the shore of Masha's island.

32 Gregg Moffitt, "The Pillage People: Swedish Warriors Amon Amarth Wage War against Misconceptions of Both Vikings and Death Metal," *Decibel* (April 2011): 58–62, at 58.

33 Eduardo Rivadavia, "Requiem Review," Allmusic.com/album, accessed 11 June 2011.

34 Details of the Viking Revival can be found in Andrew Wawn, *The Vikings and the Victorians: Inventing the Old North in Nineteenth-Century Britain* (Cambridge: D. S. Brewer, 2000), as well as his *Northern Antiquity: The Post-Medieval Reception of Edda and Saga* (Enfield Lock: Hisarlik, 1994).

35 Gregg Moffitt, "The Pillage People," 58.

36 Gregg Moffitt, "The Pillage People," 58.

37 Gregg Moffitt, "The Pillage People," 58. Hegg cites anthropological evidence that Viking skeletons became smaller after the advent of Christianity to justify this argument, claiming that once the Church began taking over, people stopped sharing as part of the ecclesiastical program. As such, he sees the Church as "so full of hypocrisy and bullshit it's unbelievable," an opinion he might be said to share with Dante, even if their philosophy and theology (and phraseology) would put them at odds.

38 Michael Alexander notes of modern historians Christine Riding and Jacqueline Riding that they found it "surprising and even implausible that in 1835 Parliament should have specified 'Gothic' or 'Elizabethan' as 'the national style' for so important a secular building" (*Medievalism: The Middle Ages in Modern England* [New

Haven: Yale University Press, 2007], xix–xx). The Ridings are the authors of *The Houses of Parliament* (London: Merrell, 2000), 15.
39 Gregg Moffitt, "The Pillage People," 59.
40 Gregg Moffitt, "The Pillage People," 59.
41 Simon Trafford and Aleks Pluskowski, "Antichrist Superstars: The Vikings in Hard Rock and Heavy Metal," *Mass Market Medieval: Essays on the Middle Ages in Popular Culture*, ed. David Marshall (Jefferson, NC: McFarland, 2007), 57–73, at 70.
42 Simon Trafford and Aleks Pluskowski, "Antichrist Superstars," 71.
43 Simon Trafford and Aleks Pluskowski, "Antichrist Superstars," 61.
44 Klaus Neumann, "Barbara Thornton, 1950–98," *Early Music* 27.1 (1999): 169.
45 Barbara Thornton and Lawrence Rosenwald, "The Voice in the Middle Ages: Poetics as Technique," *A Performer's Guide to Medieval Music*, 264–92, at 264.
46 Barbara Thornton and Lawrence Rosenwald, "The Voice in the Middle Ages," 269.
47 Barbara Thornton and Lawrence Rosenwald, "The Voice in the Middle Ages," 271.
48 Barbara Thornton and Lawrence Rosenwald, "The Voice in the Middle Ages," 275.
49 Barbara Thornton and Lawrence Rosenwald, "The Voice in the Middle Ages," 285.
50 Mary McAleer Balkun, *The American Counterfeit: Authenticity and Identity in American Literature and Culture* (Tuscaloosa: University of Alabama Press, 2006), 5.
51 "Antioch Chalice," The Metropolitan Museum of Art, metmuseum.org/Collections/search-the-collections/70008320, accessed 22 March 2012.
52 Miriam Murphy, review of Gustavus Eisen's *The Great Chalice of Antioch on Which are Depicted in Sculpture the Earliest Known Portraits of Christ, Apostles, and Evangelists*, *Catholic Historical Review* 11.1 (1925): 137–38, at 138.
53 The Antioch Chalice is not the only medieval cup that is thought to have been the Holy Grail. The Genoa Chalice and the Valencia Chalice, both in the cathedrals in those cities, still attract pilgrims because they are considered to be authentic vessels that caught Christ's blood at the crucifixion.
54 Michael Alexander, *Medievalism*, xxii.
55 Walter Benjamin, "The Work of Art in the Age of Mechanical Reproduction," *Illuminations*, ed. Hannah Arendt, trans. Harry Zohn (New York: Schocken, 1968), 217–51, at 220.
56 Walter Benjamin, "The Work of Art," 220.
57 Walter Benjamin, "The Work of Art," 221.
58 Walter Benjamin, "The Work of Art," 221.
59 Walter Benjamin, "The Work of Art," 223.
60 Walter Benjamin, "The Work of Art," 223.
61 Walter Benjamin, "The Work of Art," 223.
62 Walter Benjamin, "The Work of Art," 224.
63 Walter Benjamin, "The Work of Art," 225.
64 Helen Evans, Curator of Medieval Art and the Cloisters, Metropolitan Museum of Art, Personal Interview, 15 June 2011. We are grateful to Helen Evans, Melanie Holcomb (Associate Curator of Medieval Art), and Dita Amory (Acting Associate Curator-in-Charge of the Robert Lehman Collection, The Metropolitan Museum of Art) for speaking in such detail and with such candor.
65 Melanie Holcomb, Associate Curator of Medieval Art, the Metropolitan Museum of Art, Personal Interview, 15 June 2011.
66 Our thanks to Melanie Holcomb for this piece of inside knowledge about the workings of the Toledo Museum.
67 Helen Evans, 15 June 2011.
68 Many thanks to Kevin Stevens and Cathryn Wiatroski, who explored in great detail the differences between the Medieval Hall, Old Master Paintings, and Greek and Roman galleries at the Metropolitan Museum in the Summer of 2010. Their analyses of these distinctions were vital in compiling these observations.
69 Walter Benjamin, "The Work of Art," 234–35.

70 This work has been variously known as the Merode Altarpiece and the Campin Altarpiece; it is a triptych painted by Robert Campin, a North Netherlandish painter, between 1425 and 1428. It depicts the annunciation in its central panel, and shows donors on the left and Joseph making mousetraps on the right. A late-medieval northern city appears outside the windows, and the house in which Mary attends the angel is in every detail from the same time.

8 Experiential Medievalisms
Reliving the Always Modern Middle Ages

"Nobody says that the Middle Ages offers a completely jolly prospect," observes Umberto Eco,[1] but, at the same time, nobody can deny the period's continued appeal in the popular imagination, and for many aficionados of the Middle Ages, the allure of the past beckons them into entertainments in which they relive the glories of yesteryear. Even if many of these enthusiasts would not enjoy the prospect of life without such modern conveniences as indoor plumbing, air conditioning, and email, the fantasy of returning to the past illuminates their avocational (and, for some, their vocational) pursuits. Opportunities abound for enthusiasts to re-create and participate in the past: in addition to the various medievalisms of literature, film, art, and music explored previously in this volume, experiential medievalisms, including games, videogames, jousting, and Medieval and Renaissance Fairs, allow one to participate in this past. Of course, such a distinction is in itself arbitrary, for a well-written novel set in the Middle Ages can feel as powerfully experiential, if not more so, than a kitschy Medieval and Renaissance Fair. Through experiences both mediated (such as videogames) and immediate (such as jousting and medieval fairs), experiential medievalisms foreground the possibility of becoming, if not being, medieval, of reliving the Middle Ages in its necessarily modern reinventions.

"Medieval" videogames rely on modern technology to re-create the past, and thus the experience of such medievalisms is grounded in the pleasures of electronic anachronism, in which technology enables a return to the past in the service of fantasy, primarily quest fantasy. As Laurie Taylor and Zach Whalen argue, "videogames operate within a rich new media ecology and inform how we think about memory, history, and nostalgia through other types of media."[2] Although a relatively recent genre in the history of narrative and entertainment, especially in contrast to medieval literature, videogames engage with previous narrative and ludic forms, creating new juxtapositions of electronic and text-based narratives. Also, while Taylor and Whalen's proposition suggests an educational potential in videogames, offering a view of the historical Middle Ages for their players to experience virtually, most medieval games suggest a very different response to memory and nostalgia, leaning heavily on a temporal fantasy that blurs boundaries of time, space, and history.

On a narratological level, many "medieval" videogames descend directly from the romance tradition, in which knightly protagonists dispatch various monsters and villains before triumphing over a final enemy. These plot devices are so foundational to medieval romance that it is instructive to look at Gawain's numerous elided adventures in *Sir Gawain and the Green Knight* as a counterexample to the genre's more typical plotlines:

> Mony klyf he ouerclambe in contrayez straunge,
> Fer floten fro his frendez, fremedly he rydez.
> At vche warþe oþer water þer þe wyӿe passed
> He fonde a foo hym byfore, bot ferly hit were,
> And þat so foule and so felle þat feӿt hym byhode.
> So mony meruayl bi mount þer þe mon fyndez,
> Hit were to tore for to telle of þe tenþe dole.
> Sumwhyle wyth wormez he werrez, and with wolues als,
> Sumwhyle with wodwos þat woned in þe knarrez,
> Boþe wyth bullez and berez, and borez oþerquyle,
> And etaynez, þat hym anelede of þe heӿe felle.

> Many a cliff [Gawain] climbed over in that strange country
> Where he rode as a foreigner, far removed from his friends.
> At every creek and crossing where that fellow coursed,
> He found—quite fantastically—some foe before him,
> One who was foul and fierce, with whom he had to fight.
> In those mountains he met with such a host of marvels
> That it would be too trying to tell even the tenth part.
> Sometimes with serpents he struggled, sometimes with wolves,
> Sometimes with troll-like creatures who camp in the crags,
> Also with bulls and with bears—and even with boars—
> And giants who jumped out at him from the jags.[3]

In this passage, the *Gawain*-Poet glosses over the vast majority of Gawain's adventures during his journey seeking the Green Knight, thereby rejecting the standard plotlines of numerous romances in which a knight encounters a string of enemies, each more terrifying than the last. The *Gawain*-Poet's rejection of this simplistic narrative strategy speaks to his literary genius, as he focuses instead on Gawain's struggles in a spiritual quest for which his previous adventuring has left him ill-prepared. In regard to "medieval" videogames, this brief passage from *Sir Gawain and the Green Knight* contains virtually a narrative précis of many of their plotlines, in which the adventurer defeats enemy after enemy, moving from level to level, until the final boss is vanquished.

One of the earliest videogames with a medieval theme, *Adventure*, designed for the Atari 2600 console and released in 1979, features a minimal plotline, as expressed in the game's accompanying instruction pamphlet: "An evil magician has stolen the Enchanted Chalice and hidden it somewhere in the Kingdom. The object of the game is to rescue the Enchanted Chalice and place it inside the Golden Castle where it belongs." The game appropriates the Arthurian quest for the Holy Grail as its defining narrative, while incorporating three dragons—"Yorgle, the Yellow Dragon, who is just plain mean; ... Grundle, the Green Dragon, who is mean and ferocious; ... and Rhindle, the Red Dragon, who is the most ferocious of all"—as obstacles for the player to overcome along the path to victory.[4] As simple as *Adventure* is technologically, with a pixelated square representing the player, it influenced numerous "medieval" questing games that followed, particularly in offering players a variety of tools—a sword, a bridge, a magnet, and keys to various castles—that they must employ to navigate the game successfully. The game is also thought to be the first to incorporate an "Easter egg," a hidden message extraneous to game play that players must discover on their own, which, in this instance, allows one to enter a secret room with the message that the game was "Created by Warren Robinett." Its scant medieval plotline notwithstanding, *Adventure* was enormously popular upon its release and established the basic parameters of "medieval" videogames, to which many of its descendant games adhere.

One of the most popular videogame series of the last twenty-five years, the *Legend of Zelda* games, including *The Legend of Zelda*, *The Adventure of Link*, *Link to the Past*, *Ocarina of Time*, *Majora's Mask*, *Twilight Princess*, *Phantom Hourglass*, *Spirit Tracks*, and *Skyward Sword*, among others, employ the quest narrative as their standard plotline: a princess is captured, or a magic jewel is lost, and the young adventurer Link must restore order to a chaotic world by defeating a series of monsters, each more deadly than its predecessor. In *Twilight Princess*, the game begins at the moment when peace is disrupted, as the instruction booklet outlines:

> One day Link is showing off his swordsmanship as usual when a monkey appears. "Hey! That's the monkey that's been causing trouble all over the village! Let's get him," cry the children. They run after the monkey into the forest. Link rushes into the heart of the woods after them and is shocked to find that the dark thickets are teeming with countless monsters. After fighting his way through their ranks, Link rescues the child and the monkey from the cage where they are held captive. Until now, the forest had always been a safe place ... [5]

From this initial adventure of the mischievous monkey, Link proceeds through the Forest Temple, the Goron Mines, the Lakebed Temple, the Arbiter's Grounds, the Snowpeak Ruins, the Temple of Time, the City in the Sky, and the Palace of Twilight, collecting the pieces of the puzzle and defeating enemies until he succeeds in his climactic battle at Hyrule Castle. As is the case with many "medieval" videogames, the story is secondary to the game play, to the extent that this narrative can be condensed into two sentences in *The Legend of Zelda: Twilight Princess: The Official Nintendo Player's Guide*: "A dark power is sweeping over Hyrule. The denizens of the twilight realm, banished long ago by the three goddesses, hold the land within their grip."[6] The experience of reading medieval romances hinges, obviously enough, on the narrative held in one's hand, but in videogames the narrative often intrudes unwelcomely into the game play, a distraction from the adventuring also held in one's hand, but, in this instance, mediated through the game's controller. Under these conditions, the narratives of many videogames offer little more than a skeletal structure upon which the game designers append various challenges and puzzles, and so the games' medieval qualities imbue the adventure with little more than appropriate thematic coloring.

Whereas *Adventure* and the *Zelda* games rely more on the narrative structures of medieval romance than on allusions to specific texts, "medieval" videogames are increasingly interweaving their storylines with those of their literary forebears. Engaging with the storylines of past narratives connects videogames to a literary pedigree, although such connections are often fleeting (as in the videogame *Dante's Inferno*, as discussed in Chapter 2). In *Sonic and the Black Knight*, one of a series of games featuring the popular hedgehog's adventures in the past, the hero must challenge King Arthur himself:

> One day while Sonic is waiting for a potentially stressful encounter with [his girlfriend] Amy, he is abruptly summoned into the book of *King Arthur and the Knights of the Round Table* by Merlina, the Royal Wizard of Camelot. She is being hunted down by King Arthur himself and begs Sonic to help her save the fabled kingdom. … Meeting familiar faces along the way, Sonic must defeat the evil Arthur and ultimately find a way to rescue Camelot.[7]

The game's plot hinges on an intriguing twist: after Arthur receives Excalibur's magic scabbard from Nimue and therefore cannot be harmed in battle, he goes mad with power, and Merlina, a female version of Merlin whose sex has been shifted for no discernible reason other than possibly to appeal to female gamers, summons Sonic from the present to save the (medieval) day. As with so many popular-culture reformulations of Arthurian tales, the superficial allusions to past legends in *Sonic and the Black Knight* do little to enhance its narrative, which consists primarily of a series of challenges to one's manual dexterity.

In many "medieval" videogames of this ilk, players experience a quasi-medieval past by directing the actions of the games' protagonists, whether those of a pixelated square in *Adventure*, of Link in the *Zelda* games, or of a hyperactive hedgehog in the *Sonic* games, whereas other "medieval" videogames invite players to join the games as themselves or as avatars whom they create. In *The Sims*^{TM} *Medieval*, players learn to rule over their own medieval kingdom. The instruction booklet exhorts players to "Get Medieval!" a phrase that cheekily refers to the sodomy scene in Quentin Tarantino's *Pulp Fiction*, in which Marsellus Wallace (as played by Ving Rhames) threatens his captor with unfathomable tortures: "I'm gonna git medieval on your ass."[8] *The Sims*^{TM}

Medieval invites its players to visit a Middle Ages in which various adventures, ranging from the humorous to the disastrous to the humorously disastrous, await:

> Hark, adventurous souls! Come forth and behold the tales of *The Sims*^{TM} *Medieval*, an all-new Sims experience filled with adventures on the high seas, scheming relatives, a fickle populace, and even Sim-eating chinchillas! Partake in quests to expand your kingdom and construct new buildings to attract more Sims to your realm. Your Sims live the lives of monarchs, knights, spies, magicians and more as you choose whether—or not—to fulfill their responsibilities and bring glory to the name of your kingdom![9]

The use of second-person pronouns in this passage emphasizes the immersive experience that the game offers: although "you" direct the characters' actions, whether those of the default monarchs (with the rather baroque names of Godwin Wahl or Kalliope Qualls) or of a ruler of your own creation, the game positions the player as the benevolent (or not) ruler of the kingdom. As your Sims prosper, so does your worth as their creator and omniscient overlord.

But to what purpose such videogame medievalism? Marcello Simonetta, author of *The Montefeltro Conspiracy* and historical consultant to the video-game *Assassin's Creed Brotherhood*, believes that historically based videogames educate their players about a particular period, but his sense that *Assassin's Creed Brotherhood* accurately depicts the architecture in Italy c. 1500 and the historical figures of Pope Alexander VI, Niccolo Machiavelli, Leonardo da Vinci, and the Borgias as its integral characters is itself a fantasy. The characters may be real in the sense of their prior existence, but they are not occupying their "real" roles or engaging in their own historical moment: Da Vinci sells the player equipment to use in his quest, and the player retrieves Da Vinci's machines that the Borgia family has stolen, while Machiavelli directs the player to undertake many of the game's missions. In *Assassin's Creed II*, Rodrigo Borgia leads the Templar Order of Italy while seeking an object of ultimate power that leads to a fistfight with the Pope. The defining features of these historical figures—the ingenuity of Da Vinci, the scheming of Machiavelli, the duplicity of the Borgias—are transposed from history to videogame, yet at a great loss to the complexity of their achievements in their contemporary periods.

Games like *Assassin's Creed* prove that history provides compelling game plots, but Simonetta's anticipation that drawing from reality may move a gamer to explore an historical subject further (and thus to stimulate the educational process) is not borne out by medieval gamers themselves.[10] Matt Honig, for instance, an avid player of several games including *Breath of Fire IV*, *Fire Emblem*, *Age of Empires I and II*, and occasionally *Assassin's Creed*, suggests that "medieval" means "anything before the Renaissance, before people were paying too much attention," essentially any period that runs in opposition to modernity, but he adds that "medieval" also is fundamentally an appealing setting, a world of castles, magic, and weapons, rather than of churches, manors, and guilds. For instance, he suggests that *Breath of Fire IV*, which offers two continents, medieval Europe and Feudal Asia, is "randomly medieval," offering an atmosphere constructed essentially out of architecture, dragon gods, and winged princesses.[11] Gesina Phillips, a medieval gamer whose games of choice include *Guild Wars*, *Baldur's Gate*, and *A Bard's Tale*, as well as the older *King's Quest*, adds, "you can't have medieval games without magic," and notes that they provide a "very artificial Middle Ages," looking to the "fun parts," such as "guys with big swords," and "traditional knights on quests and fairy tales" rather than any real sense of the period. She observes particularly that the games offer a "clean Middle Ages," in which values of good and evil are laid out in strict contradistinction. Games like *Majesty*, which allows players acting as regents of the realm to construct the kingdom and to generate heroes to kill the monsters ravaging the land, pose no questions of moral ambiguity that might disrupt one's game play.[12]

David Marshall's discussion of the videogame *Dungeons and Dragons*, an electronic version of the dice-and-graph game, reveals a medieval world that does not merely incorporate certain kinds of fantastic and magical elements, but also collapses time: "medieval," he notes, ranges "from late antique to early modern, so characters typed as centurions, Vikings, knights, and cavaliers can all make appearances." Geography collapses as well: "near-and far-Eastern elements" are incorporated so that "samurai or Persian warriors join forces with those European heroes to thwart the plots of monstrous evils." He adds, "two contradictory impressions of these Middle Ages strike the casual observer: that the Middle Ages still thrive and that no time ever looked quite like this recent vision of them."[13] Fantasy, tautologically yet intrinsically, produces its own world within a system of meanings that overrides the rules of realism while still remaining believable as fantasy, and so the worlds of these games are not simply preposterous pastiches of medieval history, but a version that picks and chooses, creating an authentic atmosphere that allows the game's story to be played out within its constructed framework. The fact that the elements beyond atmosphere need not be strictly medieval (such as Merlina of *Sonic and the Black Knight* or the disruptive monkey in *Twilight Princess*) shows the extent to which this is merely a framework onto which one can hang various sorts of fantasy. The medieval tropes that succeed within this framework are incorporated, often those that make it look and feel right, although "right" is primarily defined through a contemporary lens, reflecting current entertainment perspectives rather than medieval ones. Those that do not are dispensed with in favor of extra-medieval inventions.

Daniel Kline suggests that videogames provide not a view into the "real" Middle Ages, but "a privileged entry into current representations (and contemporary understandings) of the medieval period."[14] After detailed examinations of several games, he notes an anecdote from his teaching, in which students discussed the technological and medieval meanings of *icon*. Kline notes that both senses of the term "are gateways into a kind of invisible, even meta-physical realm; both require a specialized knowledge to understand and properly implement; both are 'overdetermined' in that they pack an entire history into a rather simple image; both enable, to the uninitiated, a kind of power, or even magic."[15] These notions of *icon* are equally those of medieval games: a magical realm requiring specialized knowledge, one that packs a complex history into an experience relying on representational and archetypal codes. Power and magic, in almost all cases, are at the heart of this representation, as these are the two characteristics of the Middle Ages (one undoubtedly authentic, the other imaginary) that inform most "medieval" videogames. As "stimulating and provocative representations of the Middle Ages" and "*digital simulacra* of the Middle Ages,"[16] they provide Baudrillard's "copy of an original that never existed."[17] And while Kline is certainly correct that any rendering (historical, scholarly, popular) of the Middle Ages is ultimately "a different kind of discursive account prone to its own ideological investments and material deficiencies,"[18] the "medieval" world of videogames offers an obviously engaging but persistent fantasy, a surface that collapses into the emptiness underneath while nonetheless providing hours upon hours of amusement for their aficionados.

While videogames allow players to experience a fantasy Middle Ages in their living rooms, other experiential medievalisms invite their aficionados to stand up from the couch and live the past anew. From the Excalibur Hotel in Las Vegas to the various adventures-for-hire listed in the Medieval Travel website in the United Kingdom including the Canterbury Tales Experience and Viking Jorvik [York], from the rebirth of jousting as a sport to the many Medieval and Renaissance Fairs that travel the western world, opportunities abound to relive a recreational version of medieval literature and history. The Medieval Times® Dinner and Tournament, with locations in California, Florida, Georgia, Illinois, Maryland, New Jersey, South Carolina, Texas, and Canada, invites potential patrons to enjoy a journey back to yesteryear in its advertisements: "You're invited to a royal feast with the king and his family. While you enjoy a fine, four-course dinner, you'll be able to watch knights compete in a jousting tournament on horseback and take in the colorful medieval pageantry." The advertisements also proclaim, "the athletic stunts, jousting, and swordplay the knights perform are not fairy tale. They are very real, as you will see." Of course, the meaning of "real" in this passage is itself dubious but no less enlightening: what does it mean for a stunt, itself a staged act intended to approximate danger but safely so, to be "real"? The pageantry of Medieval Times® invites one back to the past, but a "stunt" Middle Ages rather than a fairy-tale one, positing the superiority of the stunt simulation over a fairy-tale re-creation, while also relying heavily on the tropes of Arthurian romance in its staged competitions.

For the employees of Medieval Times®, the journey to the past necessitates quick switches between the past and the present. Eveleena Fults, who has worked as a Princess at Medieval Times® in Orlando for nine years, describes the necessity of performing as a caricature rather than a character: not to act her role as a particular character with an individual personality but to symbolize and iconographically communicate princesshood through gesture, posture, and poise. While auditioning for the role at the age of sixteen, she realized that the Princess needed to exude sufficient stage presence for an audience of twelve hundred people. Fults readily admits the show's historical lapses, but finds the pleasure of the performance in the audience's reactions. After each tournament, the performers meet and greet the audience, and Fults recalled a particular instance when a young girl, terrified of the male characters and in tears because she thought her beloved Princess had left the castle, became elated when Fults approached her. As Fults explains, "creating the fantasy is my favorite part of the job," and part of this fantasy depends on embodying the past in these interactions: "you have to say My Lord and My Lady, you can't use slang, but always maintain the fantasy of the past for our guests." Such a "fantasy of being transported to another time and place" creates the allure of Medieval Times®, as Fults suggests, such that the patrons' themselves take on the archetypal roles of yesteryear. "Now, wench, when we get home..." Fults remembered one guest saying to his wife, who responded tartly yet good-naturedly to her partner's new sense of lordly authority, and, one assumes, who remained quite capable of ending this medieval masculine fantasy of willing wenches should he push matters too far.[19]

Such medieval tropes as evident at Medieval Times®, both in their stunt and fairy-tale enactments, migrate into some unlikely places, often for somewhat unclear purposes. For instance, in an episode of the television reality competition *Amazing Race*, the teams engaged in a weirdly anachronistic version of the Middle Ages, beginning at Stonehenge, where they were instructed to determine directions to Eastnor Castle, famous for being the seat of King Richard III.[20] Once there, they stormed the castle, climbing ladders while raucous peasants hurled buckets of sludge at them in a (likely intentional) re-enactment of the French castle scene in *Monty Python and the Holy Grail*. They next crossed a small lake in curricles tied to ropes, and then participated in a so-called joust, although how jousting is constituted by firing watermelons from a ballista (a giant sling-shot; not, one notes, a trebuchet) at an empty suit of armor is anyone's guess. The greatest similarity may be in the level of physical risk, as one contestant was hit with a watermelon when the ballista failed to release it, an accident that may also define the medievalness of the episode in its unexpected danger. As with "medieval" videogames, the Middle Ages, which is cobbled together from a variety of historical moments, impulses, and images, provides nothing more than atmosphere for this reality-television competition. From the pre-historical Stonehenge, to the fifteenth-century Wars of the Roses, to the Tournament as archetypal experience of the medieval, history collapses into a unified "past" in which diverse monuments suddenly relate meaningfully to one another, with contemporary ideas about competition and skill crystallizing these various elements into a game, if a disjointed one. Instead of the prizes of romance—a grail or a lady—the rewards of engaging successfully with these skills become less awe-inspiring and more pecuniary: if not exactly victory over one's pagan enemies, at least a pass into the next round of the competition, the ousting of the weakest link, and the hope of the program's cash prize promised to its winning team.

The primary action of this episode of the *Amazing Race* takes place in the foreground, while a more traditional jousting tournament proceeds simultaneously, although it functions primarily as a source of clues that direct the racers to their watermelon patches. Despite its marginalization in this episode, jousting is enjoying a revival, at least in part because "there's a real possibility of getting hurt," as a spectator at the Gulf Coast International Jousting Championships noted in anticipation.[21] Here, the Middle Ages represents the possibility of authorized violence and the spectacle of witnessing its combatants injuring one another. When jouster Rhos Tolle was "struck squarely in the chest ... and sent flying from his horse," Dashka Slater notes in her exposé of the sport's modern reemergence, "it was as if someone had sent an electric current through the arena's aluminum bleachers. Men leapt to their feet with their fists in the air. Teenage girls clutched one another's arms ... 'I want to see another guy get paralyzed,' a boy in front of me squealed, waving a toy sword."[22] This gleeful spectacle of destruction is echoed in the National Geographic program on jousting, *Knights of Mayhem*, whose premiere episode, "First Blood," featured numerous jousters spitting up blood, breaking bones, and lying knocked out cold in the lists.[23] These jousting tournaments herald the sport's reemergence in the modern world, and other such events include the Longs Peak Scottish-Irish Highlands Festival in Estes Park, Colorado; the Sword of Honor in Leeds, England; the Tournament of the Phoenix in San Diego; and the Tournois du Lys d'Argent in Québec. Worldjoust Tournaments[TM] sponsors such events, as it claims to be "dedicated to the creation of historical tournaments and their development into an upscale, modern international sport."[24]

These jousting events enact an odd engagement with and rejection of the Middle Ages. One of the world's leading jousters (from a group of about two hundred), Charlie Andrews claims to know and care nothing for history; he "doesn't joust because he's attracted to romantic notions of honor and chivalry or because he has an affinity for the medieval period. He does it because he considers jousting one of the most extreme sports ever invented."[25] While he and another top-ranked jouster, Shane Adams, began with theatrical jousting, the performances commonly seen at Medieval and Renaissance Fairs, they both turned to "full-contact" jousting, although both men still perform at fairs and festivals. While Adams performs as part of a troupe called the Knights of Valor, suggesting at least a gesture toward some medieval values, Andrews is the leader of the Knights of Mayhem, who now have their own television series. Jousting, for him at least, is not primarily an attempt to return to medieval values or ideologies, in which the competition functions as a means of displaying prowess and chivalry; rather, it appears in this modern incarnation to develop a new version of Ultimate Fighting on horseback. Knights they may claim to be, but their goal is not the order of chivalry but the chaos of

Mayhem. Indeed, the National Geographic program *Knights of Mayhem* features interpersonal clashes to accompany the jousting battles, foregrounding tension and conflict over the kind of order tournaments were designed to provide. Viewers might recall that the jousting tournament in Chaucer's *Knight's Tale* is called by Theseus to control the violence of the private battle between Palamon and Arcite for Emily's hand by imposing a set of ordered rules upon it, but in the world of reality television, increasing the conflicts, both physical and interpersonal, stands as a primary goal for generating higher ratings (and thus higher advertising revenues).

Tobias Capwell, curator of Arms and Armour at the Wallace Collection in London, views winning a medieval tournament as the equivalent of a great actor winning an Academy Award.[26] Yet, for current jousters, the rewards seem somewhat unclear. As Andrews and Adams point out, there is little money in the sport beyond performing at fairs. Many of the tournaments' purses are small, for they are usually drawn from a percentage of the participants' entry fees, although Charlie Andrews and his fellow Knights compete for $20,000 at the Sherwood Forest Faire in McDade, Texas, in the "Big Money, Big Pain" episode of *Knights of Mayhem*.[27] Opportunities for sponsorship and endorsements are limited, and the dangers of critical injury are obviously significant. Despite the plate armor and chain mail that jousters wear, broken bones, concussions, dislocated shoulders, and gashes are expected repercussions of these events, and most jousters continue to fight with broken hands, cuts, and multiple bruises. Indeed, *Knights of Mayhem* suggests that the culture of full-contact jousting expects "playing hurt"; each episode displays knights choosing to continue their combats despite significant injury, while those who surrender to their wounds (and thus their foes) are often taunted, unless they are so badly concussed they can barely stand up. Failure to compete, even for these reasons, often results in expressions of self-doubt and humiliation, a sense of failure comparable to Sir Gawain's sense of his abrogation of his chivalric responsibility at the end of *Sir Gawain and the Green Knight*, although he has clearly succeeded in the martial elements of his quest.

Oddly, this arguably more authentic version of jousting, with real (rather than balsa-wood tipped) lances is a particularly American phenomenon. European jousters, who have adopted a less violent version of this medieval sport, enjoy longer and healthier careers, and they persistently reject the "American style," often refusing to come to tournaments despite offers of free airfares.[28] Slater notes that jousters like Andrews believe that "the broken bones are what tell the crowd that the sport is real. Jousting may be wrapped in the trappings of fantasy, but those who do it want to make certain no one thinks they're pretending. 'I'm not an actor,' Andrews says, 'I don't do this to play knight.'"[29] Of course, this declaration is inherently misleading: while some jousters may see their pastime more as a sport than as a re-enactment, it is ultimately impossible to separate the two. Most European jousters come to the sport as a method of historic performance, aiming for more authentic armor representing specific historical moments, rather than the hodgepodge favored by American jousters. For instance, at the tournaments sponsored by TournamentJousts, which are approved by the International Jousting League and the Royal Armouries Museum in England, competitors are "[r]equired to wear historically accurate fifteenth-century armor, clothing and accessories, including arming doublets and hose."[30] Jeffrey Hedgecock, who earns his living as an armorer for museums, films, re-enactors, and, of course, jousters, notes that "it makes no sense to joust while ignoring the past," and adds, "without the history, you might as well do it on motorcycles."[31] For the European enthusiasts, jousting is something like the Sienese *Palio*, a way to preserve some of the livelier elements of one's cultural history within the safe (or safer) confines of the modern age.[32]

The fact that there are competing styles of jousting is hardly surprising, and the contempt that the practitioners of each express for the opposing teams sounds almost like the insults hurled by opposing camps in the bohorts represented in medieval romance. Slater comments that "lurking underneath the surface of the debate over jousting styles are deeper questions about masculinity itself." Fantasies of gender flourish in "medieval" experiences, often pining back to stereotypes of chivalrous knights and their maidens fair, yet such gender roles demand rigorous adherence to their traditional parameters. Indeed, as Clare Lees observes of medieval masculinity, "the burden of masculine potency (symbolic or real), shadowed by impotence, exacts a heavy price,"[33] an observation applicable as well to many masculinities of today. It is perhaps over-reading to understand this particular return to medievalism as an attempt to reinscribe traditional notions of gender against the anxieties of a shifting modern world, especially since, for the American jousters at least, it is a return to a masculinity that more resembles the cowboy aesthetic (a notion that itself has been significantly challenged) in medieval trappings. Jousting nonetheless encodes a desire for raw virility and aggression, albeit one with significant physical cost, that cannot be divorced from performances of gender transposed across the centuries.

In comparing European to American jousting, rhetorics of masculinity are defined alternatively by violence with manners and violence for the sake of violence. If European jousting is concerned with preserving the continent's medieval history, American jousting values the ferociousness and masculine bravado that comes with that history while divesting its meaning. If the former privileges authentic armor and fighting technique along with pageantry, the latter seems to prefer collisions, flying knights, and smashed lances. While no jouster has expressed such a sentiment in so many words, American jousting seems to add an additional conflation into the mix, making jousting into a kind of Viking frenzy, an authorized form of unbridled violence within the boundaries of a competition. This attitude introduces a version of medievalism in which the Middle Ages stands for an authorized lawlessness and abandon; within the structure of the tournament, the most dangerous, the most violent, and the most aggressive is also the most rewarded. What differentiates this aggression from, for example, American Football may be clear from George Will's famous quotation about the latter sport, "Football combines the two worst things about America: violence, punctuated by committee meetings."[34] Jousting becomes popular because it takes away the rules, the committee meetings, leaving only the violence behind. American jousting makes a masculine fantasy of the past, drawing on medieval elements (armor, fighting) but assembling them together in ways that serve purposes beyond a desire for authenticity. Although the Europeans are more overtly concerned with such a desire, they still, ultimately, achieve a mitigated experience that cannot re-create the past other than as a reflection of their own desires for this past.

As jousters seek to return their sport to cultural preeminence because it offers real violence, if conflicting visions of history, LARPers, or live-action role players, and members of the Society for Creative Anachronism understand that their combats offer a purely fantasy vision of the Middle Ages. In the film *Monster Camp*, a documentary detailing the behind-the-scenes maneuvers of a Seattle-based group of LARPers, J. P., who plays under the name of Sir Gregor, summarizes the allure of the game in contrast to the players' real lives: "There's a lot of people who [live-action role play] to try—you know, the theme of 'be all you *can't* be.' So, they're trying to be something they normally aren't in their lives to one extent or another."[35] The pleasure of the game arises in the possibility of social communion predicated more on a love for dungeons-and-dragons fantasy than for the Middle Ages, although the Middle Ages lurks in the background of their play. Kelly, a LARPer who takes his daughter to the games, affirms that LARPing creates lifelong memories to share with her: "It's something that she's going to remember for the rest of her life—'Hey, my dad was pretty neat. He took me to this really bizarre, medieval fantasy game.' Not a lot of dads do that!" The medievalism of much LARPing is often overshadowed by its role-playing fantasy element, but this panoply of tropes, while diluting its medieval traditions, instills in the game the endless possibility of new envisionings of the past, including those based in reality, history, fantasy, and individual imagination. As Michael Cramer concludes of the Society for Creative Anachronism, "members view ... [t]heir Current Middle Ages [as] a cornucopia of tropes and signs drawn from several different Middle Ages, which exists to help them negotiate their existence in the contemporary world."[36] In this manner, participants in Medieval and Renaissance Fairs share with jousters and LARPers an attempt to make available and alive certain elements of medieval culture, offering an alternative to the modern world that nonetheless takes advantage of its advancements.

The popularity of Medieval and Renaissance Fairs is evident from a perusal of *Renaissance Magazine*, which lists multiple events in thirty-six states and six countries, and whose diverse advertising highlights the vast industry catering to these fairs and their patrons. Clothing, shoes, weaponry, armor, jewelry, tableware, mead kits, artworks, books, pigments, and music are all advertised in its pages, which combine reviews of various festivals with articles on the restoration of Norman Castle Keep, the truth about Vikings, and how to make authentic May Day cider and Cornish pasties. Reviews of art shows at major museums share the same pages with discussions of the authenticity of the chastity belt, and a group-insurance plan is offered to those who earn their living at these festivals. An article on the Medieval Fair of Norman, Oklahoma, opens with an overview of its offerings:

> Inspired by the Middle Ages (approximately 600–1495) and set in April to celebrate Shakespeare's birthday, the Medieval Fair of Norman has grown to be the third largest event in the state of Oklahoma, attracting over 300,000 visitors during its three-day run. Sponsored by the University of Oklahoma and hosted in a public park, the fair is free and open to all.
>
> A living history event, the Medieval Fair of Norman features over 200 art and craft booths, 38 food vendors, games, and six stages with con-tinuous entertainment for all ages. Highlights include jousting tournaments with knights on horseback and human chess games. The kingdom comes alive each spring at Reaves Park in Norman, Oklahoma. ... [37]

The pictures accompanying the article feature ironwork forks and swords, people singing, jousters (male and female), Celtic jewelry, a giant stuffed bear, falcons, patrons dressed as pirates, women on stilts, and even fringed and coined scarves for belly-dancing on sale. This eclectic mix draws from tradi-tions well beyond the Middle Ages and Renaissance that the fair claims to represent; it shows an inclusionary and unifying past that allows everyone to "be themselves" by dressing up as someone else. Furthermore, any distinction between the Middle Ages and the Renaissance is obscured to meaninglessness in many of these events. Why, for instance, should the Medieval Fair of Norman commemorate Shakespeare's birthday in its April setting rather than the historically medieval Chaucer and his "Aprill with his shoures soote"?[38]

Many exhibitors at Medieval and Renaissance Fairs approximate as much as possible the medieval crafts they make, demonstrate, and sell. The Fort Tryon Park Medieval Festival, held each October in the park surrounding the Cloisters in New York City, includes a representative mix of artisans in its attempt "to bring to life the customs and spirit of the Middle Ages." The organizers describe the event as a transformative one:

> Manhattan's Fort Tryon Park is transformed into a medieval market town decorated with bright banners and processional flags. Performers, guests and festival goers dress in medieval costume. Visitors are greeted by authentic medieval music, dance, magic, and minstrels, as well as jugglers and jesters. The afternoon is concluded with a thrilling joust between four knights on horseback. Costumed vendors will be on hand to demonstrate and sell a wide variety of medieval crafts as well as food and drink.[39]

At the South Lawn Village, members of the Society for Creative Anachronism and the Adrian Empire (a group of enthusiastic Parks Department employees working the fair, and charmingly named for "Emperor" Adrian Benapee, New York City Parks Commissioner) present educational demonstrations of combat, music, dance, and arts. The craftspeople there demonstrate authentic blacksmithing techniques in their production of authentic weapons, although these items represent a wide range of times and places within a medieval context, as do the calligraphy, glass-blowing, embroidery, and basket weaving. Many items are available for purchase, from highly authentic weaponry and ironwork, forged on sight, to racy underwear and fairy statues. Much (although not all) of the music heard throughout the fair is played on medieval instruments and represents medieval forms: contemporary monks intone authentic chant, while choral groups sing melodies from both East and West. Yet even the most convincingly real of these performances nods to both past and present. For instance, at the 2010 fair, medieval secular songs were sung by the "Machaut Men," whose name and slogan "Machaut must go on!" riff on multiple contemporary references, including the "Macho Men" of the Village People's disco standard and the classic "show must go on" adage of Broadway. What constitutes "medieval" food is mostly emancipated from culinary history, as turkey legs are sold alongside Ye Olde Medieval Fried Dough, gingerbread baked in the shape of monks, and empanadas more reflective of New York City's cultural diversity than medieval cuisine.

It matters little whether the spirit that is brought to life by such contrasts is essentially "medieval," for these fairs create a shared space for a popular experience of a unifying fantasy of the past. After all, the website reminds us, patrons can choose to dress as a peasant or a noble; the nobles wear fancier clothing, but the peasants' attire is better suited for walking and sitting on the hay bales provided in lieu of chairs or benches.[40] It is possible to hear someone dressed in furs run up to greet a stilt walker crying, "I'm a barbarian today!"[41] However authentic the fair's offerings, this choice is the essence of its fantasy, and a stroll around the grounds demonstrates how once "medieval" becomes a choice, it comes to mean anything past, whether decorative, fantastic, or historical, as medieval lords, Renaissance ladies (and dogs), pirates, belly-dancers, fairies, demons, and others populate the grounds. If a lady dressed as a princess rides by on a pony dressed as a unicorn that seems to have stepped out of the Cloister's Unicorn Tapestries, a more authentically medieval feeling may well be generated by members of the New York Police Department's mounted unit, parting the crowd with their large, powerful draft horses that need only stride forward to create order and to control the populace. The attraction of these events, therefore, may be in the experience of a simpler time, when pleasures were tied more to the physical than to the technological. This is a cleaned-up medievalism; after all, the fantasy does not include any of the darker elements of the past, such as plague, infection, danger, violence, filth, intolerance, or torture. Weapons, all the advertisements in *Renaissance Magazine* remind its readers, must be "peace-tied" (that is, tied so they cannot be drawn) and only for peaceful purposes (as paradoxical a proclamation as this may be), and torture can only be construed as arising in the ubiquitous port-o-potties.

In his discussion of "Enchanted Castles," Umberto Eco might well be encountering the Medieval and Renaissance Festival in his understanding of the "nonchalance with which the artificial tissue seamlessly connects fake and genuine," creating what he calls "a sense of fullness, the obsessive determination not to leave a single space that doesn't suggest something, and hence the masterpiece of bricolage" that these constructions of the past produce.[42] He also suggests that the "industry of the Absolute Fake gives a semblance to the truth of the myth of immortality through the play of imitations and copies, and it achieves the presence of the divine in the presence of the natural."[43] As a "reassurance through Imitation," these constructed medievalisms attempt to connect past and present, suggesting that while we have transcended many of the horrors of the past, its pleasures remain evocative and exploitable for contemporary experience. In constructing the "spirit" of the medieval world but not its reality, patrons reach for an experience of authenticity, and therefore an escape from our mass-produced, time-bound lives and natures.

Medieval people may well have sought an escape from their own time-bound experience through religious rituals that tied the present to both past and future. The most literal escape route of the Middle Ages from real life came through pilgrimage, which allowed pilgrims to leave the familiar to seek the eternal experience of penance and salvation. Contemporary seekers looking for a similar escape can relive the Pilgrimage to Santiago de Compostella each summer, walking the same route (or parts of it) as medieval men and women, or they can choose more contemporary forms of pilgrimage, to sites as diverse as Elvis Presley's Graceland, the National Baseball Hall of Fame in Cooperstown, New York, or the Field of Dreams in Dyersville, Iowa. They may walk labyrinths such as the famed pair at Grace Cathedral in San Francisco, seeking the mystical connection to transcendence through a nexus of meditation, sacred space, and movement in a replication of a medieval replication of pilgrimage itself. These sites are often invested with similar miraculous and curative powers, and certainly the intention is that they will change the pilgrim and bring meaning to his or her existence.[44] Indeed, any of the various Hard Rock Cafes throughout the globe, featuring memorabilia including rhinestone costumes that adorned glam rockers and guitars "blessed" by being handled by rock 'n' roll musicians, enable a mini-pilgrimage for those seeking to experience pop-culture transcendence.

The impetus to experience a modern-day pilgrimage was readily apparent at the Welcome to Pilgrimage Festival at St. John's Episcopal Church in New York City on 6 November 2010, which invited parishioners and friends to "take an imaginary journey to medieval England to visit the Canterbury Cathedral and the shrine of St. Thomas Becket [sic], who was martyred there on Dec. 29, 1170." The flyer for this event offered several artifacts for contemporary pilgrims to enjoy, such as a "name tag," because "Medieval pilgrims collected badges from each site they visited." Visitors were also encouraged to collect stickers from the various stalls at the Street Fair, located in the church hallway. Each stall represented a medieval craft with a contemporary project. At the Calligrapher's Stall, visitors could create seals out of clay that were mounted on clothes pins and hardened in a toaster oven, or they could build a puppet wearing medieval costume at the Clothier's Stall. A harper played medieval music, and medieval food was provided, along with displays about Canterbury Cathedral, Thomas à Becket, and medieval guilds. At the Needle Worker's Stall, participants decorated banners that were later carried in the Pilgrimage, a walk around the block surrounding the church led by a bagpiper, which ended with a worship service in the sanctuary, in front of a replica of the Shrine of St. Thomas à Becket, made of a cardboard box painted gold and decorated with stick-on jewels.

While it is easy to point out the ways in which the event was not particularly medieval, nor particularly representative of Chaucer's Canterbury Pilgrimage, the event flyer's concluding commentary—"we hope that you enjoy your medieval experience today and that what you learn will say something to you about your own pilgrimage and search for what is meaningful and holy in your life"[45]—may best understand the function of experiential medievalism as drawing connections between the meaningful qualities of the lost past and our present experiences. We cannot, in contemporary New York City or Maldon or Florida, relive the Middle Ages. It is impossible even to make the attempt without the intrusion of the present into any fantasy of the past. However inauthentic these experiential attempts to re-create the Middle Ages may be, they tell us that there is something inherently engaging and valuable in looking back to the past for certain elements of popular experience: of the possibility of reliving a quest narrative, even if mediated through a videogame controller; of the handmade over the mass produced; of the function of the communal experience in our individual and often isolated lives; of the artifacts that draw people together and how they might still bring us together for the kinds of experience that take us to the edge of transcendence. While we do not need to play medieval videogames, take up jousting, attend Medieval and Renaissance Fairs, or embark on constructed pilgrimages to accomplish these goals, the wide range of experientially "medieval" activities available bespeaks the continued allure of past historical moments, which we desire to reclaim because they speak insistently about ourselves in the present.

Notes

1 Umberto Eco, *Travels in Hyperreality: Essays* (San Diego: Harvest, 1983), 85.
2 Laurie Taylor and Zach Whalen, "Playing the Past: An Introduction," *Playing the Past: History and Nostalgia in Video Games*, ed. Laurie Taylor and Zach Whalen (Nashville: Vanderbilt University Press, 2008), 1–15, at 9.
3 J. R. R. Tolkien and E. V. Gordon, ed., *Sir Gawain and the Green Knight*, 2nd ed., ed. Norman Davis (Oxford: Clarendon, 1967), 20, lines 713–23. The translation is from James J. Wilhelm, *Sir Gawain and the Green Knight*, from *The Romance of Arthur: An Anthology of Medieval Texts in Translation* (New York: Garland, 1994), 399–466, at lines 713–23.
4 "Adventure," atariage.com, accessed 1 November 2011.
5 "*The Legend of Zelda: Twilight Princess* Instruction Booklet" (Redmond, WA: Nintendo, 2006), 6.

6 *The Legend of Zelda: Twilight Princess: The Official Nintendo Player's Guide* (Redmond, WA: Nintendo, 2006), 4.
7 "*Sonic and the Black Knight* Instruction Booklet" (San Francisco: Sega, 2006), 3.
8 *Pulp Fiction*, dir. Quentin Tarantino, perf. John Travolta and Samuel L. Jackson (Miramax, 1994). For a masterful reading of the allure of the phrase "Getting medieval" in contemporary culture, see Carolyn Dinshaw, *Getting Medieval: Sexualities and Communities, Pre- and Postmodern* (Durham: Duke University Press, 1999), 183–90.
9 "*The Sims*™ *Medieval* Instruction Booklet" (Austin, TX: Entertainment Arts, 2011), 3.
10 Marcello Simonetta, "Assassin's Creed," Lecture at Seton Hall University, South Orange, New Jersey, 18 April 2011.
11 Matt Honig, Personal Interview, 29 June 2011.
12 Gesina Phillips, Personal Interview, 10 June 2011.
13 David Marshall, "A World unto Itself: Autopoetic Systems and Secondary Worlds in *Dungeons and Dragons*," *Mass Market Medieval: Essays on the Middle Ages in Popular Culture*, ed. David Marshall (Jefferson, NC: McFarland, 2007), 171–85, at 171.
14 Daniel Kline, "Virtually Medieval: The *Age of Kings* Interprets the Middle Ages," *Mass Market Medieval*, 154–70, at 155.
15 Daniel Kline, "Virtually Medieval," 167–68.
16 Daniel Kline, "Virtually Medieval," 168.
17 Daniel Kline, "Virtually Medieval," 170.
18 Daniel Kline, "Virtually Medieval," 170.
19 Eveleena Fults, Personal Interview, 15 November 2011.
20 *The Amazing Race*, Season 17, Episode 1, aired 26 September 2010, CBS Television.
21 Dashka Slater, "Can a Band of American Knights Turn 'Full Contact' Jousting into the Next Action Sport?" *New York Times Magazine* (11 July 2010): 24–29, at 25.
22 Dashka Slater, "American Knights," 25.
23 *Knights of Mayhem: First Blood*, Season 1, Episode 1, aired 15 November 2011, National Geographic Television.
24 Worldjoust Tournaments website, worldjoust.com, accessed 12 October 2011.
25 Dashka Slater, "American Knights," 26.
26 Dashka Slater, "American Knights," 27.
27 *Knights of Mayhem: Big Money, Big Pain*. Season 1, Episode 3, 22 November 2011, National Geographic Television.
28 Dashka Slater, "American Knights," 28.
29 Dashka Slater, "American Knights," 27.
30 Dashka Slater, "American Knights," 28.
31 Dashka Slater, "American Knights," 28. The concept of jousting on motorcycles is the premise of George Romero's film *Knightriders*, as discussed in Chapter 6.
32 The *Palio* is a horse race, held twice a year in Siena, in which riders representing the original ten contrade (neighborhoods, or bands) race around the dirt-covered Campo in the center of the city. Riders are often thrown, and horses sometimes finish the race without them. The origins of the event date back to the Middle Ages, and it reached its height in the sixteenth century.
33 Clare Lees, "Introduction," *Medieval Masculinities: Regarding Men in the Middle Ages*, ed. Clare Lees (Minneapolis: University of Minnesota Press, 1994), xv–xxv, at xxii.
34 George Will, *International Herald Tribune*, 7 May 1990.
35 *Monster Camp*, dir. Cullen Hoback, prod. Aaron Douglas Enterprises, 2007.
36 Michael Cramer, *Medieval Fantasy as Performance: The Society for Creative Anachronism and the Current Middle Ages* (Lanham: Scarecrow, 2010), 175.
37 "The Medieval Fair of Norman," *Renaissance Magazine* 72 (2010): 50–62, at 50.
38 Geoffrey Chaucer, *The Riverside Chaucer*, ed. Larry Benson, 3rd ed. (Boston: Houghton Mifflin, 1987), 23, line 1.

39 "The Medieval Festival at Fort Tryon Park," Washington Heights and Inwood Development Corporation, whidc.org/home.html, accessed 25 September 2011.

40 "Fort Tryon Park Medieval Festival: Costumes," Washington Heights and Inwood Development Corporation, whidc.org/costumes.html, accessed 25 September 2011.

41 Overheard at the Fort Tryon Park Medieval Festival, New York City, 2 October 2011.

42 Umberto Eco, *Travels in Hyperreality*, 23.

43 Umberto Eco, *Travels in Hyperreality*, 56.

44 For a fuller discussion of this phenomenon, see Angela Jane Weisl, *The Persistence of Medievalism: Narrative Adventures in Contemporary Culture* (New York: Palgrave Macmillan, 2003).

45 "Welcome to Pilgrimage" flyer, St. John's Episcopal Church in the Village, New York City, 6 November 2011.

9 Political Medievalisms
The Darkness of the Dark Ages

"My God, man, that's medieval!": thus Dr. "Bones" McCoy exclaims, with righteous indignation, while encountering the treatment practices of a 1984 hospital in *Star Trek IV: The Voyage Home*,[1] and it is evident that "medieval," in this example, stands for all that is primitive, violent, and, in terms of medical care, painful. In this science-fiction fantasy of an everyday future, the phrase "that's medieval" alludes to a dark time when irrationality ruled, and, from McCoy's perspective, when what counted as modern medical practice was essentially a kind of dismemberment. It also points to a sense that all pasts are the same past: what counted as up-to-the-minute practice in the 1980s, we are reminded, will ultimately become as distant and archaic as whatever now seems distant, and chemotherapy and funduscopic examination will someday seem as remote as the treatments recommended in the *Trotula*. Umberto Eco offers a political formulation of the medieval qualities of the contemporary world similar in sense, if not in tone, to McCoy's expression of future shock at the past. In Eco's terms, the medieval qualities of the present are evident in the potential for modernity to be irrevocably lost, as he explores in response to his provocative query, "What is required to make a good Middle Ages?":

> First of all, a great peace that is breaking down, a great international power that has unified the world in language, customs, ideologies, religions, art, and technology, and then at a certain point, thanks to its own ungovernable complexity, collapses. It collapses because "barbarians" are pressing at its borders; these barbarians are not necessarily uncultivated, but they are bringing new customs, new views of the world. These barbarians may burst in with violence, because they want to seize a wealth that has been denied them, or they may steal into the social and cultural body of the reigning Pax, spreading new faiths and new perspectives of life.[2]

It is tempting to tabulate Eco's ideas by associating each one with a troubling feature of modern political medievalism: the great international powers of globalization unify the world through totalizing corporations, while the terrorist barbarians seek to press at the borders of the West. When one dreams of the

Middle Ages, to borrow Eco's evocative image, it is always possible that one's dreams will turn to darkness.

Whereas medievalism in many areas of cultural production is ultimately a positive fantasy of inclusion and unity, of benevolent magic and the triumph of a transcendent Golden Age, in politics, such medieval fantasies are often inverted into an horrific nightmare, a symbol for pessimistic, primitive, violent, tribal, barbaric, and irrational actions, tyrannical systems of government, and uncivilized ways of living—the very medieval against which Dr. McCoy rails. A deeper reading of Eco, however, shows the deceptive nature of this reduction. Indeed, although "medieval" has been used, and continues to be used, to make the "Other" into a dark and dangerous force (that thus must be countered by violence of our own), or an all-consuming corporate machine ready to turn individuals into serfs to advance its greedy ends, Eco suggests the potential as well that out of these darker notions emerges an alteration, the "new perspectives of life" that revivify rather than reduce, and create potential for enlightenment rather than limitation. Certainly, positive notions of "medieval" exist within political discourse, such as the optimistic image of the Kennedy administration as a reincarnation of Camelot, a rebirth of Arthurian values in early 1960s America (that coincided with Alan Jay Lerner and Frederick Loewe's Broadway musical *Camelot*). Also, in the contemporary rhetoric of globalization, the Middle Ages is often held up as a time when multiple centers of power co-existed before the limiting emergence of superpowers in the Early Modern period, an example of the potential (as well as the potential for conflict) of a more equally balanced economic universe. Yet the short-lived nature of the American Camelot, and the frequent calling for a "new Renaissance" in global studies, suggest that even in the most productive notions of political medievalism, the specter of a primitive past lurks behind any positive assessments of the medieval qualities of contemporary politics. Although the unity of Golden Age rhetoric with political medievalisms is not an impossibility, it is a relative rarity.

As we explore in this chapter, political medievalisms frequently concentrate on the menace prevalent in conceptions of the medieval era as the Dark Ages, positioning the past as a threat to which the future may return us. The long shadow of the Crusades informs many modern discussions of contemporary politics and international affairs, most notably in reactions to the tragedy of September 11th, inflecting contemporary analysis of geopolitics with a medieval lexicon. Furthermore, numerous reactionary political and social organizations, including the Ku Klux Klan, claim the Middle Ages as the site of their foundational "virtues." Blended with other more contemporary fictions, medieval language and metaphor often function both as surface dressing and as more penetrating modes of construction. If chivalry is the defining virtue in many of these rhetorical ploys, the emptiness of chivalry as a signifier registers in contrast to the aggression and violent demands of war.

For as much as medievalism speaks to a desire for a Golden Age past, it is often used with surprising frequency to justify violence. Such violence may be ludic in spirit and structure, such as the reinvention of jousting in modern times, and in these instances, "medieval" games provide an outlet for sanctioned violence (as explored in the previous chapter): players may be hurt, but they should not, one hopes, be killed. In other examples of medievally inspired violence in modern times, the violence may be very real, such as in the various traditions of dueling that are dated to the Middle Ages yet have long survived this era's passing. Ute Frevert traces the history of dueling to its medieval roots, distinguishing among feuds, judicial duels, and tournaments, and notes the congruence between medieval and post-medieval combats. As Frevert observes, an essential component of medieval and post-medieval dueling was "the equal social standing of the participants," such that, if a duel were to be undertaken, "it was essential that [the combatants] should possess the same values and behavioural patterns."[3] Dueling also allowed for its participants to claim the aspects of medievalism that most appealed to them while ignoring more troublesome aspects of its history. For example, Kevin McAleer documents that, despite Germany's fractious history with France, German dueling practice descended from medieval French traditions: "German chivalry owed a great deal to French knighthood, and the German concept of the knight during the High Middle Ages is, in fact, inconceivable without this French impulse."[4] German dueling may be inconceivable without its French roots, yet Germans need not recognize such debts, for history can always be rewritten in a manner to promote the nationality and purported chivalry of its adherents. The violence of dueling in its post-medieval rebirth is presumably couched within such a presumptive sense of honor, but the connection between medieval honor and modern violence nonetheless becomes horrific when used to justify the execution of a human being with whom one has quarreled. Furthermore, when practiced on a larger scale, the turn to medieval dueling and violence, as mediated through ideals of masculine honor and chivalry, can be deployed to truly nefarious ends when practiced by ideologies of hatred, such as the Nazis and the Ku Klux Klan.

Within the cultural imaginary of the U.S. South, chivalric performances of masculine virtue purportedly represent the finest values of white southern men, but reincarnations of knighthood also serve much darker purposes, which is flagrantly evident in the manner in which the Knights of the Ku Klux Klan adopted medieval models of knighthood for their racist purposes.[5] In this instance, the disorienting effect inherent in reconstructing chivalry arises in the disjunction between the historical circumstances of its enactment and a modern-day perspective that renders this version of "chivalry" morally grotesque. In terms of the Klan's literary history, one of its most ardent supporters, Thomas Dixon, Jr., equates this racist organization with medieval chivalry in his *The Clansman: An Historical Romance of the Ku Klux Klan* (1905). Dixon's subtitle links his novel to the medieval romance tradition, as well as to the nineteenth-century rebirth of medieval romances in the novels of Sir Walter Scott. *The Clansman* records an affirmation of moral principles that the Klan claims to defend in its "Prescript of the Order of the Invisible Empire": "This is an institution of Chivalry, Humanity, Mercy, and Patriotism: embodying in its genius and principles all that is chivalric in conduct, noble in sentiment, generous in manhood, and patriotic in purpose."[6] Within this highly sentimentalized novel, chivalry courses through the bloodstreams of southerners, as northerner Elsie Stoneman realizes of her southern admirer Ben Cameron: "His love for his native state was so genuine, his pride in the bravery and goodness of its people so chivalrous, she began to see for the first time how the cords which bound the Southerner to his soil were of the heart's red blood."[7] President Abraham Lincoln is also cast as a southern knight in *The Clansman*, albeit in muted tones. He claims his southern heritage ("Why, didn't you know that my parents were Virginians, and that I was born in Kentucky?"),[8] and Phil Stoneman remarks that Lincoln hides "an iron will and lion heart" under a genial surface, an obvious allusion to Richard the Lionheart.[9] Lincoln models chivalric values during his meeting with Margaret Cameron: "this man who sprang to his feet from the chair of State and bowed to a sorrowing woman with the deference of a knight."[10] The medieval coloring of *The Clansman* grows most dramatic at the climactic unveiling of the Ku Klux Klan: "The moon was now shining brightly, and its light shimmering on the silent horses and men with their tall spiked caps made a picture such as the world had not seen since the Knights of the Middle Ages rode on their Holy Crusades."[11] Within this cultural logic, the equation of the Klan to medieval crusaders establishes their moral superiority to those who would allow their southern heritage of white privilege to be lost.

From this perspective, Klansmen necessarily assume a romantic persona that makes them attractive to women, with chivalry accentuating their masculinity. Protagonist Ben Cameron's mother praises the Klan to Elsie as a model of southern manhood: "Your lover's men will be riding to-night—these young dare-devil Knights of the South, with their life in their hands, a song on their lips, and the scorn of death in their souls!"[12] The Klan's reign of terror against African Americans, who are almost uniformly depicted as animalistic rapists (e.g., "A single tiger-spring, and the black claws of the beast sank into the soft white throat and she was still"),[13] is lauded as a proper corrective against a social epidemic of degeneracy. Crusaders against blackness, the Klansmen embody a vision of chivalric medievalism taking arms against black men degraded into the physical manifestation of disease when the chaplain prays to God to "deliver us from the body of the Black Death."[14] The sharp irony of the chivalric identities displayed in *The Clansman* does not appear in the novel itself but through the passage of time, as readers, after the successes of the Civil Rights Movement, have increasingly found this display of "chivalry" abhorrent. Such grotesque turns to medievalism to justify violence underscore the malleability of past ideals, for chivalry is perverted into a cruel enactment and defense of violence: the darkness of the Dark Ages, in such instances, arises not in the Middle Ages but in modernity's trotting out of old tropes to whitewash its own moral failings.

More recent events continue to bear out the association of the medieval past with irrational and violent acts in the present, although the accusations of "medievalism" often end up implicating the accusers as deeply as those whom they accuse. After the 8 January 2011 shooting of U.S. Congresswoman Gabrielle Giffords in Tucson, Arizona, many pundits and commentators decried the inflammatory rhetoric that characterized national politics, especially Republican rhetoric against Democrats whose districts might be swayed in upcoming elections. Particularly notorious was former Governor of Alaska and 2008 Vice-Presidential candidate Sarah Palin's webpage, which showed various politicians and their seats in the crosshairs of a hunting rifle. Responding to criticism of her rhetoric, Palin insisted she was a victim of "blood libel." Specifically, she commented: "If you don't like their ideas, you're free to propose better ideas. But, especially within hours of a tragedy unfolding, journalists and pundits should not manufacture a blood libel that serves only to incite the very hatred and violence they purport to condemn. That is reprehensible."[15] The term *blood libel*, in brief, refers to medieval Christian allegations that Jews killed Christians, particularly Christian children, as part of their religious rituals; these allegations often included suggestions that the Jews used the blood of Christian children for various nefarious purposes, including the making of Passover matzah, in a weird perversion of the idea of communion. For Palin to align journalists with medieval Christian bigotry, slander, and violence as they carry out their journalistic responsibilities evokes a series of ironies: a woman who claims to uphold traditional religious values, who enjoys hunting and killing animals, and whose rhetoric about her opposition is hardly "fair and balanced," essentially labels her opponents "medieval Christians," a rhetorical ploy with a grimly comic quality, for it concomitantly casts her, not as *a* medieval Jew, but as *all* medieval Jews who suffered expulsion and execution due to Christian hysteria. However, the function of medievalism in Palin's accusations and in the responses they elicited demonstrates a complex sense of the Middle Ages as a political tool, one that often implicates the accuser within the "medieval" world with which they (mis)characterize their opponents.

Palin likely believed that her rebuttal would quell criticisms of her, but, not surprisingly, her use of the charged phrase *blood libel* generated renewed interest in the story. An archaic and unfamiliar term for many Americans, the words required explanation and further commentary in attempts to understand how Palin viewed it as relevant to her own experience as a Christian politician in the twenty-first-century United States of America. Many explanations of blood libel followed, all of which cast the Middle Ages into darkness. As Ishaan Tharoor notes in *Time Magazine*, blood libel has roots in the Christian New Testament and is connected as well to the Christian practice of venerating relics:

> The advent of Christianity forever twinned Jews with blood. In the Gospels, Pontius Pilate publicly washes his hands of the guilt of committing Jesus to death, letting the assembled Jews take on the burden. "His blood be on us and on our children," they declare in Matthew 27.25. These were words that stuck. Christendom grew rich by encouraging pilgrimages to venerate

the purported remains of saints—bones, fingers, ears—but the Jews living in its midst were often openly faulted for bloody, occult practices, all of which were false.

Indeed, charges of blood libel played a key role in developing new legends of martyred saints, such as that of Little St. Hugh of Lincoln and young St. Simon.[16] As Tharoor details, narratives denigrating Jews provided fertile ground for celebrating Christian triumph:

> Medieval lore abounds with tales of Jews in towns across Europe, from England to modern-day Slovakia and lands farther east, stealing young Gentile children for blood sacrifices. Invariably, such sensational stories were told to justify mass executions and pogroms of Jewish communities. According to some histories, a two-year-old named Simon in the Italian town of Trento disappeared in 1475 and was found in the basement of a Jewish family, his body drained of blood so that the Jews could make matzah bread for Passover. Records show that at least eight Jews in the town were subsequently executed; Simon would be canonized as a saint a century later. Fears of Jewish baby snatching were raised by the Spanish Inquisition, leading in part to the expulsion of the entire Jewish community from Spain in 1492.[17]

From these brief examples, it is apparent that charges of blood libel played out with political repercussions across western Europe and that the charges, although often directed against a particular Jewish person or family, resonated throughout the entire Jewish community. Indeed, Chaucer's *Prioress's Tale* highlights the suppleness of the blood libel tradition, for in this instance, the Jews kill a young child for merely singing a Christian hymn; the boy's murder leads to the execution the entire Jewish community, which appears to be the narrative's darker purpose: "With torment and with shameful deeth echon,/This provost dooth thise Jewes for to sterve [die]/That of this mordre wiste [knew], and that anon."[18] As Adam Server explains, "For hundreds of years, particularly during the Middle Ages, [charges of blood libel were] used to justify the slaughter of Jews in the street and their expulsion from entire countries. 'Blood libel' is not wrongfully assigning guilt to an individual for murder, but rather assigning guilt collectively to an entire group of people and then using it to justify violence against them." Calling Palin's defense of herself while invoking blood libel "a new low for Palin," and adding that "outsize comparisons of partisan political conflict to instances of historical oppression is a fairly frequent rhetorical device among conservative medieval figures,"[19] he suggests a particular history of medievalism that allows it to be used as a charge to demonize one's opposition through condemnations of primitivism and closed-mindedness, without recognizing the ways in which such an accusation reflects back upon the accuser him- or herself. A revealing incident for the ways that medievalism continues to occupy an unstable and shifting place in the political vocabulary, Sarah Palin's charge of blood libel illuminates the power of the Middle Ages in contemporary political discourse, especially in the ways in which medieval history is obscured and corrupted to level charges steeped in violence (and possibly willful ignorance of Christian violence) that, in this instance, redound upon the accuser.

As Palin's citation of blood libel showcases, medievalism in political discourse fluctuates in its effects, and contemporary medievalism in politics exemplifies these disjointed strategies. Three separate but overlapping fields—the resurgence of crusader rhetoric following September 11th, the rise of diverse commercial impulses referred to as a "New Feudalism," and the use of "medieval" to explain certain qualities of globalization—jointly work to bring the past into the present in complex ways, often coloring the present with a fear of the Middle Ages. The violence of the past threatens to reemerge in the present, erasing the achievements of modernity as western society regresses to its pre-modern roots.

Language invoking the Crusades percolates throughout international political rhetoric: Bruce Holsinger, in *Neomedievalism, Neoconservatism, and the War on Terror*, notes multiple uses of this medievalizing impulse, including Slobodan Milosevic's recollection of the defeat of the Serbs by the Ottoman Turks as a reason for anti-Islamic sentiment against Kosovars and Bosnians; Saddam Hussein's production of a stamp with images of himself and Saladin; and Osama Bin Laden's own crusade-heavy rhetoric after the terrorist attacks of September 11th, when both sides constructed each other, and conversely themselves, as medieval.[20] As Bin Laden's followers claimed that they "would not allow that tragedy of Al-Andalus to be repeated," evoking the reconquest of Spain that began in 770 C.E. and continued until 1492, George W. Bush responded in kind that the United States and its allies were on a "New Crusade." On rhetorical grounds, both sides fought medievalism with medievalism.[21] As Holsinger observes, the construction of Al-Qaeda terrorists as "medieval" was part of a strange set of tactical opportunities. If "Medieval man is to be feared, imprisoned, and, most importantly of all, learned from, precisely for his perceived ability to render irrelevant the authority, territorial integrity, and jurisdictions of modern nations,"[22] the only appropriate response the Bush administration could make was an equally medieval Crusade. Holsinger also suggests that the events of September 11th "immediately began to function as a kind of medievalizing engine in American Political discourse," creating a dualism that attempted to separate the modern West from the "premodern world that had finally responded to the long arm of modernity with a morning of cataclysmic violence," although he also notes that the medievalizing rhetoric freed "its users from the demands of subtlety, nuance, and a rigorous historical understanding of the nature of inter- and supra-national conflict in the era of globalization."[23] It also allowed for behaviors that might be called "medieval" in themselves, the most notable being the systematized torture of prisoners that became public in the Abu Ghraib scandal. Thinking of one's enemies as "medieval," it seems, allowed "us" to void all notions of "modern" civil and individual rights: Steve Guthrie avows that commentators frequently referred to the Taliban as "medieval" and to Afghanistan as a place where they "had stepped back in time," language that was echoed after the invasion of Iraq as well.[24] Guthrie wisely notes that "our use of torture is indeed medieval," although it is rather disingenuous of modernity to allege that violence carries a taint of medievalism in the present because "physical brutality itself is not especially medieval—it seems to be an inclination of the species." For how and why are the Middle Ages complicit with violence in the present? As Guthrie further distinguishes, "the political and emotional climate of the phenomenon, and the legal policies it rests on ... have counterparts in late medieval and renaissance Europe."[25] His examination of the specifics of the *Guantanamo Guidebook* and Abu Ghraib shows the ways in which they recall medieval precedents (as well as others), and his examination of the Inquisition-like tactics used to "extort from Iraq, in the person of Saddam Hussein, a confession of heretical practices and designs against the orthodox community of nations led by the United States" demonstrates the ways that the language that began the war, the language of crusade, made possible a series of medieval (or, better, "medievally inspired") activities unfathomable under other conditions.[26]

Guthrie expands the sense of what "medieval" might mean in the context of the effects of September 11th, and as Holsinger suggests, "The War on Terror has transmogrified the medieval into something well beyond the grasp of our expertise and, in many cases, even our comprehension."[27] In many ways Holsinger is correct: any recourse to the "real" Middle Ages will fail to explain the meanings of "medieval" in the ways it is used politically as part of this rhetoric. Furthermore, medieval scholars find little that coheres between the Middle Ages we study and teach and the Middle Ages presented iconographically in the media after September 11th as solely a time of brutality. Within the wider cultural imaginary, this sense of the medieval, although very much a reduction of a complex history, takes a baggy historical period loosely defined by geography and with as many diversions as similarities, and turns it into a single entity, a signifier of irrational, violent darkness.

One similarity of this medievalism and other, more positive forms of medievalism, is its unitary nature, the sense of the past (or, better, of pre-modernity) as an unchanging, stable space. With the conflict between two distinct kinds of fervor—religious (or whatever one wants to call Al-Qaeda's horrific brand of violent zeal) and imperialist—Holsinger again points out that "the effect has been a mass enlistment of all things medieval into a global conflict in which the Middle Ages function as a reservoir of unconsidered analogy and reductive propaganda."[28] In much of the surrounding discourse, it was possible to hear the rallying call from the *Chanson de Roland*, "paien unt tort e chestiens unt dreit!" ("Pagans are wrong and Christians are right!").[29] As Jeffrey Jerome Cohen notes, Christians of the Middle Ages, particularly those imbricated in the Crusades, neither acknowledged their own differences, "promulgating instead a transnational, transtemporal myth of essential unity and sameness," nor recognized any diversity in the Islamic world, instead representing its "lack of interior variation," particularly through the homogenizing term "Saracen," which condensed "everything inimical to the fragile Christian selfsame into monstrous, racialized flesh."[30] Of course, any unifying taking place in the understanding of "them" (a homogenizing impulse that today leads to consequences for many American Muslims and Americans who look Middle Eastern) requires a consequential unifying of "us." As Cohen points out, during the Crusades "the Christian body did not have a race, because the body of the Other always carried that burden on its behalf," and a "medieval logic is being reenacted" in the construction of a homogeneous Arab "Other" who, irrespective of individual identity, represents that which against the West must defend itself.[31] If Geraldine Heng is correct that racial identification is already fully worked out by 1215, which coincides with a "juridical intervention obsessed with disciplining bodies and making difference immediately visible upon them,"[32] its effects continue in the New Crusade of the War on Terror, whose concomitant Patriot Act allows spying on and racial profiling of those who resemble "them," making them "enemy combatants" whose civil rights can be suspended in a particularly pre-modern, unconstitutional manner. Ask any Middle Eastern or South Asian American about navigating through airport security, and the broad range of these unifying assumptions becomes instantly clear. To quote Cohen again, "too many inheritances of the crusades endure."[33]

The Middle Ages, it seems, spreads its dark net into the realms of international commerce as well as international conflict, and such anxiety is keenly expressed in Jello Biafra and the Guantanamo School of Medicine's song, "The New Feudalism," which appears on their album *The Audacity of Hype*. With its parodic take on Barack Obama's autobiography *The Audacity of Hope*, Biafra signals that no sacred cows will be respected in his devastating satire of contemporary American and international politics and commerce. "The New Feudalism" opens with a description of a signed treaty, one that constructs nations as "corporate colonies" so that "Robber barons/In high castles" live luxuriously while their commercial exploits are labeled as "free trade," a label, the song suggests, appreciated without irony from the perspectives of these robber barons, but with acid irony from the songwriters' perspective. The chorus pillories international treaties, including the North American Free Trade Agreement (NAFTA) and the General Agreement on Tariffs and Trade (GATT) for enslaving the masses:

> Now it's signed
> Text classified
> Nations are now corporate colonies
> Robber barons
> In high castles
> Have the nerve to call this free trade
> Unh Unh
>
> DDT
> Gill net kills

Fought so hard to stop it all for years
Sweatshop kids in Nike Town
Globalize means downsize
Your rights to theirs

Tweet-tweet-tweet-tweedle-da-da
Tweet-tweet-tweet-tweedle-da-da
A ha-ha-ha!
NAFTA GATT-cha
"We are being farmed"
NAFTA GATT-cha
"Every time we buy"
NAFTA GATT-cha
"We are their serfs"

New Feudalism
Remember the name

Forced loans from the World Bank
Soon your countries sank
No food or medicine
Just factories, mines and dams

Peasant revolts arise
Like pesky little flies
We swat 'em down
Pull off their legs
One by one

NAFTA GATT-cha
"We are being farmed"
NAFTA GATT-cha
"Every time we buy"
NAFTA GATT-cha
"We are their serfs"

New Feudalism
Remember the name[34]

In Biafra's conception, "New Feudalism" encodes a world in which corporations transform individuals into serfs whose lives are subsumed by corporate desire for profit, a desire that takes precedence over all other concerns, including human rights, environmental destruction, outsourcing of labor, economic justice, and physical health. The inevitability of this system is emphasized in the lines linking "every time we buy" to "we are their serfs." In such a manner, the New Feudalism is inescapable and constricting, and any attempts at resistance are futile (*pace Star Trek: The Next Generation*'s alien Borg Collective, the extreme representation of corporate drive consuming individuals). The very name of Biafra's Guantanamo School of Medicine band suggests the specter of post-September 11th rhetoric (just as his former group, the Dead Kennedys, suggested the end of the Camelot era and its positive medievalizing potential), and the song "New Feudalism" intertwines these two medieval impulses of international geopolitics with that of corporate commercialization.

The term "feudalism" itself, in its current understanding, seems to emerge not from the Middle Ages, where it was a strictly legal term referring to the concerns of the fief as a specific piece of property, but from the 1700s, when it referred to the distribution of power rather than its consolidation. As Marc Bloch argues, "the most striking characteristic of the Middle Ages was the parceling out of sovereignty" within feudal regimes, albeit strictly among the aristocracy.[35] The defining characteristic of medieval feudalism was not so much the control at the top but the interdependence that a political system emerging from an agrarian economy required. While immobility and oppression were inevitable features for many, the awareness of the impossibility of its existence and survival without any of its constituents was also strong. The near decay of feudalism when the laboring classes were decimated by the plague is often credited with the rise of capitalism, since the reduction in a significant portion of the operation made its continuity impossible. The New Feudalism may rely on the same principles of interconnection, but it seems less aware of them.

The "New Feudalism," as it is most often defined, suggests an economy driven by corporate interest at the expense of individual liberty. Jerry West argues, in this regard, that

> The idea that corporate groups have rights equal to those of real persons in a society is a threat to any form of democracy based on the equality of the individual, and is a step in social evolution backward towards the structures of the Middle Ages. Recognizing the rights of corporations as equal to those of actual persons increases the power of accumulated wealth to decide what the rules are that govern how we can live our lives. When corporations exercise their influence there is little doubt that when the question is between corporate interest and the well-being of society, which way they will influence the decision.[36]

Corporate power, in West's understanding, is a direct threat to personal freedom. As corporations grow in size and financial clout, people increasingly find themselves hampered in any attempt to escape their power because of their dependence on these structures. "As corporate power grows, corporations absorb more and more of our infrastructure, buying up businesses and property and taking over government services. The end result could be a return to a feudal system where most of the population are serfs in the service of one corporation or another," West posits. As the Middle Ages are reborn in feudalism's return, West concomitantly identifies a key difference in the centralization of power: "unlike the older feudal structures, however, instead of the ruler being at the top of the pile, in today's developing feudal society the corporations own the rulers who are being reduced to corporate functionaries. The real power lies in the board rooms."[37] Bob Johnson's more inflammatory rhetoric in *The Daily Kos* summarizes a similar point: "It's *The New Feudalism*. Those of us not at the top of the income/land ownership scale wait outside the castle/estate walls to catch whatever crumbs are so generously tossed our way by the elite lords of industry. Even worse, we pay our tithes to these masters in hopes of getting a small portion of our tithing returned."[38] Such a vision of modern-day feudalism belies a tendency to assume the passivity (or perhaps worse, mindlessness) of the modern-day masses, but the critical question of who wields governing authority in nations that profess democratic values needs to be addressed, if democracy is not to lose the many basic rights inscribed in the western legal tradition since the Magna Carta in 1215.

The anti-feudal voices of West, Johnson, and others sound surprisingly medieval, demonstrating the pervasiveness of socio-economic critique across numerous centuries. Contrast, for example, Johnson's language to that of the Townley cycle *Second Shepherds' Play*, in which the eponymous shepherds lament their treatment at the hands of the gentry:

"Bot we sely [simple] shepardes that walkys on the moore,
In fayth we ar nere handys outt of the doore.
No wonder, as it standys, if we be poore,
For the tylthe of oure landys lyys falow as the floore,
As ye ken [know].
We ar so hamyd [hamstrung]
For-taxed and ramyd [oppressed],
We ar mayde hand tamyd
With thys gentlery men.
Thus thay refe [steal from] us oure rest, oure Lady theym wary [curse]!"[39]

The similarity between medieval and modern objections to the operations of the monied classes suggests the real potential of a New Feudalism, if not the proposition that the Old Feudalism never really left. The lower classes lie at the mercy of the financial interests of those who rule them, and the shepherds' complaint of being overtaxed and tithed is not so different from current attempts to undo the pensions of public workers (such as teachers and police), calling their expectations for a comfortable retirement after years of public service greedy, self-serving, and undeserved. Medieval unhappiness of the kinds the shepherds talk about led to the Peasants' Revolt of 1381, which was sparked by the sense that the aristocracy were exploiting the masses, as recorded in the revolutionary jingle, "When Adam delved and Eve span/Who was then the gentleman?" This rhyme crystallizes similar sentiments expressed elsewhere, as in the following verse believed to have been written by Richard Rolle: "When Adam delf & Eue span, sir, if thou wil spede,/Whare was than the pride of man that now merres [spoils] his mede?"[40] Likewise, contemporary discontent of a similar kind may be seen in the "Occupy" movements begun in 2011 that cast the "99%" at the mercy of the "1%" whose control and abuse of the financial system has created joblessness and impoverishment. The similar tactics of medieval peasants and of Occupy Wall Street ally both cause and response: a system that loses sight of the necessary contributions of the lower (and middle) classes, and which cuts off its responsibility to them, can only be addressed through the confrontations of the one percent by the many.

That said, if loss of individual rights to life, liberty, and the pursuit of happiness stokes apprehension concerning this New Feudalism, how these rights are abrogated, and by whom, is not a matter of consensus. While the ideologies put forward by West and Johnson voice common criticism against corporate feudalism, charges of "New Feudalism" can also be levied in a manner critical of presumably socialist endeavors. John McClaughry, retired Vermont State Senator and then President of the Ethan Allen Institute, "Vermont's independent, nonpartisan, free-market-oriented public policy think tank,"[41] suggests in "Social Property and the New Feudalism" that feudalism is returning, but for the explicit purpose of curbing, rather than accelerating, capitalism:

> Today, however, feudalism is coming back in a different guise. A growing body of legal theorists, allied with activist organizations and congenial political leaders, has been working very hard to replace the long-cherished concept of freehold property and land with the old feudal concept of social property. The essence of that theory is the contention that property and land cannot be owned by anyone. It can merely be held, on a temporary basis, subject to the overriding views of society. The ancient maxim, *sic utere tuo ut alienum non laedas*, "use your own so as not to injure that of another," is now held to be insufficient as a maxim for the proper use of land. Under the new feudalism, land must be used as society prescribes, or, at the very least, in ways not objectionable to society.[42]

McClaughry, then, sees the New Feudalism impinging on individual rights by the precise kinds of environmental protections that Biafra, West, and Johnson see being abrogated by major corporations. While this notion of New Feudalism maintains a medieval sense of the importance of land as essential to the feudalist equation, it also shows the fluidity of the term: what is at stake is not a medieval form of government replacing what might be called a modern one, but a way of talking about the role of the individual within society. The loss of the rights of the middle class (a predominantly post-medieval group) comes at both the hands of regulation and the acceptance of a kind of authoritarianism (whether such authoritarianism is defined as corporations or special interests), which renders them dependent on systems in which they can only participate and never control. For West and Johnson, such "medieval" systems benefit from demonizing workers and constructing them as greedy and needy, whereas for McClaughry, the desire to use accumulation to move out of one's socially defined and socially restricted positions is hampered by a quasi-feudalistic endeavor to accelerate communal responsibilities in contrast to individual property-holding.

In concert with the New Feudalism, since large corporations lie at the heart of both narratives, are the medievalizing treatments of globalization and its associated phenomena. It seems fashionable for contemporary scholars of the increasingly global economy and its accompanying cultural shifts to consider the contemporary world in light of a past with which it seems to share the most similarities: the Middle Ages. Parag Khanna, author of *How to Run the World: Charting a Course to the Next Renaissance*, declares in an interview in *Saudi Aramco World*, "We are again, in the 21st century, entering a multipolar landscape—one in which China, India, and Arab-Islamic countries, Europe, the United States, Brazil and others are all able to call their own shots, to determine what they want and the policies they want to pursue, without any one power dominating over the others—and that is exactly what the world was like during the Middle Ages."[43] His sense of the Middle Ages as a time when "the World was Western and Eastern *at the same time*" shows the interconnectedness of various discourses of medievalism, a discourse of interconnectedness itself.[44] If the Western/Eastern divide is essential for understanding post-September 11th crusader rhetoric, it is equally essential for understanding the global sense of the Middle Ages. Focusing on multiple centers of power, from Europe to the Middle East to China to India, Khanna also notes the ways in which these civilizations "came in to direct, sustained contact with each other in history's first world system." Noting the rise in exploration after the Crusades, he points out that, ironically, these conflicts "made civilizations cognizant of one another's grandeur."[45] Khanna notes that, during the Middle Ages, distinctions of religion, race, and nation mattered very little in conjunction with matters of trade and profit. He describes the Silk Road as particularly "amazing" because, in its emphasis on trade above all other concerns, cultural markers were overlooked:

> Whether it was Marco Polo or Ibn Battutah, whether it was the bazaars of Samarkand or Jerusalem or France, it's really remarkable how multiethnic and multicultural these were, how trade managed to transcend all of those divisions. And that continued for such a long time. This is why I believe that we are building new Silk Roads through modern infrastructure.[46]

In the current globalizing world, "one another's grandeur" may be supplanted by "one another's economic potential," but Khanna's point is well taken: if political power is still brokered primarily in the hands of the traditional post-Renaissance superpowers, economic power is increasingly, and necessarily, shared. However, the inevitable ideological conflicts that characterize today's international political and commercial relationships are hardly new, in Khanna's understanding. He calls the "sense of diverse powers and civilizations coexisting, with none dominating over the others but starting to interact—trade and commerce, but also tension and conflict—" a "very medieval phenomenon." This complicated coexistence of multiple powers thus becomes "a telltale sign of a new medievalism."[47]

Khanna views the Middle Ages as "Globalization 1.0" because of the "sustained, intercontinental contact between Western Europe and China and all of the various civilizations and empires in between," which was necessary for trade to flourish. He notes that this "constant connectivity across geography" was created both by the Silk Road and by the Crusades, an intersection of trade with violent conflict, similar to the contemporary qualities of the current global economy, and he also recognizes the shift in importance from nations to multinational corporations, which he compares to medieval merchant families such as the Medicis.[48] Their financing of the first stock exchanges and development of long-term credit, Khanna believes, reflect current events on a much more intense and rapid scale, and it is this in particular that makes the current economic situation reflective of a new medievalism, that is, the exchange of ideas, money, and power between "merchant families" (*qua* today's corporations) as well as between states.[49]

One might ask, given this somewhat optimistic view of the Middle Ages, why Khanna sees his job as preparing readers for a "new Renaissance," which, of course, is the period that moves away from his vision of the multi-centered medieval world into the more contemporary capitalism of the nation states he critiques. Citing the London Food Riot (the Peasants' Revolt in 1381) and post-revolutionary Iran, which moved quickly from a modern and developed state into chaos and violence due to civil war, he avows "there are some unfortunate parallels between what we think of when we hear the word *medievalism* and what we see happening in the world today: the fact that we can slip so quickly from a pristine model of modern nation-states into something that looks far more fragmented, dangerous and unpredictable."[50] Again, the Middle Ages is both a promise and a threat: the possibility of a reemerging time of trade irrespective of national difference and of the very breakdown of civilization as we know it.

In "The Meaning of the New Medievalism," Jörg Friedrichs suggests a possible use for the Middle Ages in contemporary politics. "At least potentially," he asserts, "the understanding of the Middle Ages can offer a background for the diagnostic of macro-historical change in the present."[51] He also cautions against the risks of this type of analysis in a particularly charming formulation: "The good news about such a detour 'back to the future' is that it will help us to avoid the Scylla of lofty postmodernism; the bad news is that it may bring us close to the Charybdis of myopic historicism."[52] The "myopic historicism" he warns against is clearly at work in the uses of medievalism to justify "a new crusade"; it unintentionally points to the ways in which post-September 11th rhetoric effaced any remembrance of the destructive, violent, irrational, and problematic nature of the Crusades themselves, and of the West's complicity in the very destruction of the plurality the "new crusade" claimed to be protecting. It also warns against a simplistic notion of the medieval world as a foundation of globalization, one that would focus only on the potential of shared power without an examination of the conflicts and repressions that very system allowed.

Yet, as Friedrichs notes, using the Middle Ages to talk about a world in which the Renaissance idea of the nation state is dissolving is to look to "a historical configuration that has indisputably worked—the Middle Ages in Western Christendom between the eleventh and the fourteenth Centuries."[53] It is possible to read this both optimistically and with caution: while for those of us interested in the Middle Ages, who see its value as a critical category, this possibility is intriguing, it is also necessary to see that the "Middle Ages," or the "medieval" as an idea is easy to appropriate, to reduce to unitary stereotypes. Using a standard notion of the political Middle Ages as a "system of overlapping authority and multiple loyalties," Friedrichs affirms that it is also a "system that is bound to be highly unstable."[54] One might say exactly the same for the medievalisms running throughout political discourse. This examination shows the ways that contemporary uses of medievalism are indeed made up of overlapping authorities—those of chivalry and crusade and globalization and new feudalism—and of multiple loyalties—to the nation and to the dissolution of the nation simultaneously. It also shows that these uses are in themselves inherently unstable, although frequently with a dark pall that carries the latent or blatant threat of a return to subjugation and/or violence. To cast the "other" as medieval requires the casting of oneself in the same light. Louise Fradenberg notes that "the past cannot continue to be treated exclusively as an apolitical and indeed ahistorical hermeneutic problem, but must be theorized concomitantly in terms of our knowledge of culturally specific needs, fantasies, fears, and practices"[55] It takes only a cursory look at political medievalism in the contemporary age to show her to be profoundly right, with such a refreshingly lucid perspective providing the only real tool to clear away the darkness.

Notes

1 *Star Trek IV: The Voyage Home*, dir. Leonard Nimoy, perf. William Shatner, Leonard Nimoy, and Nichelle Nichols (Paramount, 1986). In pop-culture parlance, this entry in the *Star Trek* annals is known affectionately as "the one with the whales."

2 Umberto Eco, *Travels in Hyperreality*, trans. William Weaver (San Diego: Harvest, 1983), 74–75.

3 Ute Frevert, *Men of Honour: A Social and Cultural History of the Duel*, trans. Anthony Williams (Cambridge: Polity, 1995), 11.

4 Kevin McAleer, *Dueling: The Cult of Honor in Fin-de-Siècle Germany* (Princeton: Princeton University Press, 1994), 16.

5 For historical studies of the Ku Klux Klan, see Nancy McLean, *Behind the Mask of Chivalry: The Making of the Second Ku Klux Klan* (New York: Oxford University Press, 1994); Richard K. Tucker, *The Dragon and the Cross: The Rise and Fall of the Ku Klux Klan in Middle America* (Hamden, CT: Archon, 1991); and David M. Chalmers, *Hooded Americanism: The First Century of the Ku Klux Klan, 1865–1965* (Garden City, NY: Doubleday, 1965).

6 Thomas Dixon, Jr., *The Clansman: An Historical Romance of the Ku Klux Klan* (1905; Lexington: University Press of Kentucky, 1970), 320. *The Clansman* is the basis of D. W. Griffith's early film masterpiece, *Birth of a Nation* (1915), and this

film's controversial reception likewise highlights the historical vagaries attached to depictions of white southern manhood.

7 Thomas Dixon, *The Clansman*, 149.
8 Thomas Dixon, *The Clansman*, 31.
9 Thomas Dixon, *The Clansman*, 72.
10 Thomas Dixon, *The Clansman*, 74.
11 Thomas Dixon, *The Clansman*, 316.
12 Thomas Dixon, *The Clansman*, 363.
13 Thomas Dixon, *The Clansman*, 304.
14 Thomas Dixon, *The Clansman*, 319.
15 Sarah Palin, qtd. in Glenn Kessler, "The Fact Checker: Sarah Palin's 'Blood Libel' Statement on the Tucson Shootings," *Washington Post* (13 January 2011).
16 For a collection of blood libel narratives, see Alan Dundes, ed., *The Blood Libel Legend: A Casebook in Anti-Semitic Folklore* (Madison: University of Wisconsin Press, 1991).
17 Ishaan Tharoor, "Sarah Palin's Claim: What is 'Blood Libel'?" *Time Magazine* (12 January 2011).
18 Geoffrey Chaucer, *The Riverside Chaucer*, ed. Larry Benson, 3rd ed. (Boston: Houghton Mifflin, 1987), 211, lines 628–30. For the anti-Semitic calumny that Jews desecrated communion wafers, see Miri Rubin, *Gentile Tales: The Narrative Assault on Late Medieval Jews* (Philadelphia: University of Pennsylvania Press, 2004).
19 Adam Server, "The Foolishness of the Blood Libel Charge," *Washington Post* (12 January 2011).
20 Bruce Holsinger, *Neomedievalism, Neoconservatism, and the War on Terror* (Chicago: Prickly Paradigm, 2007), 21.
21 See, for example, Susan Sachs, "Bin Laden's Images Mesmerize Muslims," *New York Times* (9 October 2001), A4, or Randy Boswell, "Medieval Crusades Revived in Terrorism-War Rhetoric," *Ottawa Citizen* (25 September 2001), A2. On a side note, Bush's possession of the presidency is not without medieval antecedents; Daniel Kline effectively compares Bush's election in 2000 to Henry Bolingbroke's accession of the throne after the deposition of Richard II in his study "The Crisis of Legitimation in Bush's America and Henry IV's England," *Cultural Studies of the Modern Middle Ages*, ed. Eileen Joy, Myra Seaman, Kimberley Bell, and Mary Ramsey (New York: Palgrave, 2007), 157–88.
22 Bruce Holsinger, *Neomedievalism, Neoconservatism, and the War on Terror*, iv.
23 Bruce Holsinger, *Neomedievalism, Neoconservatism, and the War on Terror*, 9.
24 Steve Guthrie, "Torture, Inquisition, Medievalism, Reality TV," *Cultural Studies of the Modern Middle Ages*, 189–216, at 189.
25 Steve Guthrie, "Torture, Inquisition, Medievalism, Reality TV," 190.
26 Steve Guthrie, "Torture, Inquisition, Medievalism, Reality TV," 208.
27 Bruce Holsinger, *Neomedievalism, Neoconservatism, and the War on Terror*, 14.
28 Bruce Holsinger, *Neomedievalism, Neoconservatism, and the War on Terror*, 15.
29 *Chanson de Roland*, ed. Pierre Jonin (Paris: Editions Gallimard, 1979), line 1015 and passim. The translation is taken from *The Song of Roland*, trans. Frederick Goldin (New York: Norton, 1978), line 1015 and passim. These words are spoken relentlessly by Charlemagne and his armies throughout the work.
30 Jeffrey Jerome Cohen, *Medieval Identity Machines* (Minneapolis: University of Minnesota Press, 2003), 191.
31 Jeffrey Jerome Cohen, *Medieval Identity Machines*, 193.
32 Geraldine Heng, "The Romance of England: *Richard Coer de Lyon*, Saracens, Jews, and the Politics of Race and Nation," *The Postcolonial Middle Ages*, ed. Jeffrey Jerome Cohen (New York: St. Martin's, 2000), 135–71, at 163; qtd. in Jeffrey Jerome Cohen, *Medieval Identity Machines*, 193.
33 Jeffrey Jerome Cohen, *Medieval Identity Machines*, 223.

34 Jello Biafra and the Guantanamo School of Medicine, "New Feudalism," *The Audacity of Hype* (Alternative Tentacles, 2009). We are most grateful to Jello Biafra for permission to quote the song in its entirety.

35 Marc Bloch, *Feudal Society, Vol. 1: The Growth of Ties of Dependence*, trans. L. A. Manyon (Chicago: University of Chicago Press, 1961), xvii.

36 Jerry West, "The New Feudalism," *OpEd News Network* (29 January 2010).

37 Jerry West, "The New Feudalism."

38 Bob Johnson, "The New Feudalism," *The Daily Kos* (16 April 2011).

39 *The Second Shepherds' Play*, in *English Mystery Plays*, ed. Peter Happé (Harmondsworth: Penguin, 1975), 265–94, at 266, lines 10–19.

40 Hope Emily Allen, *Writings Ascribed to Richard Rolle, Hermit of Hampole, and Materials for His Biography* (New York: MLA, 1927), 296. For the definitive study of the writings of the Peasants' Revolt of 1831, see Steven Justice, *Writing and Rebellion: England in 1381* (Berkeley: University of California Press, 1994).

41 The Ethan Allen Institute is essentially a libertarian organization, emphasizing individual liberty and free-market economy; see ethanallen.org. McClaughry, as with more liberal users of this medievalizing terminology, can hardly be said to present an unbiased, nonpartisan point of view.

42 John McClaughry, "Social Property and the New Feudalism," *Proceedings of the Second Annual New York Conference on Private Property Rights* (PRFA, 1996), accessed 1 December 2011.

43 Tom Verde, "The Multipolar Picture: An Interview with Parag Khanna," *Saudi Aramco World* 62.3 (May/June 2011): 40–43, at 40. Our thanks to Fredrica M. Brooks for providing us with this interesting resource.

44 Parag Khanna, *How to Run the World: Charting a Course to the Next Renaissance* (New York: Random House, 2011), 11; his italics.

45 Parag Khanna, *How to Run the World*, 11.

46 Tom Verde, "The Multipolar Picture," 43.

47 Tom Verde, "The Multipolar Picture," 40.

48 Tom Verde, "The Multipolar Picture," 40.

49 Tom Verde, "The Multipolar Picture," 41.

50 Tom Verde, "The Multipolar Picture," 41.

51 Jörg Friedrichs, "The Meaning of the New Medievalism," *European Journal of International Relations* 7.4 (2001): 475–501, at 476.

52 Jörg Friedrichs, "The Meaning of the New Medievalism," 477.

53 Jörg Friedrichs, "The Meaning of the New Medievalism," 482.

54 Jörg Friedrichs, "The Meaning of the New Medievalism," 482.

55 Louise Fradenberg, "Voice Memorial: Loss and Reparation in Chaucer's Poetry," *Exemplaria* 2.1 (1990): 169–202, at 192–93.

Bibliography

Aberth, John. *A Knight at the Movies: Medieval History on Film.* New York: Routledge, 2003.

"Adventure." Atariage.com. Web. 1 November 2011.

Aldgate, Anthony, and Jeffrey Richards. "Why We Fight." *Best of British: Cinema and Society from 1930 to the Present.* London: Tauris, 1999. 57–78.

Alexander, Lloyd. *The Book of Three.* New York: Henry Holt, 1964.

Alexander, Lloyd. *The Black Cauldron.* New York: Henry Holt, 1965.

Alexander, Lloyd. *The Castle of Llyr.* New York: Henry Holt, 1966.

Alexander, Lloyd. *Taran Wanderer.* New York: Henry Holt, 1967.

Alexander, Lloyd. *The High King.* New York: Henry Holt, 1968.

Alexander, Michael. *Medievalism: The Middle Ages in Modern England.* New Haven: Yale University Press, 2007.

Allen, Hope Emily. *Writings Ascribed to Richard Rolle, Hermit of Hampole, and Materials for his Biography.* New York: MLA, 1927.

Altcappenberg, Hein-Thomas Schulze. *Sandro Botticelli: The Drawings of Dante's Divine Comedy.* London: Royal Academy of Arts, 2000.

The Amazing Race. CBS Television. Season 17, Episode 1. 26 September 2010.

"Antioch Chalice." The Metropolitan Museum of Art. metmuseum.org. Web. 25 July 2011.

Aronstein, Susan. *Hollywood Knights: Arthurian Cinema and the Politics of Nostalgia.* New York: Palgrave Macmillan, 2005.

Aubrey, Elizabeth. "Non-Liturgical Monophony." Duffin 105–14.

Bahri, Hamid, and Francesca Canadé Sautman. "Crossing History, Dis-Orienting the Orient: Amin Maalouf's Uses of the 'Medieval.'" Davis and Altschul 174–205, 2009.

Bain, Jennifer. "Hooked on Ecstasy: Performance 'Practice' and the Reception of the Music of Hildegard of Bingen." *The Sounds and Sights of Performance in Early Music.* Ed. Maureen Epp and Brian Power. Farnham, Surrey: Ashgate, 2009. 253–73.

Balkun, Mary McAleer. *The American Counterfeit: Authenticity and Identity in American Literature and Culture.* Tuscaloosa: University of Alabama Press, 2006.

Barnhouse, Rebecca. *The Coming of the Dragon.* New York: Random House, 2010.

Barnhouse, Rebecca. "Of Trenchers and Trestle Tables: Recent Young Adult Novels Set in the Middle Ages." *Medieval Academy News* (September 2009): 8.

Barnhouse, Rebecca. *Recasting the Past: The Middle Ages in Young Adult Literature.* Portsmouth, NH: Boynton/Cook, 2000.

Barr, Mike, and Brian Bolland. *Camelot 3000: The Deluxe Edition.* New York: DC Comics, 2008.

Barron, T. A. *The Lost Years of Merlin.* New York: Philomel, 1996.

Barron, T. A. *Merlin's Dragon*. New York: Philomel, 2008.

Benjamin, Walter. *Illuminations*. Ed. Hannah Arendt. Trans. Harry Zohn. New York: Schocken, 1968.

Beowulf. Ed. Franz Klaeber. Lexington, MA: Heath, 1950.

Bergeron, Katherine. "Finding God at Tower Records: The Virtual Sacred." *The New Republic* (27 February 1995): 29–35.

Besserman, Lawrence. "Chaucer and Dickens Use Luke 23.24." *Chaucer Review* 41.1 (2006): 99–104.

Biafra, Jello, and the Guantanamo School of Medicine. "New Feudalism." *The Audacity of Hype*. Alternative Tentacles, 2009.

Biddick, Kathleen. *The Shock of Medievalism*. Durham: Duke University Press, 1998.

Birk, Sandow, and Marcus Sanders. *Dante's Inferno*. San Francisco: Chronicle, 2004.

Birk, Sandow, and Marcus Sanders. *Dante's Paradiso*. San Francisco: Chronicle, 2005.

Birk, Sandow, and Marcus Sanders. *Dante's Purgatorio*. San Francisco: Chronicle, 2005.

Black Knight. Dir. Gil Junger. Perf. Martin Lawrence, Tom Wilkinson, and Marsha Thomason. Fox, 2001.

Blatanis, Konstantinos. *Popular Culture Icons in Contemporary American Drama*. Cranbury, NJ: Associated University Presses, 2003.

Bloch, Howard, and Stephen Nichols, ed. *Medievalism and the Modernist Temper*. Baltimore: Johns Hopkins University Press, 1996.

Bloch, Marc. *Feudal Society, Vol. 1: The Growth of Ties of Dependence*. Trans. L. A. Manyon. Chicago: University of Chicago Press, 1961.

Bloom, Harold. *The Anxiety of Influence: A Theory of Poetry*. 2nd ed. New York: Oxford University Press, 1997.

Boccaccio, Giovanni. *Boccaccio's Expositions on Dante's* Comedy. Ed. and trans. Michael Papio. Toronto: University of Toronto Press, 2009.

Borchardt, Alice. *The Dragon Queen*. New York: Del Rey, 2001.

Borchardt, Alice. *The Raven Warrior*. New York: Del Rey, 2003.

Boswell, Randy. "Medieval Crusades Revived in Terrorism-War Rhetoric." *Ottawa Citizen* (25 September 2001): A2.

Bradley, Marion Zimmer. *The Mists of Avalon*. New York: Del Rey, 1982.

Braida, Antonella. *Dante and the Romantics*. Basingstoke: Palgrave Macmillan, 2004.

Brauneiss, Leopold. "Arvo Pärt's Tintinnabuli Style: Contemporary Music toward a New Middle Ages?" Utz and Swan 27–34.

Brooks, Chris. *The Gothic Revival*. London: Phaidon, 1999.

Brown, Catherine. "In the Middle." *Journal of Medieval and Early Modern Studies* 30.3 (2000): 547–74.

Brownlee, Marina, Kevin Brownlee, and Stephen Nichols, ed. *The New Medievalism*. Baltimore: Johns Hopkins University Press, 1991.

Cadmun, Michael. *Book of the Lion*. New York: Viking, 2000.

Cart, Michael. *Young Adult Literature: From Romance to Realism*. Chicago: American Library Association, 2010.

Castronovo, David. *The English Gentleman: Images and Ideals in Literature and Society*. New York: Ungar, 1987.

Chalmers, David M. *Hooded Americanism: The First Century of the Ku Klux Klan, 1865–1965*. Garden City, NY: Doubleday, 1965.

Chanson de Roland. Ed. Pierre Jonin. Paris: Editions Gallimard, 1979.

Chaucer, Geoffrey. *The Riverside Chaucer*. Ed. Larry Benson. 3rd ed. Boston: Houghton Mifflin, 1987.

Chickering, Howell, ed. and trans. *Beowulf: A Dual-Language Edition*. New York: Doubleday, 1977.

Chrétien de Troyes. *Arthurian Romances*. Ed. D. D. R. Owen. London: Everyman, 1993.

Chrétien de Troyes. *Lancelot, or the Knight of the Cart*. Ed. and trans. William W. Kibler. New York: Garland, 1984.

Classen, Albrecht. *The Medieval Chastity Belt: A Myth-Making Process*. New York: Palgrave Macmillan, 2007.

Cohen, Jeffrey Jerome. *Medieval Identity Machines*. Minneapolis: University of Minnesota Press, 2003.

Coleridge, Samuel Taylor. *The Collected Works of Samuel Taylor Coleridge*. Ed. Carl Woodring. Princeton: Princeton University Press, 1990.

Conlee, John, ed. *Prose Merlin*. Kalamazoo: Medieval Institute Publications, 1998.

Cooper, Susan. *The Dark Is Rising*. New York: Atheneum, 1973.

Cowell, Cressida. *How to Train Your Dragon*. New York: Little Brown, 2004.

Cramer, Michael. *Medieval Fantasy as Performance: The Society for Creative Anachronism and the Current Middle Ages*. Lanham: Scarecrow, 2010.

Crocker, Holly. *Chaucer's Visions of Manhood*. New York: Palgrave Macmillan, 2007.

Crompton, Anne Eliot. *Gawain and the Lady Green*. Naperville, IL: Sourcebooks Fire, 2010.

Curta, Florin. "Pavel Chinezul, Netru Vodă, and 'Imagined Communities': Medievalism in Romanian Rock Music." Utz and Swan 3–16.

Cushman, Karen. *Catherine, Called Birdy*. New York: Clarion, 1994.

Cushman, Karen. *The Midwife's Apprentice*. New York: Clarion, 1995.

Dante Alighieri. *The Divine Comedy: Inferno*. Trans. Mark Musa. Bloomington: Indiana University Press, 1996.

Dante Alighieri. *The Divine Comedy: Paradise*. Bloomington: Indiana University Press, 2004.

Dante Alighieri. *The Divine Comedy: Purgatory*. Bloomington: Indiana University Press, 2000.

Dante Alighieri. *Literary Criticism of Dante Alighieri*. Ed. and trans. Robert S. Haller. Lincoln: University of Nebraska Press, 1973.

Davidson, Roberta. "The Reel Arthur: Politics and Truth Claims in *Camelot, Excalibur*, and *King Arthur*." *Arthuriana* 17.2 (2007): 62–84.

Davis, Kathleen, and Nadia Altschul, ed. *Medievalisms in the Postcolonial World: The Idea of "the Middle Ages" Outside Europe*. Baltimore: Johns Hopkins University Press, 2009.

Demaray, John. *Cosmos and Epic Representation: Dante, Spenser, Milton, and the Transformation of Renaissance Heroic Poetry*. Pittsburgh: Duquesne University Press, 1991.

Dinshaw, Carolyn. *Getting Medieval: Sexualities and Communities, Pre- and Postmodern*. Durham: Duke University Press, 1999.

Di Renzo, Anthony. *American Gargoyles: Flannery O'Connor and the Medieval Grotesque*. Carbondale: Southern Illinois University Press, 1993.

Dixon, Jr., Thomas. *The Clansman: An Historical Romance of the Ku Klux Klan 1905*. Lexington: University Press of Kentucky, 1970.

Dobson, R. B., and J. Taylor, ed. *Rymes of Robin Hood: An Introduction to the English Outlaw*. Pittsburgh: University of Pittsburgh Press, 1976.

Donaldson, E. Talbot. *The Swan at the Well: Shakespeare Reading Chaucer*. New Haven: Yale University Press, 1985.

Donne, John. *The Complete Poetry and Selected Poems of John Donne*. Ed. Charles Coffin. New York: Modern Library, 1952.

Doughty, Oswald, and John Robert Wahl, ed. *Letters of Dante Gabriel Rossetti.* Oxford: Clarendon, 1965–67.

Driver, Martha, and Sid Ray. "Preface: Hollywood Knights." *The Medieval Hero on Screen.* Ed. Martha Driver and Sid Ray. Jefferson, NC: McFarland, 2004. 5–17.

Dryden, John. *King Arthur, or The British Worthy: A Dramatick Opera. Dryden: The Dramatic Works.* Ed. Montague Summers. New York: Gordian, 1968.

Duffin, Ross, ed. *A Performer's Guide to Medieval Music.* Bloomington: Indiana University Press, 2000.

Dundes, Alan, ed. *The Blood Libel Legend: A Casebook in Anti-Semitic Folklore.* Madison: University of Wisconsin Press, 1991.

Durant, Will, and Ariel Durant. *The Story of Civilization, Vol. 4: The Age of Faith.* New York: Simon & Schuster, 1950.

Eco, Umberto. *Travels in Hyperreality.* Trans. William Weaver. New York: Harcourt, Brace, 1986.

Edgar, Madalen. *The Boy's Froissart: Selected from Lord Berners' Translation of the Chronicles.* London: Harrap, 1912.

Eliot, George. *Middlemarch.* 1872. Oxford: Oxford University Press, 1998.

Eliot, T. S. "Dante." *Selected Essays.* 1932. New York: Harcourt, Brace, 1950. 199–327.

Eliot, T. S. *The Sacred Wood: Essays on Poetry and Criticism.* 1920. London: Methuen, 1967.

Eliot, T. S. "What Dante Means to Me." *To Criticize the Critic.* New York: Farrar, Straus, & Giroux, 1965. 125–35.

Ellis, Steve. *Dante and English Poetry: Shelley to T. S. Eliot.* Cambridge: Cambridge University Press, 1983.

Enzensberger, Hans Magnus. *Zig Zag: The Politics of Culture and Vice Versa.* New York: New Press, 1997.

Evans, Helen. Curator of Medieval Art at the Cloisters, Metropolitan Museum of Art. Personal Interview. 15 June 2011.

Everling, Wolfgang. *Dante Alighieri's* Divina Commedia *Illustrated by Salvador Dalí.* Hamburg: Verlag Dante, 2003.

Fay, Elizabeth. *Romantic Medievalism: History and the Romantic Literary Ideal.* Basingstoke: Palgrave Macmillan, 2002.

Finke, Laurie, and Martin Shichtman. *Cinematic Illuminations: The Middle Ages on Film.* Baltimore: Johns Hopkins University Press, 2010.

Flahiff, F. T. "'Mysteriously come together': Dickens, Chaucer, and *Little Dorrit.*" *University of Toronto Quarterly* 61.2 (1991–92): 250–68.

"Fort Tryon Park Medieval Festival: Costumes." Washington Heights and Inwood Development Corporation. whidc.org/costumes.html. Web. 25 September 2011.

Fradenburg, Louise. "Voice Memorial: Loss and Reparation in Chaucer's Poetry." *Exemplaria* 2.1 (1990): 169–202.

Fredeman, William, ed. *The Correspondence of Dante Gabriel Rossetti: The Formative Years, 1835–1862: Vol. I, 1835–1854.* Cambridge: D. S. Brewer, 2002.

Frevert, Ute. *Men of Honour: A Social and Cultural History of the Duel.* Trans. Anthony Williams. Cambridge: Polity, 1995.

Frey, Charles, and Lucy Rollin, ed. *Classics of Young Adult Literature.* Upper Saddle River, NJ: Pearson, 2004.

Friedrichs, Jörg. "The Meaning of the New Medievalism." *European Journal of International Relations* 7.4 (2001): 475–501.

Friesner, Esther. *The Sherwood Game.* New York: Baen, 1995.

Fults, Eveleena. Personal Interview. 15 November 2011.

Ganim, John. *Medievalism and Orientalism: Three Essays on Literature, Architecture, and Cultural Identity.* New York: Palgrave Macmillan, 2005.

Gaudenzi, Cosetta. "Dante's Introduction to the United States as Investigated in Matthew Pearl's *The Dante Club.*" *Italian Culture* 26 (2008): 85–103.

Geoffrey of Monmouth. *Historis Regum Britanniae of Geoffrey of Monmouth.* Ed. Acton Criscom. Trans. Robert Ellis Jones. Geneva: Slatkine, 1977.

Geoffrey of Monmouth. *The History of the Kings of Britain.* Ed. and trans. Lewis Thorpe. London: Penguin, 1966.

Geoffrey of Monmouth. *The History of the Kings of Britain.* Ed. Michael Reeve. Cambridge: Brewer, 2007.

Gikandi, Simon. "Africa and the Signs of Medievalism." *Medievalisms in the Postcolonial World.* Altschul and Davis 369–82.

Gilbert, Creighton. *How Fra Angelico and Signorelli Saw the End of the World.* University Park: Pennsylvania State University Press, 2003.

Ginés, Montserrat. *The Southern Inheritors of Don Quixote.* Baton Rouge: Louisiana State University Press, 2000.

Gottfried von Strassburg. *Tristan.* Trans. A. T. Hatto. London: Penguin, 1967.

Gottfried von Strassburg. *Tristan.* Ed. Karl Marold. Leipzig, 1906.

Gray, Elizabeth Janet. *Adam of the Road.* New York: Viking, 1942.

Gray, Thomas. "The Bard: A Pindaric Ode." *The Works of Thomas Gray.* Ed. William Mason. London: J. F. Dove, 1927. 382–87.

Greene, Thomas. *The Vulnerable Text.* New York: Columbia University Press, 1986.

Guthrie, Steve. "Torture, Inquisition, Medievalism, Reality TV." Joy, et al. 189–216.

Guy-Bray, Stephen. *Loving in Verse: Poetic Influence as Erotic.* Toronto: University of Toronto Press, 2006.

Haahr, Berit. *The Minstrel's Tale.* New York: Delacorte, 2000.

Handler, Daniel (as Lemony Snicket). *A Series of Unfortunate Events: The Bad Beginning.* New York: HarperCollins, 1999.

Handler, Daniel (as Lemony Snicket). *A Series of Unfortunate Events: The End.* New York: HarperCollins, 2006.

Harty, Kevin. "Cinema Arthuriana: A Comprehensive Filmography and Bibliography." *Cinema Arthuriana: Twenty Essays.* Ed. Kevin Harty. Rev. ed. Jefferson, NC: McFarland, 2002. 252–301.

Harty, Kevin. *The Reel Middle Ages.* Jefferson, NC: McFarland, 1999.

Havely, Nick. "Introduction: Dante's Afterlife, 1321–1997." *Dante's Modern Afterlife.* Ed. Nick Havely. London: Macmillan, 1998. 1–14.

Heldris of Cornwall. *Silence.* Ed. and trans. Sarah Roche-Mahdi. East Lansing: Colleagues, 1992.

Heng, Geraldine. "The Romance of England: *Richard Coer de Lyon*, Saracens, Jews, and the Politics of Race and Nation." *The Postcolonial Middle Ages.* Ed. Jeffrey Jerome Cohen. New York: St. Martin's, 2000. 135–71.

Hillman, Judith. *Discovering Children's Literature.* 2nd ed. Upper Saddle River, NJ: Merrill, 1999.

Hoenselaars, Ton, ed. *Shakespeare's History Plays: Performance, Translation, and Adaptation in Britain and Abroad.* Cambridge: Cambridge University Press, 2004.

Holcomb, Melanie. Associate Curator of Medieval Art, the Metropolitan Museum of Art. Personal Interview. 15 June 2011.

Hollander, Robert. "Milton's Elusive Response to Dante's *Comedy*." *Milton Quarterly* 45.1 (2011): 1–24.

Holsinger, Bruce. *Neomedievalism, Neoconservatism, and the War on Terror*. Chicago: Prickly Paradigm, 2007.

Honig, Matt. Personal Interview. 29 June 2011.

Howard, Donald. "Flying through Space: Chaucer and Milton." *Milton and the Line of Vision*. Ed. Joseph Wittreich. Madison: University of Wisconsin Press, 1975. 3–23.

Jinks, Catherine. *Pagan in Exile: Book 2 of the Pagan Chronicles*. Cambridge, MA: Candlewick, 1994.

Jinks, Catherine. *Pagan's Crusade: Book 1 of the Pagan Chronicles*. Cambridge, MA: Candlewick, 1992.

Jinks, Catherine. *Pagan's Vows: Book 3 of the Pagan Chronicles*. Cambridge, MA: Candlewick, 1995.

Jinks, Catherine. *Pagan's Scribe: Book 4 of the Pagan Chronicles*. Cambridge, MA: Candlewick, 1997.

Johnson, Bob. "The New Feudalism." *The Daily Kos* (16 April 2011).

Johnston, Judith. *George Eliot and the Discourses of Medievalism*. Turnhout, Belgium: Brepols, 2006.

Jones, Terry. *Chaucer's Knight: The Portrait of a Medieval Mercenary*. Baton Rouge: Louisiana State University Press, 1980.

Jones, Terry, Terry Dolan, Juliette Dor, Alan Fletcher, and Robert Yeager. *Who Murdered Chaucer? A Medieval Mystery*. New York: St. Martin's, 2004.

Joy, Eileen, Myra Seaman, Kimberley Bell, and Mary Ramsey, ed. *Cultural Studies of the Modern Middle Ages*. New York: Palgrave, 2007.

Justice, Steven. *Writing and Rebellion: England in 1381*. Berkeley: University of California Press, 1994.

Kaufman, Amy. "Medieval Unmoored." *Studies in Medievalism* 19 (2010): 1–11.

Keats, John. *The Complete Poems*. Ed. John Barnard. New York: Penguin, 1973.

Keats, John. "Robin Hood: To a Friend," *John Keats*. Ed. Elizabeth Cook. Oxford: Oxford University Press, 1994. 82–84.

Kennedy, Mike Dixon. *The Robin Hood Handbook: The Outlaw in History, Myth, and Legend*. Phoenix Mill: Sutton, 2006.

Kessler, Glenn. "The Fact Checker: Sarah Palin's 'Blood Libel' Statement on the Tucson Shootings." *Washington Post* (13 January 2011).

Khanna, Parag. *How to Run the World: Charting a Course to the Next Renaissance*. New York: Random House, 2011.

King, Andrew. The Faerie Queene *and Middle English Romance: The Matter of Just Memory*. Oxford: Clarendon, 2000.

King Arthur. Dir. Antoine Fuqua. Perf. Clive Owen, Keira Knightley, and Ioan Gruffudd. Touchstone, 2004.

King Arthur Was a Gentleman. Dir. Marcel Varnel. Perf. Arthur Askey and Evelyn Dall. Gainsborough Pictures, 1942.

Kline, Daniel. "The Crisis of Legitimation in Bush's America and Henry IV's England." Joy, et al. 157–88.

Kline, Daniel. "Virtually Medieval: The *Age of Kings* Interprets the Middle Ages." David Marshall 154–70.

Knight, Stephen. "'Meere English flocks': Ben Jonson's *The Sad Shepherd* and the Robin Hood Tradition." *Robin Hood: Medieval and Post-Medieval*. Ed. Helen Phillips. Dublin: Four Courts, 2005. 129–44.

Knight, Stephen, and Thomas Ohlgren, ed., *Robin Hood and Other Outlaw Tales*. Kalamazoo: Medieval Institute Publications, 2000.

Knightriders. Dir. George Romero. Perf. Ed Harris and Tom Savini. Laurel, 1981.

Knights of Mayhem. Dir. Max Landes. Season 1, Episode 1. 15 November 2011. Season 1, Episode 3. 22 November 2011. National Geographic Television.

Kreutziger-Herr, Annette. "Imagining Medieval Music: A Short History." Shippey and Arnold 81–109.

Kritzeck, James. *Peter the Venerable and Islam*. Princeton: Princeton University Press, 1964.

Lanier, Sidney. *The Centennial Edition of the Works of Sidney Lanier*. Ed. Clarence Gohdes and Kemp Malone. 10 vols. Baltimore: Johns Hopkins University Press, 1945.

Lasky, Kathryn. *Hawksmaid: The Untold Story of Robin Hood and Maid Marian*. New York: HarperCollins, 2010.

Lees, Clare, ed. *Medieval Masculinities: Regarding Men in the Middle Ages*. Minneapolis: University of Minnesota Press, 1994.

"*The Legend of Zelda: Twilight Princess* Instruction Booklet." Redmond, WA: Nintendo, 2006.

The Legend of Zelda: Twilight Princess: The Official Nintendo Player's Guide. Redmond, WA: Nintendo, 2006.

Lerer, Seth. *Children's Literature: A Reader's History, from Aesop to Harry Potter*. Chicago: University of Chicago Press, 2008.

Littleton, Scott, and Linda Malcor. *From Scythia to Camelot*. New York: Garland, 1994.

Lurie, Alison. *Boys and Girls Forever: Children's Classics from Cinderella to Harry Potter*. New York: Penguin, 2003.

Luzzi, Joseph. "The Rhetoric of Anachronism." *Comparative Literature* 61.1 (2009): 69–84.

Mallory, J. P. *In Search of the Indo-Europeans*. New York: Thames & Hudson, 1991.

Malory, Thomas. *Works*. Ed. Eugène Vinaver. 2nd ed. London: Oxford University Press, 1971.

Mann, Jill. "Sir Gawain and the Romance Hero." *Heroes and Heroines in Medieval English Literature*. Ed. Leo Carruthers. Cambridge: D. S. Brewer, 1994. 105–17.

Marshall, David, ed. *Mass Market Medieval: Essays on the Middle Ages in Popular Culture*. Jefferson, NC: McFarland, 2007.

Marshall, David. "The Haze of Medievalisms." *Studies in Medievalism* 20 (2011): 21–34.

Marshall, David. "A World unto Itself: Autopoetic Systems and Secondary Worlds in *Dungeons and Dragons*." David Marshall 171–85, 2007.

Marshall, John. "Riding with Robin Hood: English Pageantry and the Making of a Legend." *The Making of the Middle Ages: Liverpool Essays*. Ed. Marios Costambys, Andrew Hamer, and Martin Heale. Liverpool: Liverpool University Press, 2007. 93–117.

Martindale, Andrew, and Edi Baccheschi, ed. *The Complete Paintings of Giotto*. New York: Abrams, 1966.

Matthews, John. "The Round Table: The 2004 Movie *King Arthur*." *Arthuriana* 14.3 (2004): 112–25.

McAleer, Kevin. *Dueling: The Cult of Honor in Fin-de-Siècle Germany*. Princeton: Princeton University Press, 1994.

McClaughry, John. "Social Property and the New Feudalism." *Proceedings of the Second Annual New York Conference on Private Property Rights*. PRFA, 1996. prfamerica. org. Web. 2 April 2012.

McDougal, Stuart, ed. *Dante among the Moderns*. Chapel Hill: University of North Carolina Press, 1985.

McKinley, Robin. *The Outlaws of Sherwood*. New York: Greenwillow, 1988.

McLean, Nancy. *Behind the Mask of Chivalry: The Making of the Second Ku Klux Klan*. New York: Oxford University Press, 1994.

"The Medieval Fair of Norman." *Renaissance Magazine* 72 (2010): 50–62.

"The Medieval Festival at Fort Tryon Park." Washington Heights and Inwood Development Corporation. whidc.org/home.html. Web. 25 September 2011.

Meredith, Sean. "Film Synopsis." www.dantefilm.com/about.html. Web. 27 November 2011.

MewithoutYou. *Catch for Us the Foxes*. Tooth and Nail Records, 2004.

Miles, Rosalind. *The Child of the Holy Grail*. New York: Crown, 2001.

Miles, Rosalind. *Guenevere: Queen of the Summer Country*. New York: Crown, 1998.

Miles, Rosalind. *Isolde: Queen of the Western Isle*. New York: Crown, 2002.

Miles, Rosalind. *The Knight of the Sacred Lake*. New York: Crown, 2000.

Miles, Rosalind. *Lady of the Sea*. New York: Crown, 2004.

Miles, Rosalind. *The Maid of the White Hands*. New York: Crown, 2003.

Miner, Earl. *The Cavalier Mode from Jonson to Cotton*. Princeton: Princeton University Press, 1971.

Mitchell, Jerome. *Scott, Chaucer, and Medieval Romance: A Study in Sir Walter Scott's Indebtedness to the Literature of the Middle Ages*. Lexington: University Press of Kentucky, 1987.

Moffitt, Gregg. "The Pillage People: Swedish Warriors Amon Amarth Wage War against Misconceptions of Both Vikings and Death Metal." *Decibel* (April 2011): 56–62.

Monster Camp. Dir. Cullen Hoback. Aaron Douglas Enterprises, 2007.

Monty Python and the Holy Grail. Dir. Terry Jones and Terry Gilliam. Perf. Graham Chapman, John Cleese, and Eric Idle. Python (Monty) Pictures, 1975.

Moreland, Kim. *The Medievalist Impulse in American Literature: Twain, Adams, Fitzgerald, and Hemingway*. Charlottesville: University Press of Virginia, 1996.

Morris, William. "The Defence of Guenevere" and "King Arthur's Tomb." *Arthur, the Greatest King: An Anthology of Modern Arthurian Poems*. Ed. Alan Lupack. New York: Garland, 1988. 56–79.

Mulryan, John. "Introduction." *Milton and the Middle Ages*. Ed. John Mulryan. Lewisburg: Bucknell University Press, 1982. 11–16.

Murphy, Miriam. "Review of Gustavus Eisen's *The Great Chalice of Antioch on Which Are Depicted in Sculpture the Earliest Known Portraits of Christ, Apostles, and Evangelists*." *Catholic Historical Review* 11.1 (1925): 137–38.

Musa, Mark. "Translator's Note: On Being a Good Lover." In Dante Alighieri. *The Divine Comedy, Vol. 1: Inferno*. Trans. Mark Musa. New York: Penguin, 2003. 57–64.

Nassar, Eugene Paul. *Illustrations to Dante's* Inferno. Rutherford: Fairleigh Dickinson University Press, 1994.

"NECA Takes You to Hell and Back with New *Dante's Inferno* Collectible Figure." Youbentmywookie.com. Web. 30 November 2011.

Nennius. *British History and the Welsh Annals*. Ed. John Morris. London: Phillimore, 1980.

Neumann, Klaus. "Barbara Thornton, 1950–98." *Early Music* 27.1 (1999): 169.

Newman, Sharan. *The Chessboard Queen*. St. Martin's, 1983.

Newman, Sharan. *Guinevere*. New York: St. Martin's, 1981.

Newman, Sharan. *Guinevere Evermore*. New York: St. Martin's, 1985.

Obey, Erica. *The Wunderkammer of Lady Charlotte Guest*. Bethlehem: Lehigh University Press, 2007.

Orme, Nicholas. "Children and Literature in Medieval England." *Medium Aevum* 68.2 (1999): 218–46.

Oxford English Dictionary. OED Online. www.oed.com. Web. 31 December 2011.

Page, Thomas Nelson. *Two Little Confederates*. 1888. New York: Grosset & Dunlap, 1916.

Pearl, Matthew. *The Dante Club*. New York: Random House, 2004.

Phillips, Gesina. Personal Interview. 10 June 2011.

Poe, Edgar Allan. *The Collected Tales and Poems of Edgar Allan Poe*. New York: Modern Library, 1992.

Pound, Ezra. *Drafts and Fragments of Cantos CX–CXVII*. New York: New Directions, 1959.

"Prime 9." Major League Baseball Productions/A&E Entertainment. Major League Baseball Network. 2009.

Pugh, Tison. *Queer Chivalry: Medievalism and the Myth of White Masculinity in Southern Literature*. Baton Rouge: Louisiana State University Press, 2013.

Pulp Fiction. Dir. Quentin Tarantino. Perf. John Travolta and Samuel L. Jackson. Miramax, 1994.

Pyle, Howard. *The Merry Adventures of Robin Hood*. New York: Scribner's, 1883.

Ramey, Lynn, and Tison Pugh. "Introduction: Filming the 'Other' Middle Ages." *Race, Class, and Gender in "Medieval" Cinema*. Ed. Lynn Ramey and Tison Pugh. New York: Palgrave Macmillan, 2007. 1–12.

Rewa, Michael. "The Matter of Britain in British and American Popular Music (1966–1990)." *Popular Arthurian Traditions*. Ed. Sally Slocum. Bowling Green, OH: Bowling Green State University Press, 1992. 104–10.

Riding, Christine, and Jacqueline Riding. *The Houses of Parliament*. London: Merrell, 2000.

Rieser, Klaus. "Icons as a Discursive Practice." *U.S. Icons and Iconicity*. Ed. Walter Holbling, Klaus Rieser, and Susanne Rieser. Vienna: Austrian Association for American Studies, 2006. 7–16.

Rivadavia, Eduardo. "Requiem Review." Allmusic.com/album. Web. 11 June 2011.

Roberts, Judson. *Dragons from the Sea: Book 2 of the Strongbow Saga*. New York: HarperTeen, 2007.

Roberts, Judson. *The Road to Vengeance: Book 3 of the Strongbow Saga*. New York: HarperTeen, 2008.

Roberts, Judson. *Viking Warrior: Book 1 of the Strongbow Saga*. New York: HarperCollins, 2006.

Robin Hood: Men in Tights. Dir. Mel Brooks. Perf. Cary Elwes, Richard Lewis, and Amy Yasbeck. Twentieth-Century Fox, 1993.

Robinson, Carol, and Pamela Clements. "Living with Neomedievalism." *Studies in Medievalism* 18 (2009): 55–75.

Roe, Albert S. *Blake's Illustrations to the* Divine Comedy. 1953. Westport, CT: Greenwood, 1977.

Rose, Jacqueline. *The Case of Peter Pan, or the Impossibility of Children's Fiction*. 1984. Philadelphia: University of Pennsylvania Press, 1992.

Rossum, Gerhard Dohrn-van. *History of the Hour*. Trans. Thomas Dunlap. Chicago: University of Chicago Press, 1996.

Rovang, Paul. *Refashioning "Knights and Ladies Gentle Deeds": The Intertextuality of Spenser's* Faerie Queene *and Malory's* Morte D'Arthur. Madison: Fairleigh Dickinson University Press, 1996.

Rubin, Miri. *Gentile Tales: The Narrative Assault on Late Medieval Jews*. Philadelphia: University of Pennsylvania Press, 2004.

Sabor, Peter. *Medieval Revival and the Gothic. The Cambridge History of Literary Criticism, Vol. 4: The Eighteenth Century.* Ed. H. B. Nisbet and Claude Rawson. Cambridge: Cambridge University Press, 1997.

Sachs, Susan. "Bin Laden's Images Mesmerize Muslims." *New York Times* (9 October 2001): A4.

Salvadori, Francesca, ed. *John Flaxman: The Illustrations for Dante's* Divine Comedy. Milan: Royal Academy of Arts, 2004.

Salway, Peter. *Roman Britain*. Oxford: Clarendon, 1981.

Samuel, Irene. *Dante and Milton: The* Commedia *and* Paradise Lost. Ithaca: Cornell University Press, 1966.

Sartre, Jean-Paul. *No Exit and Three Other Plays*. New York: Vintage, 1955.

The Second Shepherds' Play. In *English Mystery Plays*. Ed. Peter Happé. Harmondsworth: Penguin, 1975. 265–94.

Server, Adam. "The Foolishness of the Blood Libel Charge." *Washington Post* (12 January 2011).

Shakespeare, William. *The Riverside Shakespeare*. Ed. Blakemore Evans, et al. 2nd ed. Boston: Houghton Mifflin, 1997.

Shakespeare, William, and John Fletcher. *The Two Noble Kinsmen. The Riverside Shakespeare.* 1689–1731.

Shelley, Percy Bysshe. *Shelley's Critical Prose*. Ed. Bruce McElderry. Lincoln: University of Nebraska Press, 1967.

Shippey, Tom. "Medievalisms and Why They Matter." *Studies in Medievalism* 17 (2009): 45–54.

Shippey, Tom, with Martin Arnold, ed. *Studies in Medievalism XIV: Correspondences: Medievalism in Scholarship and the Arts*. Cambridge: D. S. Brewer, 2005.

Silverman, Rabbi Morris, ed. *Machzor: High Holiday Prayer Book*. Hartford, CT: Prayer Book, 1951.

Simmons, Clare. "Introduction." *Medievalism and the Quest for the "Real" Middle Ages*. Ed. Clare Simmons. London: Cass, 2001. 1–28.

Simonetta, Marcello. "Assassin's Creed." Seton Hall University, South Orange, NJ. 18 April 2011. Lecture.

"*The Sims*^{TM} *Medieval* Instruction Booklet." Austin, TX: Entertainment Arts, 2011.

Sir Gawain and the Green Knight. Ed. J. R. R. Tolkien and E. V. Gordon. 2nd ed. Ed. Norman Davis. Oxford: Clarendon, 1967.

Sir Gawain and the Green Knight. Trans. James J. Wilhelm. *The Romance of Arthur: An Anthology of Medieval Texts in Translation*. New York: Garland, 1994. 399–466.

Slater, Dashka. "Can a Band of American Knights Turn 'Full Contact' Jousting into the Next Action Sport?" *New York Times Magazine* (11 July 2010): 24–29.

Sobchack, Vivian. "The Insistent Fringe: Moving Images and Historical Consciousness." *History and Theory* 36.4 (1997): 4–20.

The Song of Roland. Trans. Frederick Goldin. New York: Norton, 1978.

"*Sonic and the Black Knight* Instruction Booklet." San Francisco: Sega, 2006.

Spenser, Edmund. *The Faerie Queene*. Ed. Thomas Roche. London: Penguin, 1987.

Spenser, Edmund. *The Yale Edition of the Shorter Poems of Edmund Spenser*. Ed. William Oram, et al. New Haven: Yale University Press, 1989.

Spinner, Stephanie. *Damosel*. New York: Knopf, 2008.

Spradlin, Michael. *Keeper of the Grail: The Youngest Templar, Book 1.* New York: Putnam, 2008.

Spradlin, Michael. *Trail of Fate: The Youngest Templar, Book 2.* New York: Putnam, 2010.

Spradlin, Michael. *Orphan of Destiny: The Youngest Templar, Book 3.* New York: Putnam, 2010.

Stafford, Pauline. "Introduction." *The Making of the Middle Ages: Liverpool Essays.* Ed. Marios Costambys, Andrew Hamer, and Martin Heale. Liverpool: Liverpool University Press, 2007. 1–14.

Staines, David. *Tennyson's Camelot:* The Idylls of the King *and Its Medieval Sources.* Ontario: Wilfred Laurier University Press, 1982.

Star Trek IV: The Voyage Home. Dir. Leonard Nimoy. Perf. William Shatner, Leonard Nimoy, and Nichelle Nichols. Paramount, 1986.

Steinbeck, Elaine, and Robert Wallsten, ed. *Steinbeck: A Life in Letters.* New York: Viking, 1975.

Steinbeck, John. *The Acts of King Arthur and His Noble Knights: From the Winchester Manuscripts of Thomas Malory and Other Sources.* Ed. Chase Horton. New York: Farrar, Straus, & Giroux, 1976.

Stewart, Susan. *On Longing: Narratives of the Miniature, the Gigantic, the Souvenir, the Collection.* Durham: Duke University Press, 1993.

Stokes, Jane. "Arthur Askey and the Construction of Popular Entertainment." *British Cinema: Past and Present.* Ed. Justine Ashby and Andrew Higson. London: Routledge, 2000. 124–36.

Summers, David. *Spenser's Arthur: The British Arthurian Tradition and the* Faerie Queen. Lanham: University Press of America, 1997.

Taylor, Laurie, and Zach Whalen, ed. *Playing the Past: History and Nostalgia in Video Games.* Nashville: Vanderbilt University Press, 2008.

Tennyson, Alfred, Lord. "Extracts from *The Foresters.*" Dobson and Taylor 243–49.

Tennyson, Alfred, Lord. *Idylls of the King.* Ed. J. M. Gray. London: Penguin, 1983.

Tharoor, Ishaan. "Sarah Palin's Claim: What is 'Blood Libel'?" *Time Magazine* (12 January 2011).

Thornton, Barbara, and Lawrence Rosenwald. "The Voice in the Middle Ages: Poetics as Technique." Duffin 264–92.

Tinkler-Villani, Valeria. *Visions of Dante in English Poetry: Translations of the* Commedia *from Jonathan Richardson to William Blake.* Amsterdam: Rodopi, 1989.

"To Hell and Back." Necaonline.com. Web. 30 November 2011.

Tolkien, J. R. R. *The Lord of the Rings.* 2nd ed. Boston: Houghton Mifflin, 1967.

Tosches, Nick. *In the Hand of Dante.* Boston: Back Bay, 2002.

Trafford, Simon, and Aleks Pluskowski. "Antichrist Superstars: The Vikings in Hard Rock and Heavy Metal." David Marshall 57–73.

Trigg, Stephanie. "Introduction: Medieval and Gothic Australia." *Medievalism and the Gothic in Australian Culture.* Ed. Stephanie Trigg. Turnhout, Belgium: Brepols, 2005. xi–xxiii.

Twain, Mark. *A Connecticut Yankee in King Arthur's Court.* 1889. London: Penguin, 1986.

Twain, Mark. *Life on the Mississippi.* The Oxford Mark Twain. Series ed. Shelley Fisher Fishkin. 1883. New York: Oxford University Press, 1996.

Tucker, Richard K. *The Dragon and the Cross: The Rise and Fall of the Ku Klux Klan in Middle America.* Hamden, CT: Archon, 1991.

Utz, Richard, and Jessie Swan, ed. *Studies in Medievalism XIII: Postmodern Medievalisms.* Cambridge: D. S. Brewer, 2005.

Verde, Tom. "The Multipolar Picture: An Interview with Parag Khanna." *Saudi Aramco World* 62.3 (May/June 2011): 40–43.

Wace. *Wace's Roman de Brut: A History of the British*. Ed. and trans. Judith Weiss. Exeter: Exeter University Press, 1999.

Watson, Donald. *Shakespeare's Early History Plays: Politics at Play on the Elizabethan Stage*. Athens: University of Georgia Press, 1990.

The Waverly Consort. "The Christmas Story." waverlyconsort.org/concerts.php. Web. 11 June 2011.

Wawn, Andrew. *Northern Antiquity: The Post-Medieval Reception of Edda and Saga*. Enfield Lock: Hisarlik, 1994.

Wawn, Andrew. *The Vikings and the Victorians: Inventing the Old North in Nineteenth-Century Britain*. Cambridge: D. S. Brewer, 2000.

Weisl, Angela Jane. *The Persistence of Medievalism: Narrative Adventures in Contemporary Culture*. New York: Palgrave Macmillan, 2003.

West, Jerry. "The New Feudalism." *OpEd News Network* (29 January 2010).

White, T. H. *The Once and Future King*. New York: Putnam, 1958.

Wilhelm, James J. "Arthur in the Latin Chronicles." *The Romance of Arthur: An Anthology of Medieval Texts in Translation*. Ed. James J. Wilhelm. New York: Garland, 1994. 3–9.

Williams, Tony. *The Cinema of George A. Romero: Knight of the Living Dead*. London: Wallflower, 2003.

Wood, Christopher. *The Pre-Raphaelites*. London: Seven Dials, 1981.

Wordsworth, William. *Translations of Chaucer and Virgil*. Ed. Bruce Graver. Ithaca: Cornell University Press, 1998.

Workman, Leslie. "Editorial." *Studies in Medievalism* 1.1. (1979): 1–3.

Index

Taylor & Francis ──────────────────

eBooks
FOR LIBRARIES

ORDER YOUR FREE 30 DAY INSTITUTIONAL TRIAL TODAY!

Over 23,000 eBook titles in the Humanities, Social Sciences, STM and Law from some of the world's leading imprints.

Choose from a range of subject packages or create your own!

Benefits for you

▶ Free MARC records
▶ COUNTER-compliant usage statistics
▶ Flexible purchase and pricing options

Benefits for your user

▶ Off-site, anytime access via Athens or referring URL
▶ Print or copy pages or chapters
▶ Full content search
▶ Bookmark, highlight and annotate text
▶ Access to thousands of pages of quality research at the click of a button

For more information, pricing enquiries or to order a free trial, contact your local online sales team.

UK and Rest of World: **online.sales@tandf.co.uk**

US, Canada and Latin America:
e-reference@taylorandfrancis.com

www.ebooksubscriptions.com

ALPSP Award for BEST eBOOK PUBLISHER 2009 Finalist

Taylor & Francis **eBooks**
Taylor & Francis Group

A flexible and dynamic resource for teaching, learning and research.